Russia's Workers
in Transition

Russia's Workers in Transition

Labor, Management, and the State under

Gorbachev and Yeltsin

Paul T. Christensen

NORTHERN ILLINOIS UNIVERSITY PRESS   DEKALB   1999

Library of Congress Cataloging-in-Publication Data

Christensen, Paul Thomas, 1963–

Russia's workers in transition : labor, management,

and the state under Gorbachev and Yeltsin / Paul T.

Christensen.

     p.   cm.

Includes bibliographical references and index.

ISBN 0-87580-253-2 (alk. paper)

1. Labor policy—Russia (Federation) 2. Working

class—Russia (Federation) 3. Russia (Federation)—

Economic policy—1991– 4. Industrial relations—

Russia (Federation) I. Title.

HD8530.2.C49   2000

331'.0947—dc21

99-30604

CIP

To My Parents, Gerrie and John Christensen,

who made everything possible, and who taught me

the value of labor and the dignity of

those who perform it.

"Blessed are those who have not seen and yet believe."

—John 21.29

They were right, my dear, all those voices were right

And still are; this land is not the sweet home that it looks

Nor its peace the historical calm of a site

Where something was settled once and for all: A backward

And dilapidated province, connected

To the big busy world by a tunnel, with a certain

Seedy appeal, is that all it is now? Not quite:

It has a worldly duty which in spite of itself

It does not neglect, but calls into question

—W. H. Auden, *In Praise of Limestone*

Contents

Acknowledgments

Like any other form of labor, this book was a collective as well as a personal project, and I am very grateful to a great many people in the United States and Russia for their help and guidance over the years as the book evolved. First and foremost, I would like to thank my friend and colleague Stephen F. Cohen for his advice and support, and for conveying to me his deep understanding of the complexities of Russian and Soviet society and history. I am also indebted to Daniel Field and William C. Wohlforth for their critical and insightful reading of the draft chapters of the book, which kept me on course on more than one occasion. I would particularly like to thank Joan Barth Urban and Valerie Bunce, the readers of the manuscript for Northern Illinois University Press, for their extremely helpful comments and critiques.

The institutional support that I received that financed my research in the Soviet Union and Russia made the empirical chapters of the book possible. I am grateful to the Center for International Studies, the Program in Russian Studies, the Council on Regional Studies, and the Department of Politics, all of Princeton University, the American Council for Teachers of Russian, the MacArthur Foundation, the Mellon Foundation, and the Maxwell School of Citizenship and Public Affairs of Syracuse University for their research and travel grants.

My research in the Soviet Union and Russia was successful only through the assistance of my many friends in the former USSR. Gennadi Bordiugov, Sergei Magaril, and Sergei Tsakunov helped me gain access to important archives and individuals in Moscow. Anna Esina and Galina Gorskaia of the Russian Center for the Preservation and Study of Documents of Contemporary History, and my colleagues at the Moscow Institute of Management were incredibly generous with their advice, contacts, time, and energy. My research in factories and mines across Russia and Ukraine was made possible by my colleagues in the regions I visited, and I cannot thank them enough: Valerii Pisigin in Naberezhnye Chelny; Oleg Aliev in Makhachkala; Zinaida Korovina and Viktor Solomikhan in Donetsk; and Aleksandr Klimov in Novosibirsk. I also owe an unpayable debt of gratitude to Tamara Aleksandrovna Gorelova, who made the Soviet system work in my favor, at least in her small corner of it.

I would like to convey a special note of thanks to all of the workers and trade union members who gave so generously of their time on and off the job to talk to me about their experiences under Gorbachev and Yeltsin, and particularly to Aleksandr Zamiatin for his help in St. Petersburg and Moscow. I am also grateful to the Moscow office of the AFL-CIO's Free Trade Union Institute, and especially its director Irene Stevenson, for giving me access to their documents and contacts.

The book has benefited immensely from the critical but sympathetic eye of my editor, Mary Lincoln, and I am very grateful to the staff at Northern Illinois University Press for the care and attention they have devoted to the manuscript.

Finally, I want to thank Richard Brody, Terry Sabonis-Chafee, and Liz McKeon, whose gentle good humor and acid wit made Moscow a wonderful place to be in winter. And most important, my love and thanks to my family: to my wife, Marjorie Howes, for her constant love and support, her peerless editing, and for reminding me through her work what scholarship should be, and to my daughter, Alexandra, for her uncritical affection and for keeping it all in perspective.

Russia's Workers
in Transition

Restructuring State Socialism

Theorizing the Political Economy of Post-Sovietism

In the fall of 1998, the political, economic, and social crisis that had been building in Russia since the abolition of the Soviet Union and the introduction of "shock therapy" in 1992 reached a critical and dangerous point. The ongoing struggle between Yeltsin's government and opposition forces in the Duma paralyzed the political system at the center, while power struggles between the central and regional governments threatened the integrity of the Russian state. Russia's seven-year economic implosion intensified as a result of the growing world economic crisis and the failure of the Russian financial system. The collapse of Russia's social safety net, rising unemployment, increasing poverty, and ubiquitous crime and corruption combined to leave Russian society demoralized, angry, and seemingly powerless to respond coherently. This was a systemic crisis, a case of demodernization not experienced by a developed industrial state except as a result of war.

How did this happen? By what path did the superpower that was the Soviet Union reach the position of being the "dilapidated province" of Europe that it had become by 1998? How did Western analyses of Russia succeed or fail in identifying the reasons for this crisis? And more important than that, how did Western analyses and advice contribute to Russia's ongoing systemic implosion? Most answers to these questions in the fall of 1998 focused as they had in recent history on immediate problems and events, such as the failure of the banking system, the difficulties with tax collection, and the ongoing problem of wage arrears. These factors, however, were merely symptoms of more enduring structural problems with the process of "transition" in Russia. The crisis Russia faced in 1998 was systemic; the factors that led to it were systemic as well, rooted in the Yeltsin era but stretching back to the Gorbachev years and the contradictions of perestroika.

This book retraces the policies of transition under Gorbachev and Yeltsin as a means of answering the questions posed above. While the answers are complicated, their basic contours are clear; there are three central arguments in this book that comprise the answers. The first is that Russia's systemic crisis was the result of the Yeltsin government's attempt to impose a socioeconomic and political system on Russia that was entirely inappropriate for a country emerging from seventy years of communism. The introduction by fiat of shock therapy and privatization, and the consequent exclusion of society at large from participation in the reform process, undermined the foundations of the economy, eroded societal support for reform, and crippled the development of civil society. The second and related argument is that Gorbachev's reforms, while contradictory, poorly implemented, and insufficiently radical, provided a better basis for an ultimately successful economic transition and for the eventual consolidation of democracy than did the policies of Yeltsin. This is not to argue that Gorbachev would necessarily have succeeded given more time, or that the economic crisis in the Soviet Union in 1991 was not disastrous. Rather, the argument is that the underlying structure of his policies was more appropriate, because Gorbachev recognized the limitations and possibilities presented by the fact that for better or worse the Soviet Union was a communist system.

The third argument is that Western analysts, advisers, and governments were too quick—as were Yeltsin and his allies—to adopt modes of analysis and to prescribe policies regarding Russia derived from the experiences of countries outside the former communist world. The result of their approach to reform in Russia has been twofold. On the one hand, it has caused many Western analysts to de-couple the political and socioeconomic aspects of reform. This in turn has led to misunderstandings about the nature of both transition and crisis in Russia. On the other hand, it has led Western advisers to give Russia precisely the wrong advice about how to proceed with transition. Single-mindedly focused on where it wanted Russia to go, the West paid little attention to where Russia was starting from and tended to disregard Russia's history, socioeconomic structure, and political culture.

The arguments put forward here are grounded in a detailed empirical analysis of the relationship among workers, managers, and the state in the former Soviet Union and Russia under Gorbachev and Yeltsin. The reason for the particular choice of subjects is that the conflicts and alliances among these forces were more pivotal to the political, economic, and social struggles in both periods than were those among any other groups, save perhaps nationalities. The narrative is constructed, if not from the perspective of Russian workers, then certainly with an eye toward presenting that perspective within the confines of the overall analysis. In specific reference to labor, the book has two distinct but interrelated purposes. The first is to explain the structure, socioeconomic position, forms of identity, and politics of the Soviet and Russian working class as they have developed in the years since the beginning of perestroika in 1985. The second purpose is to examine the general processes of change that have taken place in Russia over the last decade through the lens of the working class's role in those processes and the state's policies toward workers. The goal of both parts is to answer the questions posed at the outset by examining the general case of Russia's systemic crisis through the specific case of labor's experience of that event. The results of this examination serve as the basis for the book's challenge to Western comparative political science assumptions about "transition politics" in postcommunist states—particularly and most emphatically the assumptions about the role of social groups in transitions and the effects of their politicization.

Among post-Sovietologists and other comparativists who have studied the changes initiated by Gorbachev, there is little agreement on any of the major analytical questions that the policies of Gorbachev and Yeltsin have brought to the fore. Was it possible to reform the Soviet system, or was perestroika doomed from the start?[1] Did the abolition of the Soviet Union and the rise to power of Yeltsin constitute a revolution, or simply a stage in the process of change? Do events since 1992 represent a breakthrough to democracy, the consolidation of "nomenklatura capitalism," or a Russia trapped in a political and economic no-man's-land?[2] And finally, the question that informs this book and to which I have already given a tentative answer: are the theoretical constructs that Western comparative political science has used to attempt to answer these questions, namely transition and democratization theory, appropriate to the Russian context, or are the structures of post-Soviet Russia different enough from those of other transitional states to invalidate explanations derived from Latin and South America, southern Europe, the Newly Industrializing Countries, or the developing world?

In one sense, the final question posed above supersedes the others, insofar as one's initial analytical assumptions condition the questions asked and the answers given. The major theoretical debates that have emerged over the past decade regarding what is actually taking place in Russia center on two major issues. First is the question of comparability versus exceptionalism, in the Russian case. Explicitly or implicitly, this debate has pitted "transitologists," who wish to engage in "conceptual traveling," against country- or region-oriented comparative specialists, who think that such theorists are mixing apples and oranges, along with other types of flora and fauna, when viewing Russia and Eastern Europe as just another set of transitional states.[3] While not wishing to reinforce a two-camp mentality, the arguments presented here place the book firmly in the latter group.

The second issue concerns democracy and markets, and therefore democratization and marketization. The debate centers on what constitutes functioning democracy and markets, what genuine democratization and marketization entail, and to what extent they are being seen in Russia. This debate is at once theoretical, empirical, and ideological, but in its essence it is a debate about institutions and procedures versus power relations. Most of the comparative politics literature on democratization posits a very narrow definition and set of tests for democracy. While there is some variation in the details, the basic features of "democracy" for these theorists are (1) free and fair elections, regularly held and conducted on a competitive basis, and (2) respect for a basic package of civil and human rights—such as freedom of the press, speech, and religion—that can be defended through recognized and agreed-to legal means and institutions against the depredations of the state or other forces in society. In a democracy, to quote Giuseppe Di Palma, "the outcomes are uncertain; the rules cannot be uncertain."[4] Democracy, then, is about rules, not *who* rules.

While not dismissing the importance of formal institutions and rules, other comparativists argue that such narrow definitions of democracy displace from the center of analysis, or elide altogether, two equally important components of democracy, namely empowered individuals or social groups and "responsive rule."[5] While rules and elections give people mechanisms to exert influence, they do not give them the material wherewithal to do so, nor do they guarantee any correspondence between people's expressed wishes and government action.[6] Whether it is money, property, trade union dues, party donations, or PACs, people must have resources to make democracy work. Likewise, the goals and interests to which those resources are directed must have genuine opportunities to be realized if a system is to be termed a democracy.[7] One can agree with Di Palma that democracy cannot guarantee outcomes, but it must provide for real contestation—not just among elites, but in society as a whole. The specter of transitions that failed because elements within the polity and society asked for too much has narrowed the notion of democracy to electoralism and truncated civil rights. This may be tactically smart, but it is theoretically unjustified. Democracy, and the study of it, must be about the *rulers* as well as the rules, whether in a transitional state or a "developed democracy."

The problem of disjuncture between the formal rules of democracy and the actual power relations within a state is nowhere more evident than in Russia, precisely because the struggles over property, control of resources, social (dis)empowerment, and state (non)responsiveness are so acute. This book focuses on the struggles of one particular social group—the working class. Its struggles have encompassed issues ranging from supplies of soap for miners to the role of the Communist Party in society, from labor relations and control of factories to payment of wage arrears and privatization, and from the nature and importance of trade unions to the future of presidents and governments. In the former Soviet Union as elsewhere, democracy is not simply a form of governance, but a system of political economy. It is only through an empirical examination of the struggles over the structure and future shape of that political economy during the perestroika and post-perestroika years that it is possible to judge what democratization means in Russia and where it stands. The following empirical analysis of industrial politics from 1985 to 1998 lays the basis for the book's critique of "transitology" as applied to the former communist states, and the notions of democracy and democratization that generally accompany transition theory.

Transitology versus Change in the Soviet Union and Russia

"A horrible end is better than horror without end."[8] Throughout the last week of April 1991, a small placard bearing this message stood propped against the wall of the Communist Party headquarters in Donetsk, where hundreds of striking miners from the Donbass coalfields had gathered to listen as their co-workers and allies demanded everything from wage increases to the resignation of the government to the abolition of the Communist Party. When asked what the sign meant, the miners responded that anything, even severe short-term economic hardship, lost wages, or the spread of civil strife was preferable to the continuation of "poor-man's communism" or the accelerating decline of their standard of living that, in their minds, Gorbachev's perestroika had wrought.

Seven years later, the miners were on the picket lines again, as they had been many times between 1991 and 1998. Among their demands were the payment of wage arrears, the improvement of economic conditions in the mining regions, and the resignation of both the government and President Boris Yeltsin.[9] It was an interesting paradox. It had been six years since Boris Yeltsin's rise to power and the abolition of the Soviet Union, along with—in theory at least—the USSR's centrally planned system. During this period, the leadership introduced a series of reforms designed to build a market economy, initiated two major cycles of privatization, and constructed at least the trappings of political democracy. Yet in spite of all this, Russian workers were still striking—not against the firms for which they worked, but against the central government and its institutions, the very government and institutions they had helped put in power. This is not to argue that nothing had changed in Russia since the end of perestroika, but rather to say that the nature of those changes was contradictory and problematic.

Take the miners' strikes as an example. Six years of reform in the Soviet Union had brought much more than an economy in crisis: perestroika had created a situation in which miners could go on strike, elect their own strike committees, and stand in the central square of a major city denouncing the system and all it represented. The level of anger, desperation, and politicization reflected in that strike graphically illustrated both the perils faced by an authoritarian regime that had set in motion a process of reform and the increased opportunities for political action that a movement away from authoritarianism provides for social groups long excluded from political processes.

The miners' strikes were only the most visible and radical manifestation of worker discontent in the Soviet Union, which by 1991 was deep and far reaching. Both the Gorbachev leadership and Soviet workers themselves had traveled a long road from 1985 to 1991. A reform leader who had made workplace democracy a cornerstone of his economic and political reform program in 1987 had not only abandoned that program entirely, but by the spring of 1991 was denouncing the labor movement as a menace to perestroika and was threatening a nationwide ban on all strike action. And large sectors of the Soviet working class, which had been skeptical but hopeful participants in perestroika, responded by turning on the Soviet political system and those striving to reform it.

In 1998, worker discontent with the government and its socioeconomic policies was equally intense. Not just miners, but metalworkers, autoworkers, textile workers, air-traffic controllers, locomotive engineers, doctors, teachers, workers in the defense industries, and even the police and military either went on strike or threatened to do so. In most cases, the immediate cause was nonpayment of wages, but the common thread that tied these disparate workers together was a sense of the government's failure to manage the economy and to make good on its promise to build a "normal, civilized" country out of the ashes of Soviet communism. In the "new Russia," the working class remains internally divided, excluded from the political system, and faced with economic turmoil and few resources to defend its economic interests. Not surprisingly, large sectors of the Russian working class, which had been enthusiastic and hopeful participants in Yeltsin's version of perestroika, responded by turning on the Russian political system and those striving to control it.

For its part, the Yeltsin government that had set out in 1992 to build "a people's capitalism" and a democratic state had by 1998 done neither. People's capitalism rapidly gave way to shock therapy, dictated from above by Egor Gaidar and his Western advisers, and to privatization programs that created a small wealthy elite of apparatchiks-turned-owners, a Russian nouveau riche, and mafiosi capitalists, while devastating the living standard of millions. Yet for all this, the Russian state was as deeply enmeshed in the socioeconomic structures of Russia as ever, and in many ways these structures remained firmly rooted in their Soviet past.[10]

Russian "democracy" exhibited similar pathologies. The rules of the democratic game—so central to democratization and transition theory—soon were replaced by tanks bombing parliament, rule by presidential decree, Kremlin intrigue worthy of the Brezhnev era, and the wanton destruction of the tiny republic of Chechnya in the name of Russian statehood. Contested elections, relatively untainted by obvious fraud, continued apace through 1998, but this fact must be balanced by the equally demonstrable fact that power remained highly concentrated in the office of the president and the regional executives, while neither the constitution of the Russian Federation nor the actual operation of politics provided substantive balance-of-power mechanisms from other branches of government or society at large.

In short, after more than a decade of tumultuous change, the question remains: what is Russia? Where does it fit on our conceptual map? The uncertainty of the issue is reflected in the terminology used by comparativists to describe it. For transitologists, Russia is either a democracy, a neo-democracy, a delegative democracy, or simply a country undergoing "peaceful revolutionary change" toward capitalist democracy.[11] A cartoon in the Russian newspaper *Izvestiia* summed up the problem: A man bursts into a room where another man is seated at a table with a bottle of vodka. The first man shouts: "Democracy has triumphed in Russia!" The second man starts from his chair with a look of horror and says, "What? Again?"[12]

The cause of this conceptual confusion lies mainly in the methodology generally used to study Russia, rather than in the contradictory nature of Russian politics and economics. In the course of a debate between Philippe Schmitter and Valerie Bunce over the appropriateness of using concepts of transition derived from the experiences of Latin America and southern Europe to study Russia, Valerie Bunce posed the central issue succinctly:

> The key question, then, is whether the differences constitute variations on a common process—that is, transitions from dictatorship to democracy—or altogether different processes—that is, democratization versus what could be termed postcommunism. Schmitter and Karl take the first position and their critics the second.[13]

While much has been written on this subject, it is worthwhile to review the main contours of transition theory—particularly those aspects concerning workers and labor relations—in an attempt to articulate an alternative perspective and to explain why transition theory is not an appropriate tool to apply to the former Soviet Union and Russia.

The core problem is that the cases from which transition theory has been derived and the cases to which it is now being applied do seem to have a striking family resemblance that makes comparison plausible and tempting. First, as transitologists point out, the Latin American and southern European cases themselves are not identical, so difference is not an a priori barrier to comparison. Research into the question of how transitions occur has demonstrated that there is no single, identifiable method for making a successful and lasting shift from an authoritarian system to a nonauthoritarian one. Every successful transition has reflected the particularities of its country's history, culture, economy, and social structure, just as the form of each country's authoritarian regime reflected these same particularities. One should expect, therefore, the same to be true in Russia and Eastern Europe. In short, differences in microprocesses do not invalidate claims about the similarity of macroprocesses. Thus, it is plausible to argue that the focus of analysis must be the broad patterns and courses of action identified in studies of transitions that seem to enable successful moves away from authoritarian structures.

The first such pattern concerns how and why transitions begin, or what the impetus is for an authoritarian system to break with what have been the mainstays of its power in the past. Alfred Stepan identifies eight possible routes to "redemocratization," of which only one reflects the process that took place in the USSR: "[R]edemocratization initiated from within authoritarian regimes" in which "the initiating group [is] drawn from the civilianized political leadership."[14] Stepan observes that this process rarely entails a "once-and-for-all decision to devolve power" but, rather, occurs when "some major institutional power holders within the ruling authoritarian coalition perceive that because of changing conditions their long-term interests are best pursued in a context in which authoritarian institutions give way to democratic institutions."[15] Even granted that a "decision to devolve power" may not be taken, Stepan's statement implies that leaders within the authoritarian system do make a conscious decision to begin a transition and that they have some sort of strategy for bringing it about.

Gorbachev and his allies did have such a strategy, which was guided by the perception that the old authoritarian structures could no longer deliver the goods economically, politically, or socially. They believed that in the long term this situation would threaten both social peace and their own positions within the system; the same can be said of Yeltsin and his allies. The ways in which these strategies succeeded or failed is the subject of subsequent chapters. While significant changes have occurred since Yeltsin's ascendance to power, even in 1998 many of the old structures, attitudes, and elites of the Soviet authoritarian system remained in place and continued to function. As some obstacles were removed, new ones arose. Although the transitional strategies of the Yeltsin leadership differed from those of the Gorbachev leadership, the collapse of the central political structures of the Soviet system did not equal the birth of a new system. The "transition" was initiated by an authoritarian regime, and it was continued by another regime that, despite a series of elections and referenda, remained authoritarian in essence and lacked a proven base of social support for its policies.

If transitions initiated by authoritarian regimes begin because certain elite groups within the regime think their long-term interests are better served by democratic institutions, the logical corollary is that certain other powerful groups within the regime do not see it that way. After reviewing a large number of cases in both Europe and South America, Guillermo O'Donnell, Philippe Schmitter, and Laurence Whitehead, writing in *Transitions from Authoritarian Rule,* came to the conclusion that "there is no transition whose beginning is not the consequence—direct or indirect—of important divisions within the authoritarian regime itself, principally along the fluctuating cleavage between hard-liners and soft-liners."[16] The distinction identifies the key originating factor in regime-led transition, from which all other components of the transition—alliances, pacts, negotiations, and so on—follow. Once the transition has been initiated by the regime, these other components of the transition process have a reciprocal effect on the policies of the regime as emergent forces within the society begin to articulate demands.

The second pattern concerns the construction of institutions to guarantee contestation. Having decided to begin a break with old authoritarian structures, a regime must design a set of institutions ensuring all relevant social and political groups the right to participate in a post-authoritarian system.

These institutions must be agreed upon by both the regime leaders and the groups concerned in order to lower the probability that any group will try to sabotage the process.[17]

If viewed from the perspective of political institution-building alone, the parallels between the Latin American and southern European cases and the Soviet/Russian case again seem conducive to comparison. Gorbachev's policy of glasnost, his introduction of competitive elections, the referendum on a reformed Soviet Union, and the negotiations surrounding the New Union Treaty appear to fit this pattern of transition. Yeltsin's policies regarding elections, the writing of a new constitution for Russia, the negotiations on autonomy between the central government and Russia's regions, among others, also seem to fall within the framework of transition theory. While one can argue about how and why these policies succeeded or failed, it is plausible to see them as comparable to other such policy initiatives in other contexts.

The conceptual stretching necessary to make transitology applicable to the Soviet/Russian case, then, appears methodologically justifiable when viewed from the perspective of elite politics and political institution-building narrowly defined. When these political factors are placed in the context of the socioeconomic structures of the Soviet Union and Russia, however, their comparability proves to be superficial, and the need for a model of postcommunist political economy becomes evident. One can see this most clearly by examining two threads of argument that run through transition theory pertaining to economic and social questions in transitional states.

The first of these arguments is that the institutions devised and the policies followed during the transition must not involve any kind of redistribution of property, wealth, or privilege vis-à-vis the major powerful interests in society, except for the diminution of political advantages that these interests agree to as part of the transition. In all of the historical cases of transition prior to those of Eastern Europe and the Soviet Union, this has meant in practical terms that neither capitalism as a system nor capitalists as a class could be directly threatened if a transition was to go forward.

Second, there must be social forces already in place that have an existing constituency—independent from the authoritarian regime—that can provide the basis for participatory politics once the authoritarian regime begins to relinquish power. It may well be that these organizations were either co-opted or crushed by the authoritarian regime; what is important is that the regime never claimed these organizations as its own, and that these organizations retained roots in society beyond the compass of the regime. Equally important, these groups must not make demands beyond the scope of political democratization—specifically, this means in most cases demands for electoralism—for the reasons outlined above. In other words, for a transition to be successful, the legal and institutional grounds for political competition must be established, and there must be groups to engage in such competition once those institutions have been organized, all the while remembering that property rights must be protected. Anything more than this is problematic.

In attempting to bring this analysis of transitions to bear on the case of the former Soviet Union and Russia, one is immediately faced with a problem arising from the difference in the nature of capitalist and socialist systems. All of the transitions on which the analysis above is based and from which the three conditions are derived took place in countries that were authoritarian and capitalist, and all of these analyses of transitions presuppose the prior existence of capitalism: private property, a market economy, functioning labor and capital markets, banking systems, and a significant level of integration into the capitalist world economy.

In the case of the former Soviet Union, capitalism, with all its attendant structures—economic, political, social, and cultural—did not exist. There were elements of coherent social groups in the sense that O'Donnell and Schmitter use the term, but in 1985 in the former USSR such elements were embedded in the statist system of the Soviet Union and could articulate their interests only in reference to the state, positively or negatively. The central argument between proponents and critics of the applicability of transition theory to the former Soviet Union is this: are these differences in degree or in kind?

At times, transitologists seem to argue the former. Philippe Schmitter and Terry Lynn Karl, for example, state that, although they recognize "significant interregional differences" between the sets of cases, their position is that transitologists "should stick to their original operating assumptions. These latter cases of regime change [in the East] can be—at least initially—treated as conceptually and theoretically equivalent to those that preceded them."[18] Although they do not explain why the burden of proof is on regional specialists to demonstrate distinctiveness rather than transitologists to demonstrate similarity, the language they use exposes a basic problem with their assumptions. In former communist states, the question is not simply *regime change,* but a fundamental change in entire socioeconomic, cultural, and ideological systems, in addition to regime change.

Adam Przeworski argued similarly that the economic problems faced by Latin American countries at the time of their transitions were every bit as serious as those of the former Soviet Union and that the changes required were every bit as radical.[19] Placing the Polish case alongside discussions of Latin America and southern Europe in *Economic Reforms in New Democracies* also seems to suggest a level of equivalence. While Giuseppe Di Palma in *To Craft Democracies* seems more skeptical, he leaves the door open when he argues that "the comparisons between transitions East and West reveal common issues and behaviors that are the more striking in view of the institutional differences between the respective regimes in each area."[20]

In spite of this, there is throughout the literature an undercurrent of recognition that these systems are basically different, and that the distinct modes and relations of production that were the hallmark of these systems are the key to that difference. Thus Schmitter argues that "what is most striking are the differences in point of departure in socio-occupational structure as the result of many years of policy measures designed to compress class and sectoral distinctions, equalize material rewards and, of course, eliminate the diversity of property relations."[21] He continues by noting that "eastern social systems seem very 'amorphous'" and unlikely to produce the types of parties and interest organizations that are the hallmark of consolidated Western democracies. But Schmitter's most telling comment is this:

> At least until the twin shocks of marketization and privatization produce more substantial and more stable class and sectoral differences, the politics of these neodemocracies are likely to be driven by other, much less tractable cleavages (i.e., ethnicity, locality, personality).[22]

This passage seems to imply that decades of communism created a set of relations unlike those found in Western capitalist countries, Latin America and southern Europe included, and that until capitalism has been re-created ("the twin shocks of marketization and privatization"), the postulates of transition theory are more likely to obscure than illuminate what is taking place in former communist states.

Likewise, Di Palma argues that "beyond a certain point, the political democratization of Communist systems cannot proceed without the other reforms. Democracy may be able to operate, and even allay disenchantment, in a socially imperfect capitalist system. But democracy cannot operate in a collective economy. It is not a conceivable trade off."[23] His argument is that democratization can only occur in a liberal economy—by which he means a market economy based on private property—because only such an economy can provide citizens with the resources to compete in the political arena. Agree or disagree, his position is that only in the context of "already existing capitalism" can a state provide its people with the political possibilities for defending their economic rights in the future—in exchange for the economic sacrifices that may be necessary during a transition period.

Di Palma's reasoning also forces one to question Przeworski's argument in *Democracy and the Market* about comparability, particularly since Przeworski states that the "central difference between Eastern Europe and Latin America was the manner of allocating resources and, to a lesser extent, the frequency of administered pricing."[24] What Przeworski is in fact arguing is that the central difference between the two sets of countries was that Latin American states had a market system already in existence under authoritarianism and Eastern European countries and the Soviet Union did not.

Control over property and resources—be they individually or collectively owned—is the mechanism through which independent groups either allied with or opposed to a regime can retain or reestablish their place in a nonauthoritarian system. At the same time, a successful transition depends upon the property and power of the dominant groups being protected from redistributive programs. Yet in the case of the former Soviet Union, any attempt to move away from authoritarianism had to do exactly what the authors cited above argue would be fatal to all other transitions: such a move had to challenge and reformulate the very structures of property and power in order to "create" identifiable, politically viable groups that would support the efforts of those figures within the regime attempting to make the transition and give such groups the resources to make that support effective. According to the postulates derived from other transitions, a successful move away from authoritarianism toward democracy in Soviet-style systems would be virtually impossible.

The Soviet system, and to a large extent the Russian system that has followed it, embodied not only state control of the economy and the political system, but also state control—either directly or through organizations such as factories, schools, trade unions, or collective farms—of housing, daycare, medicine, social welfare, and other aspects of what in the Soviet Union was called "the social sphere." As a result, not only people's material interests, but their social values, cultural norms, and even their notions about acceptable forms of change were and remain connected to the state writ large. This being the case, any attempt to reform the Soviet system had to include redistributive mechanisms that simultaneously embraced the political, economic, social, and cultural spheres if they were to succeed. These spheres of Soviet life were thoroughly interdependent, as they are in any system; unlike in capitalist systems, however, the state claimed all these spheres as its own and provided the sole framework for most of the major political struggles concerning them. Sovietology and comparative communism as particular fields of study were predicated on the fact that communism represented a historically unique political economy and social formation. It is precisely in the relationship of these spheres to each other and to the state that the uniqueness of both of these systems and their transitions is located. It was only by transferring property and power from the state to society in all these areas that a move away from authoritarianism could succeed in Russia. Gorbachev never managed to implement such a program; as of 1998, Yeltsin had failed to do so as well.

Transition theory, too, seems unable to provide an analysis that embraces the interconnections of the political, economic, social, and cultural aspects of the Soviet Union's and Russia's movement away from communist authoritarianism. As Valerie Bunce noted,

> in southern Europe and Latin America, *the* issue was democratization; that is, a change in political regime. Indeed, the circumscribed character of political change in southern Europe and Latin America is one reason why students of comparative democratization could reduce democratic transitions to a process involving interactions among a handful of political elites. By contrast, what is at stake in eastern Europe is nothing less than the creation of the very building blocks of the social order.[25]

Creating these building blocks demands drastically changing the lives of millions of people in the former Soviet Union and Eastern Europe.

As careful and nuanced as any specific analysis of transition in a *capitalist* state may be, reforming an economy along existing principles or changing only a political regime is not equivalent to the simultaneous transformation of the political, economic, and social foundations of a system. Among scholars of the former communist world, and among comparativists who have turned their analytical focus east since the collapse of communism, the debates over transition and democratization theory acknowledge at some level that these cases are different. The question is how different. While not wishing to caricature the literature, models of regime change that are subsumed under the rubric of transition theory are ill equipped to analyze the changes taking place in Russia, and the effects and implications of these changes on the theoretical or practical level. The basis for this general critique is reinforced by examining the arguments of transition theory on more concrete subjects: in this case, on the role of social groups in transition and of labor in particular.

Antiauthoritarianism and Labor Politics

One of the central questions during transitions is what policy the regime will adopt concerning labor, and what the workers will do in response. The primary reason that this issue is so important is that in virtually all authoritarian systems—capitalist and noncapitalist alike—the labor relations system is highly skewed against labor, and therefore the level of worker resentment against the regime and the managerial elites is likely to be relatively high. Consequently, labor's demands for redress in the form of both political and economic redistribution of powers are also likely to be far reaching.[26] After examining the experiences of a number of countries, analysts of transitions have concluded that this situation must be mitigated, because if the expectations of labor were met the potential for a backlash would be greatly increased. These analysts argue that workers must be convinced of the need to put their economic demands on hold and to moderate their political demands if the transition is to succeed.[27] This is of course the logical concomitant of the injunction discussed above to focus on institutions and avoid policies that threaten the vested interests of powerful economic actors that support the authoritarian regime.

The underlying assumptions of this argument mirror those made at the macrolevel. The argument assumes the existence of an authoritarian capitalist system, in which neither labor nor business is entirely subsumed by the state. While state-owned industries may exist in capitalist states (and may even constitute a fair percentage of the industrial sector),[28] state-run companies still function within a capitalist market system, and the market system and private property are supported and defended by the state. Workers are subject to the vagaries of this system, but they also retain some independence from the authoritarian regime as such. Even if the authoritarian regime takes on certain corporatist traits,[29] such as co-opting unions and business organizations into state-sponsored mechanisms for conflict resolution, there is still a recognition that these organizations have an existence apart from the state (otherwise there would be no need to co-opt them). The same would hold if the authoritarian regime acted to crush union resistance or ban unions altogether. Neither authoritarian leaders nor analysts of these systems assume that the interests of the state, business, and labor are coterminous; both do assume, however, that labor will be an important, independent political force during a period of transition.

The general prescription among analysts in favor of limiting transitional policies to the design of political institutions logically implies that the question of altering existing labor relations systems should be left off the agenda, even if labor organizations raise it. The potential for conflict over this issue is substantial, given that attempts to alter the labor relations system invariably challenge management's traditional rights in a capitalist system to control the organization of the workplace.[30] Thus, it is not surprising that radical proposals for worker representation or self-management reforms are so problematic for transitions in this context.

On the other hand, most discussions of labor rights imply that there is both a "historical memory" of the rights that previously did exist and a recognition—no doubt a grudging one on the part of economic elites—that at least some of these rights must be restored if a transition of any kind is to move forward. Due to the structures of authoritarian capitalism, however, it is possible to make at least a formal distinction between political rights in the system as a whole (that is, contestation and participation) and economic rights affecting the workplace (that is, redistributive mechanisms). The first are permitted, the second are not. In what one analyst describes as the "greatest challenge to the transitional regime,"[31] the leaders within the regime who are pushing the transition must control and channel labor activism in "acceptable" directions and labor must agree to limit its demands in order to avoid a potential backlash from regime hard-liners, economic elites, or a combination of both.

In the context of the system of labor relations and worker politics that existed in the Soviet Union, the above propositions are inapplicable because most of the assumptions on which they are based were false. First of all, workers, capitalists, and the state did not appear as separate entities with diverse interests and varying but independent resources on which to base collective action. In the Soviet case, virtually everyone worked for the state, and their resources depended on maintaining their positions within that apparatus. Take Soviet trade unions as an example: they were neither co-opted by the state nor repressed by it. The Soviet regime very early on destroyed what independent unions there were; in the late 1920s, Stalin executed the independently minded leadership of the Soviet-era unions, and then re-created unions whose only legitimacy derived from delivering whatever benefits the party/state allowed. In addition, the unions were reorganized by place of work rather than by craft, and everyone became a union member—including the enterprise director and all members of management. Finally, the ideological claim made by the regime that the dictatorship itself was the leading representative of the proletariat was pounded into the heads of Soviet workers with the full force of the regime's formidable propaganda apparatus, and any organizing of "oppositional" workers was considered traitorous by definition. In light of this, it is not hard to understand why workers found it difficult to construct a "usable past" on which to base collective action in the present.

Second, if workers in authoritarian capitalist systems have good reasons to assume that they will be better off after the transition and, therefore, that supporting it is the logical choice, workers in Soviet-style systems find reasons and choices that are not so clear. As a result, worker mobilization in favor of a transition from authoritarianism, which analysts of the authoritarian-capitalist system describe, is not a foregone conclusion in state-socialist systems. While it is true that the labor relations system was just as tyrannical in Soviet-style systems as in authoritarian capitalist ones, Soviet workers had guaranteed employment and many—particularly in the heavy and extractive industries—were relatively well off compared to others in their society. This complicates matters. In authoritarian capitalist systems, workers have to put economic demands on hold during a transition in order to secure political rights, which they can then use to struggle for economic gains they had no hope of achieving under the authoritarian system. In Soviet-style systems, workers have to sacrifice economic security even to gain the political rights necessary to struggle for their economic interests.

By far the most striking difference between labor politics in the two types of systems is that in both the Soviet system and in postcommunist Russia, it is difficult for labor to know whom to fight in the first place. Should workers direct their efforts against local management, the central ministries, the Party (in the case of the Soviet Union), the state institutions, the official trade unions? All of the above? Are the radical reformers or the conservative elements more likely to serve workers' interests? The cause of the confusion is the nature of the labor relations system itself. In the Soviet case, there was not a bourgeoisie, supporting and supported by an authoritarian regime in a market system, as distinct from the state as both are from labor. In the Soviet industrial system all workers, as well as managers, bureaucrats, party bosses, and trade union officials, ostensibly had the same boss: the state. So, where should opposition be directed?

It was difficult to determine from the shop floor exactly who within the elites controlled resources, just as it was difficult to determine what the interests of various groups were, and what power they had to subvert or support the process. In the post-Soviet case, some of the players have changed, but the problem remains. The Communist Party bosses are gone, but the representatives of the new party of power are no less a problem. And it is still no clearer whom one is dealing with now that there are scores of directors of pseudoprivatized but quasi-governmental enterprises and joint-stock companies, many of whom are directly involved in the central governing apparatus of the ruling elite. Given the particularities of the labor relations system under state socialism and in the later period, one cannot necessarily make the same assumptions about the role of labor in a transition process that are made by transition theorists using models derived from the experience of authoritarian capitalist regimes. Conditions in authoritarian capitalist regimes and Soviet-style regimes are fundamentally different, and the regime's approach to these issues and the workers' responses and initiatives reflect these differences.

Gorbachev, who intended to make a transition to "democratic socialism," tried to empower workers in factories at the expense of managerial and ministerial elites. Emphasizing political inclusion at the workplace would make workers feel they had a stake in the economic well-being of their factories, thus encouraging workers to give up a tendency to "withdraw their efficiency"—that is, the control they had over the shop floor and the pace and quality of production[32]—in exchange for such inclusion. No less important, the leadership adopted this program in order to establish a new foundation for the legitimacy of the Soviet system and its leaders, based on the reformers' sponsorship of the transition process. When Soviet leaders came to the conclusion that this was unworkable, they tried to give the old managerial elites more power vis-à-vis both the central authorities and the workers that they managed.

On the other hand, the Russian government since 1992 has managed to consolidate the power of the old Soviet industrial nomenklatura through its shock therapy and privatization policies. Even as it tried to disempower portions of the old elites in favor of new private interests, domestic and foreign, it left much of the old industrial system and its structures ailing but intact. At the same time, Yeltsin's government has virtually ignored workers and shut their organizations out of any meaningful participation in the process of change. Workers have responded by becoming more and more polarized regarding democratization and economic reform, because none of the programs has succeeded in extricating Russia from its economic and political crisis.

The fundamental reason that both Gorbachev's and Yeltsin's policies failed to pull Russia out of its economic and political crises was that these policies never resolved the problem of who would control large-scale, nationalized property and the socioeconomic infrastructure that was rooted in this property and depended on the goods and services produced by it. From the drafting and implementation of the *Law on the State Enterprise (LSE)* in 1987 through the strikes of 1989–1991 and beyond into the post-Soviet conflicts over privatization and control of social insurance funds, who would have the final say on the disposition of the products, wages, social welfare benefits, profits, and the actual plant and equipment of Soviet factories has defined the politics of industrial reform.

Although I will argue in subsequent chapters that labor radicalism in reference to issues of property rights was beneficial rather than problematic for democratization in Russia, the central point here is that for transitology as regime change, this should never have been an issue in the first place. For transitology as a model of economic reform strategy, the issue of property was of course central. But herein lies the problem. The connection between these two versions of transitology, and more importantly their connection to the underlying issue of what either model means for society, is either not made or is seriously underanalyzed.[33] This is not to argue that the wide range of research that goes by the name transition theory does not address social questions, but rather that how it addresses them is determined by the nature of the cases and the theoretical assumptions guiding the work. As the preceding discussion on labor in transition illustrates, transition theory's view of labor and what labor should do simply does not make analytical sense in the Soviet and Russian case.

From Transitology to Post-Soviet Political Economy

The preceding analysis of the changes taking place in Russia, predicated on the idea that it is necessary to examine simultaneously the political, economic, social, and cultural elements of these changes, is grounded in recent scholarship on the political economy of transitions. This literature is based on a series of assumptions concerning the close relationship between politics and economics that attempt to counterbalance transition theory's overemphasis on the political and the contingent.[34] The first assumption is that the socioeconomic structure of any system "constitutes an essential point of departure for understanding politics, including the politics of regime change"; second, that support or opposition to change "will depend upon how economic policy and performance affect the income of different social groups"; and third, that "it is impossible to derive political or policy outcomes from economic cleavages and interests without consideration of the institutional context in which groups operate."[35] While these assumptions may seem obvious, they have not in fact been made by many transitologists studying Russia. Adopting such assumptions, however, makes it possible to avoid the dual reductionism that comes from focusing too narrowly on either "politics" or the "economy" decontextualized from the system as a whole. In the Russian case, examining either the formal institutions of electoralism, branches of government, and the constitution or the aggregate indices on privatization, monetary policy, and investment might lead one to conclude that Russia is a democratic capitalist state. Analyzing the way these discrete parts function to structure political and economic life, particularly in this case the life of Russia's workers, severely undercuts the notion that Russia is either democratic or capitalist.

The problem with much of the literature on Russia's transition is its teleology. There is an embedded assumption that to analyze Russia is to analyze the political economy of *democratic* transitions rather than the political economy of postcommunism. The question of what kind of political economy and social formation is in fact emerging in Russia should be a matter for analysis, not faith.[36] In order to determine where Russia is coming from and where it might be going, this book examines the political economy of the Soviet Union and Russia, and in particular its labor relations system, over time. The chapters that follow look at the question of how the socioeconomic conditions of the Soviet Union and Russia affected the timing and content of policies designed to alter the old regime, not only from the perspective of how these conditions affected elite behavior, but also how they conditioned social responses to the policies adopted—particularly working-class responses. The focus of the analysis is industrial policy, which in the Soviet Union and Russia has been, from the time of the Bolshevik revolution onward, the example par excellence of "politicized" economy. Examining the shop-floor effects of industrial policy, in addition to its design and implementation, will provide a much clearer sense of whether and to what extent putatively transformative policies had transformative effects. Beginning in the Stalin period and continuing through the Yeltsin years, the analysis will focus on those policies—political, social, and economic—that structured and attempted to alter the political economy of the industrial sector. In each period, strong ideological models and presuppositions guided the design of policy, but the institutional context in which the policies had to be implemented led to serious unintended consequences. In the pre-perestroika period, industrial policy, guided by an authoritarian-statist ideology,[37] was intended to control labor while maintaining the stability and viability of the system as constructed in the Stalinist period. Under Gorbachev, industrial policy was guided by Gorbachev's own brand of democratic-socialist ideology and was intended to create a sort of Soviet socialist-style state corporatism. Under Yeltsin, policy in this area, guided by an almost Friedmanesque version of "liberal capitalism," was intended to create simultaneously the conditions for "primitive capitalist accumulation" *and* the bases for workers to defend their interests in a "normal" way—that is, through contracts and collective bargaining.

The chapters that follow provide the empirical basis for a critique of transition theory and for an alternative view of the political economy of post-Sovietism. Chapter 2 is a historical analysis of the labor relations system from Stalin to Brezhnev. The chapter shows that although the old Soviet system remained stable and viable for many years, by the early 1980s the warning signs of decline were increasingly evident to the Soviet leadership. The economic and social system became sclerotic, and workers, while outwardly controlled, took advantage of their institutional position and withdrew their efficiency from production. Chapters 3 through 5 cover the Gorbachev period and its attempts to reform the labor relations system. The central arguments in these chapters reveal that when Gorbachev took over the Soviet Union and tried to reform it, he weakened the central planning system through democratization but did not succeed in replacing the old system with anything coherent. Gorbachev's industrial policies did empower workers to a certain degree and politicized them even more, but did so without actually giving them enough power to overcome those who opposed Gorbachev's ideas, much less to serve as the foundation of a democratic socialist state. Gorbachev ended up creating a kind of negative state corporatism, in which all sides had sufficient power to paralyze the reform process without having any strong incentives to cooperate in bringing it to fruition. Gorbachev's policies also set in motion a struggle within the working class over the nature of labor organizations, and this has had an enduring effect on working-class identity in Russia.

Finally, chapters 6 and 7 examine Yeltsin's industrial policies, which by 1998 had created an odd hybrid of new pseudocapitalist structures grafted onto old Soviet ones. What appeared to be evolving was a type of authoritarian, truncated, and anarchic state capitalism. On the one hand, political, economic, and social struggles became ever more concentrated within enterprises, localities, regions, and industrial sectors, all of which were engaging in beggar-thy-neighbor policies. On the other hand, due to the specificities of privatization and other policies, all of these actors remained closely bound to the state through subsidies, state shareholdings in enterprises, and political connections. The evidence suggests that Yeltsin's government attempted to construct a version of state corporatism, but if corporatism in the political science sense is defined as a system designed to control or eliminate conflict and chaos, in the Russian case it has rather become the framework for the continuation and intensification of conflict and chaos. This hybrid system created a bifurcated mode of production, not capitalist but no longer Soviet, that led to differentiated relations of production within and among sectors of the economy. Such duality accounted in large part for the volatility and contradictory nature of labor politics in Russia by the fall of 1998.

The institutional realities of the Soviet and Russian labor relations system remain grounded in the ambiguous and politically charged history of labor in the former Soviet Union. Equally, the reaction of workers to these realities remains conditioned by their understanding of the system in which they live. This understanding, in turn, is derived not only from their own life experiences, but also from "history" as they learned it in school, from older generations of workers, and from others in their social milieu. In order to understand events since 1985, it is essential to know the history of the Soviet labor relations system and the broader historical context in which that system developed.

CHAPTER TWO

The Dictatorship and the Proletariat

The Political Economy of Labor Relations from Lenin to Brezhnev

T he Soviet political economy, which has structured and limited the changes that have taken place in Russia since 1985, was the result of a combination of ideologically driven policies and unforeseen circumstances. The very terminology used to describe it—"command-administrative system," "totalitarianism," "state socialism"—was in some ways misleading, and at times ideologically driven, but nevertheless indicated that this system represented a historically new social formation. While analysts of Russia's transformation recognize at some level the difference in starting points between postcommunist and other transitional states, the central issue is the content of that difference. Examining the effect of the Leninist legacy on the political economy of an industrial relations system is crucial to demonstrating the particularity of post-Sovietism.

When the Bolsheviks took power in 1917, revolutionizing the industrial relations system was high on their list of priorities. The Party guarded its control over the industrial sector with vehemence: heavy industry was, more than any other sector of society, the key to building socialism. At the same time, the realities of production and politics on the factory floor were a constant reminder that having formal control was one thing, exercising that control to carry out industrial policy was another.

Throughout Soviet history, such control was the central problem of labor relations. The party/state's articulation of programmatic goals was an attempt to "control" the nationalized industrial sector and labor force, but there remained the basic question of how to get workers to produce. Building social-ism demanded sacrifices from the workers. As trade union leader Mikhail Tomsky stated at the seventh Trade Union Congress in 1926: "[T]he interests of today must be subordinated to the general class interests of tomorrow."[1] Because workers were concerned primarily about the interests of today, the party leadership faced a serious problem. Through what set of incentives and sanctions could the Party advance "the general class interests of tomorrow" without alienating the workers in whose name it claimed to rule?

The questions for workers proved no less vexing. How was it possible for workers to defend their interests and improve their lot given the demands of the party/state system? Labor politics in the 1920s and 1930s dealt as much with establishing the institutional context and the political boundaries within which this question could be answered as it did with methods of raising pro-duction. From the 1920s to Gorbachev's rise to power in 1985, labor politics consisted of an ongoing struggle between workers and the party/state system over the preservation or alteration of those institutions and boundaries to the advantage of one side or the other.

Understanding the Soviet labor relations system and the reasons it proved so difficult to change demands much more than a knowledge of the institu-tions that formally constituted this system. The informal structures that work-ers and managers used to play the system and the attitudes about work that became ingrained over time are equally important. The behavior of Soviet workers and managers was the result of both the institutions of the labor rela-tions system and the chaotic circumstances of Soviet industrialization, partic-ularly during the Stalinist period. The habits and attitudes that constituted shop-floor culture in Soviet factories have proved as difficult to eradicate as the institutions themselves.

"Face to Production": Labor Relations and Stalinism

As tumultuous and difficult as the first decade after the revolution was for Soviet workers, it was the Stalinist period that saw the creation of the labor relations system that would last until Gorbachev came to power in 1985. Af-ter the Russian Civil War and throughout the 1920s, the party leadership was deeply divided over the question of how to industrialize Russia. By 1928, some in the leadership continued to support the market-oriented structures of Lenin's New Economic Policy (NEP), which was introduced in 1921 and served as the basis of party policy throughout the 1920s, while others ques-tioned the legitimacy of the NEP altogether. The outcome of these "industri-alization debates" is well known. Stalin defeated Bukharin and set in motion the crash industrialization drive that threw the labor relations system into tur-moil: the all-out push for industrialization, the sudden influx of millions of peasants into old and new factories, and the atmosphere of constant suspicion that accompanied the introduction of the first five-year plan left nothing of the NEP system intact. The immediate effects of Stalin's industrialization drive on the working class were dramatic. During the years of the first five-year plan the number of workers in heavy and light industry doubled, and the number of construction workers increased fivefold.[2] As millions of peasants were forced into factories and new construction projects began around the country, the workforce became highly mobile both geographically and within the factory. Older, skilled workers improved their positions and young, better-educated workers—many of whom were zealous Party and Komsomol members—took over "leading positions in production."

Stalin's industrialization drive diluted the core of the old proletariat and "ruralized" the factory, wreaking havoc on productivity and discipline and causing what Hiroaki Kuromiya has called a "crisis of proletarian identity."[3] If during the NEP many workers resented the management-oriented policies of the Party that were primarily geared to increasing production, at least they knew who played what role in the labor relations system.[4] Under Stalin, the roles were challenged and frequently changed as the regime struggled to find a system of labor relations that would help accomplish the miracles required by Stalin's obsession with forced-pace industrialization.[5] As was the case with the Stalinist system more generally, two competing strands of labor policy—the drive for productivity and the ideologically driven programs to include workers in management—were taken to extremes.

The Party began to attack managers during the Shakhty affair of 1928, in which a number of foreign and "bourgeois" Soviet engineers were accused and convicted of sabotage. Relations on the shop floor deteriorated because many workers saw the Shakhty affair as a signal from the Party to launch an all-out assault on management. At the same time, however, the Central Committee of the Party in 1929 passed a resolution reaffirming the policy of one-man management, with Lazar Kaganovich saying that "the earth should tremble when the director walks around the plant."[6] Directors were given sweeping new powers to discipline workers, and the unions—firmly under Stalin's control since the purging of Tomsky—were instructed to "turn their face to production," which meant among other things explaining to workers the necessity of one-man management.[7]

Institutionalizing this policy, however, proved much more difficult than promulgating it. During the early years of the industrialization drive, control over the localities was far from perfect. In 1930, party documents spoke of "continuing anarchy in enterprises" and of "direct interference of social organizations in the work of directors and attempts of the administration to avoid responsibility." In many factories, the directive on one-man management was virtually ignored.[8]

Avoiding responsibility did not save managers from the first wave of purges in the early 1930s. The ease with which a person could be denounced as a "wrecker" undermined the effectiveness of the directive. It was not difficult for a disgruntled worker to charge an engineer with malfeasance in response to the latter's attempt to exercise his new powers of command in the factory. In spite of the official policy against "spets-baiting" (specialist baiting) many managers felt harassed, and this encouraged them not to take responsibility lest the situation worsen further. Stalin made temporary peace with the technical intelligentsia from 1932 to 1935,[9] but attacks on them started up again with the onset of the Stakhanovite movement in the autumn of 1935, only to change again in 1941 due to the exigencies of war.

Finally, the involvement of the Party in industry continually undermined one-man management. While local Party committees interfered in directors' business, it was the central authorities who produced the taut plan targets that managers had to meet, who pressured and at times removed managers for actual or perceived failures, and who either initiated or encouraged policies such as the shock-work movement and Stakhanovism that disrupted production and forced directors to alter factory operations. Having eliminated the market and incentive structures of the NEP, Stalin in effect encouraged directors to rule as despotic "little Stalins" through one-man management. This policy remained the official line throughout the Stalinist period, and even after Stalin's death the power of the Soviet factory director remained immense. At the same time, the Party had to pressure managers to use their powers as the Party saw fit, and this required constant violations of one-man management. It was not until after World War II that something of a stable condominium was reached. The prewar Stalinist system was a period of mass mobilization, not only in the political sense as commonly understood, but also in the sense of mobility—upward, downward, and sideways. In equal measure, Stalinism on the shop floor meant pressure from all sides to produce more and to cut costs; and when all else failed it meant unvarnished coercion of the kind most commonly associated with the period as a whole.

If, as William Chase suggests,[10] the Party opened Pandora's box by encouraging worker activism, the Party also spent the 1930s trying to structure that activism through a series of campaigns aimed at increasing productivity. Whereas all of these campaigns—shock work, socialist competition, the collective contract campaign, counterplanning, Stakhanovism—had their own particularities, they were all of a piece in the goals they tried to accomplish. These mobilization campaigns strove to increase productivity by breaking down what Stalin and his supporters throughout the industrial system saw as the main obstacles to industrialization: industrial bureaucrats, recalcitrant managers, the older generation of skilled workers, and the "backward" workers recently arrived from the countryside.[11] And these campaigns were not mere creations of the Party's economic departments and propaganda machinery: many workers, mostly young, better educated than their peers, and relatively highly skilled, initiated these movements and were their most avid supporters.[12]

The Stakhanovite movement, initiated by the record coal production shift of a Donbass miner, was the last great worker mobilization drive of the Soviet era and, like the shock-work movement before it, was a political and cultural phenomenon as well as an economic one. Stakhanov's record shift was almost immediately surpassed, and soon record shifts were being set in different industries all across the country. In economic terms the movement as a whole was of questionable effectiveness, just as shock work and socialist competition were, and it created unique problems in industries where it was introduced.

Stakhanovism was politically important, however, not only as an alleged example of the superiority of the Soviet system, but also as a means through which Stalin revived his drive against managerial and technical cadres in 1935. The renewed pressure on scientific and technical workers was different in political terms from the specialist baiting of the late twenties and early thirties, insofar as it was directed against the "red" specialists, who were presumably more loyal to the regime than the old "bourgeois" managers. If even those who were products of the Stalinist system were not safe, then no one was secure.

Stakhanovism coincided with the height of the Terror of 1936–1939, and in one important sense the Terror and Stakhanovism were two sides of the same coin. Stakhanovism was designed to encourage increased productivity from below, while the Terror hung like the sword of Damocles over the head of any manager, technical specialist, party official, or trade union functionary who stood in the way of workers that adopted Stakhanovite methods. Stakhanovites, whose prestige and privileges were totally dependent upon the goodwill of the Stalinist regime, were particularly vociferous in their support of the purges.

There is little evidence regarding the attitudes of ordinary workers to the purges, but large numbers of workers took advantage of the atmosphere of denunciation and fear to get back at their bosses. Although the attacks on specialists may have induced in workers the feeling that they had a new means of altering the power structure on the shop floor, such attacks also had the effect of reinforcing fear of responsibility. This fear, in turn, served to undercut the goals that Stakhanovism was meant to achieve.

Finally, the Stakhanovite movement can be seen as yet another chapter in the development of working-class differentiation in the Soviet Union. Both the shock-work movement and Stakhanovism were a means through which the "new proletarian forces"[13] brought forward by Stalin's revolution from above moved from the shop floor into management, the Party apparatus, or other professional work—helping to strengthen the social base of the Stalinist system in the process. This upward social mobility and the prestige that accompanied it were supplemented by direct material rewards, the importance of which were considerable in a society of scarcity such as the Soviet Union in the 1930s.[14]

If the ideal type of labor relations system in this period was strong one-man management combined with mass worker involvement through mobilization campaigns, joined in the cause of socialist construction, the reality on the shop floor was quite different. The one economic effect of these movements that most students of the subject seem to agree on is that they disrupted the economic functioning of the shop floor, long-term effects notwithstanding. Organizing such campaigns in most cases required special preparations, such as making sure that the shock workers had all the supplies necessary to engage in continuous production. Due to the tautness of plans and supplies at the factory level, this usually meant that other workers on the same shift did not have adequate means at their disposal.[15] The problem was compounded by the fact that in the course of these movements, machines and tools—not to mention workers—were overtaxed, leading to breakdowns, delays, and increased injuries, all of which had detrimental effects on productivity.

Managers and workers adopted various strategies for dealing with the pressures of mass mobilization. As Lewis Siegelbaum noted of Stakhanovism, this movement "evoked not only enthusiasm and resistance" but also "maneuvering and accommodation,"[16] and it is this latter element that had the most lasting effect on Soviet labor relations. Maneuvering took many forms, including the misrepresentation of enterprise activities as socialist competition or shock work, the exhibition of initial enthusiasm followed by the quiet abandonment of the movement, and the outright falsification of results. While the evidence is not exhaustive, reports from the period suggest that such maneuvering was widespread.[17]

In spite of the terroristic nature of Stalin's regime, there was also a measure of overt resistance to these mobilization campaigns in addition to the more subtle forms described above. Throughout the period there were verbal and physical attacks on shock workers, on managers who zealously pushed the programs, and on Stakhanovites, although the frequency of these types of events is unclear from the documentary record.[18] Given the dangers inherent in overt resistance, it is not surprising that for workers the most common way of dealing with these campaigns was to adapt. While there were many workers who were genuinely part of the vanguard of the mobilization campaigns, others simply declared that they, too, were shock workers. In so doing, they made the designations less meaningful. According to available statistics for the Soviet Union as a whole, at the beginning of the shock-work movement in 1929, 10 percent of workers were involved. Three years later, the number was near 71 percent; by 1932, being a shock worker was the norm rather than the exception. The increase in numbers coincided with the rise of complaints in Party and trade union documents about high levels of phony shock work.[19]

Available evidence demonstrates that there were massive numbers of workers who throughout the 1930s violated the norms of labor and conduct established by the regime. These workers were confronted by a considerable number of their fellow laborers and by citizens who, urged on by the regime, struggled to enforce these same norms. Such confrontations reflected the intensity of the politics of production during these years. Workers, managers, and the authorities all attempted to structure the labor relations system to their advantage, adopting multiple strategies in their attempts to accomplish this task. Workers were constantly reminded of their duty to help build socialism and were exhorted to expend every effort in the cause of socialist construction. The central focus of their lives, however, was the shop floor, the construction site, or the mine where they worked, and therefore the politics of the time were manifested first and foremost through the policies, campaigns, and conditions that affected life on the shop floor. The political meaning of what workers did and did not do must be judged in that light.

Workers under Stalinism responded to the policies of the regime by buying in and by bailing out. They bought in by becoming shock workers, engaging in socialist competition, making suggestions at production meetings, and adopting Stakhanovite methods. Workers bought in for a variety of reasons: revolutionary idealism, a belief in Stalin and his policies, simple materialism, expediency, and fear. Buying in also gave them a measure of bargaining power on the shop floor. Managers who made life difficult for workers or treated their attempts to participate with contempt could be and often were derided, pressured, denounced, fired, purged, and even shot. Such threats often resulted in a worker or group of workers securing something they wanted.

Similarly, workers bailed out in a variety of ways. Bailing out did not mean quitting the system, for that was not an option; rather, it meant refusing to accept the norms and standards of the system and the regime's justification for them. To be sure, much of the evidence of poor labor discipline, low productivity, and high labor turnover is explicable simply in terms of the chaos of the time, but such an explanation is much more compelling for the early post-NEP period than for the years that followed. Leaving jobs, "withdrawing efficiency,"[20] missing work, even drinking to excess both on and off the job were also signs of protest. They were not direct political challenges to the regime, but they were challenges to the system of labor relations that the regime was trying to create.

In this sense such actions served as indirect challenges to the legitimacy of the system, and the intensity with which the regime struggled against these phenomena is a good indication that it had correctly assessed the situation. "They tell us that we are the masters of the enterprise," said workers in the Lenzavod factory in Rostov-on-Don in 1930, "but on the shop floor they pressure us and command us. What the hell kind of masters are we then?"[21] By bailing out in all the varied ways they did, workers throughout the 1930s continued to ask that same question, as the disjuncture between the claims of the system and the reality of shop-floor life became ever more embedded during the days of Stalinism. As is the case with all systems of labor relations, the Soviet system under Stalin employed coercion—physical, material, social, and ideological—and, through a variety of institutions and policies, attempted to manufacture consent.[22] The specificities of the Soviet system, and consequently the particular problems that faced Soviet leaders when they tried to change this system, were grounded in the type of centrally directed economy that the Stalinist regime created, the methods used to build it, and the ideology called on to justify it.

By the time of Stalin's death, the boundaries within which workers and managers could engage in the "politics of production" had been set. In the labor relations system, the Party's bias in favor of hierarchy over inclusion, which first emerged during the NEP, was finally institutionalized by the end of the Stalinist period after the wild pendulum swings of the 1930s. The Party and the central planning apparatus defined the economic priorities. Managerial authority was reaffirmed, but unlike during the 1930s, the absence of any further mobilization campaigns made this authority somewhat more meaningful. This left workers with little room to maneuver, as the mechanisms for social mobility and the means to challenge perceived managerial abuses became increasingly less available.

The trade unions had long before ceased to be meaningful centers for the defense of workers' rights, having lost whatever claim to independence they had had when Mikhail Tomsky resigned from their leadership in 1929. Throughout Stalin's reign, the unions became progressively less responsive to workers' concerns and turned toward partnership in the regime's program of industrialization at any cost. The unions' main tasks were the mobilization and disciplining of their members, and the provision of social and material benefits to those who did what they were told.

For all this, however, the labor relations system by the end of the Stalinist period had also incorporated and routinized many of the features of the industrial system of the 1930s that undercut the effectiveness of that system and gave workers some leverage of their own. The emphasis on an ever-increasing industrial base, which drove the authorities to continue building large industrial enterprises, led to a perpetual shortage of workers. This problem was exacerbated by the taut planning system and ongoing supply difficulties, which led managers to hoard labor. Managers were therefore reluctant to use their authority to fire or otherwise discipline workers. This led predictably to the reappearance of high turnover rates, absenteeism, and other long-established forms of violations of labor discipline. The ability of workers to withdraw their efficiency was not only retained, it became the cornerstone of a negative form of workers' control on the shop floor, made all the more effective due to guaranteed wage rates and the lack of unemployment.

The regime continued to make demands on industry that both managers and workers somehow had to accommodate, and this led to a measure of collusion between management and labor reminiscent of that which drew the ire of the authorities in the prewar period. For example, the use of "ratchet planning" meant that neither workers nor managers had an interest in overfulfilling the plan targets by too much.[23] And because managers knew that the end of the month would bring with it the need to engage in "storming," they would often wink at violations of labor discipline by workers the rest of the time.

The labor relations system that had emerged by 1953 was made up of an odd amalgam of competing, and at times conflicting, elements: authoritarianism, inclusion, and collusion. Stalin's elimination of market mechanisms and of semiautonomous social groups and organizations that characterized the NEP necessitated the search for new mechanisms to force managers to direct and workers to produce. The mechanisms chosen were by no means the only ones possible, nor was the way they were combined the only option. Given the murderous nature of Stalin's authoritarianism, the frenetic pace of industrialization, and the legitimating ideology of the system in power, however, there was a certain grim logic to the choices and the combination.

Under Stalin, the authorities relied on the Terror and the draconian labor laws that went with it to compel industrial workers and managers to produce. These methods proved increasingly ineffective as the reconstruction period after World War II came to a close. The labor relations system might have been formally centralized, hierarchical, and authoritarian, but the politics of production on the shop floor were guided by the fact that the tenuous security enjoyed by management and the limited means of resistance available to workers meant that neither side could push the other too far without damaging the ability to satisfy the demands of the regime that ruled them both.

From "Normalization" to "Stagnation": Change and Continuity in Labor Relations under Khrushchev and Brezhnev

Upon Stalin's death in 1953, workers, managers, and the institutions of the party/state system were faced with the task of working, producing, and living in an industrial system born in revolution, devastated by war, and rebuilt at great cost in the twilight years of Stalin's increasingly rigid regime. In the area of labor relations, Stalin's death raised new questions: how would the system function without the Terror, without the breakneck pace, without the Stakhanovs, without Stalin as the driving force of Soviet power? Khrushchev and Brezhnev faced the same dilemma when attempting to make labor relations policy: how was it possible to spur economic growth, raise productivity, ensure innovation and simultaneously maintain political control in the absence of the coercive policies of the Stalin era?

Both Khrushchev and Brezhnev were equally dedicated to maintaining the main structural features of the Soviet economic system, but their perceptions of how best to improve that system differed in fundamental ways. Khrushchev embarked on a path that featured moderate economic reform combined with populist politics; the goal was to give workers material and ideological reasons to support the system. Brezhnev, on the other hand, initially favored a policy of technological modernization and increased managerial power, but as the Brezhnev period wore on, technocratic reform was replaced by benign neglect of the economy and tolerance of widespread corruption.[24]

Neither Khrushchev nor Brezhnev proved able or willing to change three basic features of the labor relations system that together combined to undermine their policies. The first was the constant labor shortage. Due to the rapid expansion of industry in the 1930s combined with the huge losses incurred in World War II, "managers were almost powerless to enforce rigid discipline" on the shop floor.[25] The second was the overcentralization of the planning system that led to constant bottlenecks and supply problems that disrupted production. This was the source of the well-known Soviet institution of "storming," which forced managers to hoard labor and gave workers some leverage over management on such issues as pay and labor discipline, since management needed workers' support to fulfill the enterprise's production plan. The third was the regime's commitment to full employment on ideological grounds; the security this gave workers was an additional obstacle to raising productivity.

The process of Stalinist industrialization and the structure of the Stalinist system created a political economy in which Soviet industrial workers lost the ability to influence, through their trade unions or any other means, the policy of the system as a whole and also lost the ability to organize independently or to pursue their interests collectively. The same process, however, had given workers the ability to withdraw their efficiency, and thereby influence the pace, quality, and growth of production on the shop-floor level. Much of the history of labor relations during the Khrushchev and Brezhnev years consists of attempts by the party/state apparatus to either harness this latter form of influence in the service of building socialism or to break it when doing so better served the regime's purposes.

With the abolition of the Terror, the Khrushchev leadership created "a climate of relative personal security" for workers and society at large for the first time since the 1920s.[26] Khrushchev's most important measure in terms of the labor relations system was the repeal of the repressive prewar Stalinist labor laws on 25 April 1956.[27] These laws had made it a crime for workers to change jobs without permission, to be absent from work, or even to be late to work, and they carried penalties ranging from reductions in pay to six months' corrective labor to imprisonment. The repeal of these laws once again made it possible for workers to change jobs legally either for personal reasons or as a means of protecting themselves from abusive managers. A new set of labor regulations in 1957 made it much more difficult for managers to fire workers without proper cause, and the trade unions were given some authority in guaranteeing the rights of workers.[28] Restrictions on workers that remained in place from Stalinist legislation after the 1957 reforms were finally repealed in 1960.

The repeal of these laws and the reestablishment of certain rights for workers helped to allay some of the resentment felt by workers toward the Soviet regime. The loss, however, of the coercive mechanisms that had driven workers to produce, however inefficiently, during the Stalinist period confronted the regime with the problem of finding something to put in their place.[29] The Khrushchev leadership followed a three-pronged strategy designed to rally the workers to the regime and improve economic performance.

The three elements of this strategy were a fundamental reform of the wage system, a restructuring of the trade unions, and a "revitalization" of mechanisms for involving workers in the management of production. Each reform had a dual nature: it was at once an act of de-Stalinization, which served a political purpose, and an act designed to stimulate labor productivity, which served an economic one. The two aspects of the reform were inseparable, for it was only by convincing workers that they had a stake in the system that the regime might succeed in convincing workers to stop withdrawing their efficiency.

The wage reform stretched from 1956 to 1962, beginning with heavy, high-priority industries and ending with light industry. It was designed to rectify the worst imbalances and inconsistencies of the Stalinist wage system, and simultaneously to create "an effective incentive system" that would permit greater control by the regime over the production process.[30] The results of the reform were mixed. It did away with some of the most glaring anomalies and injustices of the Stalinist wage system, and it increased the standard of living for some groups of workers.[31] The reform also succeeded in attenuating some aspects of the "essentially coercive" character of Soviet wage policy not only by raising base wages but also by eliminating progressive piece rates almost entirely.[32]

The wage reform made life somewhat easier for workers, but failed almost entirely as an economic stimulus. Managers and workers had developed systems of collusion that enabled managers to fulfill plans and workers to maintain earning levels in spite of low base wage rates and ostensibly high norms. Donald Filtzer compellingly argues that during the wage reform, management continued to act on the assumption that "earnings must not fall below 'established' levels—that is, those levels that prevailed before the reform or had come to be expected as normal over the ensuing years."[33] Maintaining wage rates was necessary to keep workers—especially skilled workers—quiescent: the continuing labor shortage, the renewed ability of workers to change jobs at will, and the persistence of supply problems and other externally generated pressures on plan fulfillment combined to force managers to find new ways around the reformed wage system. Maintenance of wage rates was achieved in countless ways,[34] and the overall effect was to create new anomalies in place of the old ones. The wage reform did little to weaken workers' control over the pace and quality of production at the shop-floor level.

As part of the wage reform, Soviet trade unions were given the right to participate in the adjudication of wage disputes and the right to approve norm revisions. This was part of a broader reform of the trade unions that was intended to make them more responsive to the needs of workers.[35] The reform of the trade unions served a number of purposes. First, the reform was part of the "democratization" process under Khrushchev: it was designed to create the impression that workers had a say in the events that governed the workplace. Second, it put more pressure on managers to adhere to established labor laws, thereby tempering one cause of worker dissatisfaction. On both counts, the reform was intended to convince workers that the new leadership was on the side of the proletariat. Although there is little agreement about how effective the unions were in reorienting their work during this period,[36] the reform clearly did serve one additional purpose: it returned the unions to an important place within the structural apparatus of the Soviet system. Like the reassertion of Party primacy after the dictatorship of the Stalin period, the reform of the trade unions served the institutional interests of an important section of the Soviet elite.[37]

The final element of Khrushchev's de-Stalinization of labor relations was the revival of mechanisms designed to increase worker participation in management. Unlike the great mobilization campaigns of the 1930s, however, the new methods of mobilization were never pushed to the point that they threatened to disrupt production seriously. The Party and state leadership under Khrushchev had witnessed the effects of mass mobilization during the 1930s and had determined that it was not an effective means of achieving the regime's objectives. As a result, these ostensibly "democratic" mechanisms became routinized and formulaic: they remained in force as levers of control, used at times by the Party, at times by management, and less frequently by workers themselves to put pressure on the other groups involved in the politics of production. The regime was loath to abandon them, for ideological and political reasons, but they lost much of their force as mechanisms for manufacturing consent or prompting opposition.

By the time of Khrushchev's ouster in 1964, a degree of normalcy had been achieved in the sphere of Soviet labor relations that had not existed in Soviet history. Wages had increased and a degree of logic had been introduced into their structure. Mass mobilizations and the political disruptions that had accompanied them were a thing of the past. Workers as individuals had regained many of the rights that had been lost under Stalin, and the trade unions had begun (if often haphazardly) to defend workers' interests in addition to carrying out production-oriented activities.

Khrushchev's reforms were inherently limited by the fact that the regime would not tolerate any form of independent collective action or organization on the part of workers,[38] and by the fact that even the "reformed" trade unions and production conferences remained under the tight control of the party/state system. In the end, these institutions reflected the elites' interests, which did not necessarily coincide with the workers' interests. The key issue remained the failure of these economic reforms to break the workers' ability to withhold efficiency. The Khrushchev leadership undermined the effectiveness of its own wage reforms by repealing Stalinist labor laws—in itself a progressive and humane act—in a labor-scarce economy governed by an ideology that refused to accept unemployment or the reestablishment of a labor market. The reforms were further weakened because the leadership rejected any form of destatization of property or other market mechanisms, continued policies that made dismissal of a worker extremely difficult, and failed to solve the pathologies of the planning system. Khrushchev's reform of the labor relations system had left workers for the most part better off, but it had failed to play its designated role in the solution of Soviet economic problems. On the contrary, the labor relations system continued to contribute to these problems in no small measure.

Whereas Khrushchev was given to sweeping reforms, Brezhnev adopted an approach that focused on gradualism and stability. The conservative reaction to Khrushchev's liberalism affected economic policy as much as any other area of policy making. The new leadership began by reversing many of Khrushchev's innovations. Most of his agricultural reforms were undone, the regional economic councils—which were the core of Khrushchev's decentralization program—were eliminated, the Party structure was reunified, and the central industrial ministries were reestablished.[39] These were the elements of Khrushchev's reforms that had most threatened the institutional interests of Soviet elites, and their reversal was the first step toward the policy of "stability of cadres."

Unlike these economic reforms, however, many of Khrushchev's reforms of labor relations remained. Brezhnev continued the effort to improve the wage system, the trade unions retained their renewed dual function of encouraging productivity and defending workers' rights,[40] and the mechanisms for drawing workers into management continued to function. These reforms had diminished worker resentment and helped to rationalize the labor relations system, but since they had not seriously threatened the power of any Soviet elites it made no sense to reverse them.

There was, however, a definite shift in emphasis concerning labor relations. Beginning with the Kosygin reforms in 1965, the leadership dropped the pro-worker rhetoric of the Khrushchev years and adopted a pronounced pro-management line. Propaganda attacks on managers declined, calls for labor discipline increased, and the Soviet leadership began to emphasis managerial professionalism and the determinative importance of science and technology for the further development of socialism.[41] In reality, the limited decentralization of authority that was actually included in the Kosygin reforms quickly undermined the reforms' effectiveness. The ministries retained effective control over enterprises under their jurisdiction and often issued orders "on a wide variety of topics supposedly within the competence of management."[42] Plans were constantly altered at the ministerial level, and because managers' and workers' bonuses continued to be based on plan fulfillment, the incentive to hide material reserves, limit plan overfulfillment, and hoard labor remained unchanged.[43] By the early 1970s, the decentralizing aspects of the 1965 reforms were a dead letter, and all that remained of the Kosygin reforms was the recentralized ministerial system.

The 1970s saw additional attempts by the leadership to improve the performance of the economy through administrative reorganizations of enterprise operations, but like their predecessors these reforms were limited in scope and ineffective. The Brezhnev leadership increasingly relied on imports to bolster the Soviet economy, using both the fortuitous rise in the price of oil and the hard currency derived from arms sales as a substitute for any further attempts to alter the basic structure of the economy or the labor relations system.[44] Massive amounts of money were invested in continued new production, which only worsened the already existing labor shortage but had no effect on the continuing downward growth rates of labor productivity and the economy.

From the 1950s, the Soviet labor force had become much more skilled and better educated, and none of these experiments addressed the problems or aspirations of Soviet workers in the 1970s. The centralized structure of the economy and the hierarchical nature of the labor relations system militated against workers being able to fully use their skills, achieve upward mobility, or use their greater education in the workplace. The increasing "hereditization" and improved education of Soviet workers encouraged them to identify themselves as workers with common interests. The continued existence of a neo-Stalinist labor relations system governing a labor force far different from the one it had been designed to control was equally conducive to increasing restiveness on the part of Soviet workers.[45]

The potential problems arising from this combination of factors did not go totally unnoticed by Soviet students of the labor relations system during the Khrushchev and Brezhnev years. There were scholars within the Soviet social science establishment who offered as a solution to these problems a more far-reaching form of workplace democratization than either the Khrushchev or particularly the Brezhnev leadership was willing to accept.[46] Debates over greater democratization of the workplace never came to dominate the political discourse on labor relations, however, and discussions about the role of the market under socialism that had taken place in the 1960s virtually disappeared from public view. Still, these debates and discussions continued, albeit quietly, throughout the Brezhnev period; by the late 1970s and early 1980s, prominent figures such as Abel Aganbegian and Tatiana Zaslavskaia had joined them.[47] By the time Gorbachev came to power, proponents of workplace democratization and markets—not necessarily the same people—had built up an impressive repertoire of arguments in support of their case.

Over the years, the Soviet leadership became more concerned with retaining power and maintaining social peace than with forcing people to work harder, and this position served as the foundation for the social contract between state and society during the late Soviet era. People worked as little as possible in the state sector and as much as possible outside it; the government did not interfere as long as people's activities were not outrageously illegal. Subsidies to state industries continued, wages increased, living standards improved, and in exchange, the vast majority of society remained quiescent and perhaps even grateful that the radical pendulum swings of the Stalin and Khrushchev years were behind them.[48]

This is not to argue that there were no workers who were conscientious, hard working, and believed in Soviet socialism, nor is it to argue that the pathologies of the labor relations system were mainly their fault. Rather, the point is that the post-Stalin leadership never found an adequate and acceptable replacement for the exceedingly coercive labor policies of the Stalin era. The Khrushchev and Brezhnev leaderships, to their credit, refused to turn the clock back to the early 1940s and its draconian labor laws. These leaders also, however, rejected two other possible options. First, they dismissed any proposals that might have led to genuine worker participation or the evolution of self-management institutions. Second, for both ideological reasons and reasons of personal power, they refused to entertain any form of marketization, which could have provided the threat of unemployment as a tool to increase worker discipline and productivity. In other words, democratic socialism was out, but so too was state capitalism. These options would have to wait for the arrival of Gorbachev and Yeltsin.

CHAPTER THREE

The Revolution Delayed

The Politics of Production Democracy, 1987–1990

The discussion of postcommunist political economy presented in chapter 1 began with the proposition that the nature and extent of party/state control over the Soviet system and the consequent need to design reform policies that redistribute power from the state to society in Soviet-style systems are what distinguish postcommunist states from other transitional systems. The emphasis on institution-building in transitology does not address the fact that social groups in postcommunist systems must in essence be reconstituted as agents and empowered through implementation of redistributive policies before institutions guaranteeing equal rights to contestation can be made effective. The content of these policies will be shaped by the ideological presuppositions of those involved in drafting them as well as by the structural and institutional context in which these policies arise.

The policy of "workplace democratization," represented by Gorbachev's 1987 *LSE* and the struggles surrounding the law's implementation illustrate the particularity of communist transitions. The Soviet Union presents an intriguing case because Gorbachev, who was not demonstrably unintelligent or unaware of the history of economic reform efforts in communist systems, decided to introduce a form of worker self-management that most analysts in the West rightly or wrongly regard as either economically unworkable, utopian, or unacceptable for ideological or political reasons. Why then did Gorbachev and his allies take this tack? The reasons were ideological, to be sure, reflecting Gorbachev's vision of "democratic socialism," but they were equally contextual and institutional, embedded in the structure of the political economy of Soviet industry described in the preceding chapter.

During the first eighteen months of his tenure, Gorbachev followed in the footsteps of his erstwhile sponsor Yuri Andropov, who forcefully advocated discipline, responsibility, and technical progress in the industrial sector. In a series of speeches in 1985 and 1986, Gorbachev and his advisers exhorted workers and managers to "accelerate economic and scientific progress" and "strengthen discipline" in the factories. This approach proved ineffective, and in early 1987 Gorbachev began to discuss seriously, in language reminiscent of Khrushchev's populism, new mechanisms to revive old ideas of "worker self-management" and "industrial democracy" as part of perestroika. The struggle over defining the limits of worker self-management became increasingly intense as political leaders, bureaucrats, managers, and workers began to realize that, in its most radical form, the policy of industrial democratization could cut to the core of managerial and nomenklatura power in the factory.

When Gorbachev came to the conclusion that reforming the Soviet system was impossible without the democratization of political and economic life at the factory level, the leadership attempted to design reforms that addressed both redistributive and institutional questions. Three key issues were involved in the design of these reforms: the type of institutions needed to guarantee workers' genuine participation; the adequacy of the empowerment mechanisms; and the level of acceptance by both elites and other social groups of the institutions and the extent of power redistribution.

The theory of workplace democracy was straightforward. Democratization at the workplace would put pressure on the recalcitrant industrial nomenklatura in the factories while ministerial inertia would be attacked from the top. Workers were to be given the right to elect their managers, a "council of the labor collective" (STK) would be established that would give workers a voice in factory management and decision making, and the rights of the trade unions would be expanded.

The debate over the provisions of the law dragged on for four months, plagued by turf battles between elites and arguments over how far democratization should be pushed. The final version of the law was basically a stalemate produced by three opposing forces: the reformers, who wanted to transfer substantial power to the labor collective; the industrial ministries, who wanted to retain their traditional control over industry; and the managers, who wanted substantial amounts of power transferred to them. Workers, who were soon to become a fourth force in this struggle, were not particularly vocal or organized, although those who did speak out generally sided with the reformers. The clearest example of this stalemate was that the new law granted various rights—to the labor collective and the enterprise council on one hand and to the administration on the other—that flatly contradicted each other. At the same time, the ministries and the Communist Party retained a myriad of mechanisms to interfere with the ability of both the labor collective and the administration to exercise those rights. The extent of these contradictions became clear when the law went into effect on 1 January 1988.

The period of 1987–1991 marked the most thoroughgoing attempt by the

Soviet leadership to reform the country's political economy based on a recognition of the particular linkage between political and economic power in a communist system. That linkage, consisting of the direct and immediate interdependence of political and economic power on a systemic level, preordained that change in these two spheres would take place simultaneously.

The dynamics of change in the political economy of communist systems is best viewed at the microlevel—in this case at the level of Soviet enterprises and the communities in which they are situated—because it is here that the building blocks of the social order take concrete form. In countries undergoing a change from authoritarian capitalism to "democratic" capitalism, such an analysis would indeed make little sense, since nothing of substance at this level is altered by the transition process. In the case of the former Soviet Union, however, the struggles and changes that have taken place at the microlevel have in profound ways structured the postcommunist political economy of Russia, its class structure, its power relations, and its politics.

The conflicts set in motion by the introduction of the *LSE* called into question the organizing principles of the Soviet socioeconomic structure as the struggle to define the meaning and set the limits of self-management shifted from the corridors of political power in Moscow to the shop floors of the industrial plants of the Soviet Union. As a mechanism to empower workers and advance the process of democratization, the enterprise law was seriously flawed: its provisions were contradictory and its language vague. The failings of the institutions included in the law were the result of the failure of the law's designers to address squarely the issue of who had ultimate control over industrial property. The law contained provisions that established who had the right to make decisions about individual enterprise operations, but no amount of tinkering with these provisions could solve the problems caused by the unresolved issue of property rights. On this point, most Western analysts of democratization and of Soviet labor politics agree. A majority of these same analysts,[1] however, make a fundamental mistake in assuming that the politics of implementing the enterprise law did not change the calculus of shop-floor power or have a long-term and ultimately positive effect on the democratization process. This assumption is demonstrably false.

At the shop-floor level, the contradictions and ambiguities of the enterprise law translated into ongoing battles for control over the institutions and procedures that were intended to make "production democracy" a reality. The analysis that follows is built around three case studies of the experience of self-management in industrial enterprises in Russia and Ukraine: the KamAZ Association, the Makhachkala Electronics Factory (Makhachkala Electric), and the Gorky mine.[2] The evidence derived from these case studies suggests that although Gorbachev's policy of self-management failed in terms of the leadership's programmatic goals, the larger goal of creating a constituency among workers for a transition from authoritarianism to democracy fared rather better. The evidence also indicates, however, that by 1991 a sub-

stantial sector of the Russian labor force remained either apathetic or antagonistic toward democratization and the market reforms to which it was increasingly linked.

Self-Management: Institutions and Issues

In all of the industrial enterprises affected by the enterprise law, the struggle over self-management focused on the same three issues that had animated
the debate over the law while it was being drafted: the relationship of the enterprise to the central ministry; the structure and authority of the enterprise
council; and the conduct of elections to managerial posts. The ideal self-managed enterprise, as seen by proponents of the policy, was one that was independent of any ministry, responsible for its own plans, finances, development,
supplies, and workforce. It was also an enterprise controlled by its collective,
through the mechanisms of the enterprise council and the election of managerial personnel. The combined effect of independence from the center and control from below would break the power of the nomenklatura at both levels and
give workers an interest in the economic well-being of their enterprise.

The imperfections in the design of the policy of self-management as reflected in the enterprise law and other official pronouncements made the effective implementation of production democracy difficult; the institutional realities of the Soviet labor relations system complicated matters still further. A
number of issues not directly related to the policy of self-management played
an important role in the fate of production democracy, the most important of
which concerned the labor code, access to information, the nature of shop-
floor culture, and property rights. Workers and other nonmanagerial members
of labor collectives were put at a serious disadvantage in the battles over self-
management because the law either did not or could not address these issues.

The Soviet labor code was more like a written form of social contract between the state and the workers than a set of laws pertaining to labor. The
code clearly delineated the rights and obligations of workers and managers,[3]
and discrepancies between provisions of the code and the enterprise law on
this point were never resolved. The code also contained provisions that
made it relatively easy for managers to discipline troublesome workers, and
there was nothing in the new enterprise law to prevent managers from using
these provisions against workers pushing for greater involvement in management.

Greater involvement in management for nonmanagerial personnel in factories required access to information on the activities of the enterprise, and
glasnost in this area was hard to find. The determining of plans, wage increases, infrastructure and social expenditures, and even the qualifications of
various candidates to managerial posts, demanded either data or someone
knowledgeable on the subjects willing to share such information with the collective or its representatives. Managers were the only people who had this information, so the success or failure of self-management in some measure

depended on their cooperation. This fact proved to be troublesome throughout the period in question.

The willingness of managers to use the labor code, combined with their monopoly on the information that allowed them to maintain control over labor collectives, led to the reluctance of many workers to challenge them. This situation reflected another reality of labor relations that the enterprise law did not, and could not, address: the tenacity of attitudes and habits that constituted "shop-floor culture" in Soviet factories. Managers were accustomed to operating in an authoritarian manner. As one Soviet economist put it: "The Soviet director is God, the Tsar, and the military commander rolled into one."[4] The workers, for their part, were used to managers behaving that way and over time had found their own methods of either buying into or bailing out of the system. The policy of self-management therefore had to struggle not only against its own inadequacies, but also against decades of tradition.

Two elements of shop-floor culture in particular militated against workers and managers accepting the reforms contained in the enterprise law, both of which grew out of the traumatic development of the Soviet industrial system under Stalin. Once again, this is a case in which the institutional context and the structure of the socioeconomic system directly affected the politics of change, and in a way that was peculiar to Soviet-style systems. The first element was an abiding distrust of any mechanism that the Party claimed was designed to enhance the "participation of the workers in management." These mechanisms—such as shock work, Stakhanovism, and the permanent production conferences—had always in the end been ineffectual in granting workers any meaningful influence. In addition, they had served to increase the pressure on workers to produce while at the same time disrupting the production process, which damaged the earning power of many production workers. Workers therefore had a built-in historical bias against structures such as the enterprise councils.

The second was the fear of losing the ability to engage in the informal types of shop-floor bargaining that the pathologies of the planning system had made a permanent feature of industrial life. The self-management provisions of the enterprise law were part of a larger reform package that promised to link wages more tightly to productivity and to change work rules, the planning system, and the wage system in such a way as to reduce workers' ability to play the system to their advantage. Furthermore, a related part of the reform program was designed to make workers, through brigade self-management councils, responsible for determining the bonus rates of their fellow workers. This kind of "self-policing" also smacked of previous campaigns to intensify labor discipline and squeeze more productivity from workers. These were formidable obstacles, indeed, particularly because workers saw few guarantees in the new law that the mechanisms would not be used against them.

The absence of such guarantees was not surprising, because the legislation did not directly confront the question of who controlled state property, and this question came to play an increasing role in the restructuring of industrial relations after 1987. The policy of self-management was included as part of a law on state enterprises, but soon after the adoption of this law the government began to experiment with a series of changes in the forms of state property. Some of these changes allowed bureaucrats and managers to argue that certain enterprises were no longer state enterprises in the technical sense. This caused further confusion regarding the rights of labor collectives, and gave management yet another mechanism to maintain control of enterprises.

The enterprise law and its self-management provisions were designed to create a new political economy in Soviet factories, one that would serve as the foundation for democratization and—once the transition was complete—for democratic socialism as the Gorbachev leadership understood that term. The issue was not whether there would be a redistribution of power in the process, for that was inevitable. The central question was who would gain and who would lose that power. And the central problem for workers was that the contradictions in the legislation, combined with the existing structures of the labor relations system discussed above, meant that self-management was open to interpretation and left in place structural biases that worked in favor of management's interpretation of the policy.

Davids and a Goliath: Workers, Self-Management, and KamAZ

The Kama Order of Lenin Association for the Production of Heavy Transport Vehicles (KamAZ for short) was a monument to the aspirations of the Brezhnev leadership: it was built with state-of-the-art German technology in the early 1970s and was an archetypical example of Soviet-style *gigantomania*. In a city of just over 200,000 people, KamAZ directly employed approximately 120,000. The collection of factories that made up KamAZ was virtually self-sufficient: raw materials came in one end, and finished trucks came out the other. It was the largest production facility of its kind, so important to the Soviet leadership that its director was on the nomenklatura list of the Politburo.

The city of Naberezhnye Chelny, the home of KamAZ, was a classic factory town. Most city services were funded by the KamAZ association; the majority of local officials at one time worked in the administration of KamAZ; even the bulk of the housing stock was owned by the giant industrial enterprise. As one worker put it, "this city was built to serve the factory. The wide boulevards you see were designed not so people could stroll after work, but so they could get back and forth from the factory more quickly. Workers were viewed as an aspect of the production process, not as residents of a city."[5] The relationship between the factory and the city defined the attitudes of workers and managers toward reform. In the Soviet and post-Soviet periods, the fate of KamAZ would determine the fate of the city and its residents.

For some, the experience of building the factories and the city around them was formative and exhilarating. The 1970s in Naberezhnye Chelny—like the 1930s in cities such as Magnitogorsk or Komsomolsk—was a decade of achievement. Nail' S. Nurmukhamedov, the Vice Director for Social Development at KamAZ, has worked in the city since 1973. He began as an engineer, became head of the KamAZ Komsomol and then moved on to the post of vice director of KamAZ. After that, he went to work for the city Party committee, and was elected president of the City Soviet before returning to KamAZ to take up the post of vice director. Describing the factory and the city during the Brezhnev years, he said "there were no conflicts because, well, we all breathed the same air. The Party led all aspects of the formation and building of KamAZ. Maybe it was an 'era of stagnation' in some places, but not here. Here it was a time of growth and development."[6] Nurmukhamedov's biography and opinions were shared by most of the city's and KamAZ's leaders. As he pointed out in the same interview, this did not mean that the KamAZ nomenklatura was necessarily against reform. But the reforms embodied in the policy of self-management were predicated on the view that the command-administrative system inherited from the Stalin era and solidified during the Brezhnev period—and by implication those who oversaw it—had failed, that radical change was necessary, and that the labor collectives had the right to carry out such change. But just as Nurmukhamedov rejected Gorbachev's diagnosis of the illness, the nomenklatura of the factory and city challenged his prescription for curing it. While the elites of KamAZ may have granted that the command-administrative system required an overhaul, they firmly believed that they had the right and the experience to control reforms that would affect life at KamAZ and throughout the city.

The close ties between the factory and Naberezhnye Chelny affected the views of workers as well. The numerous grievances that workers had about working conditions and other aspects of factory life were compounded by the fact that the city itself scarcely functioned. Public transportation between the factory and the city, as well as inside the city, was overcrowded, underfinanced, and irregular; stores were empty; violent crimes per capita were high (the city's gangs were nationally known); and streets and apartments were, to put it mildly, in disrepair.[7] All of these problems fueled worker discontent and found their way into the arguments over self-management. The policies and priorities—particularly financial—that were adopted by KamAZ influenced not only the life of a worker on the shop floor, but also the lives of workers and their families outside of work. Such a reality, so palpable in a city like Naberezhnye Chelny, was the subtext that framed the reform debate and process at KamAZ.

The fact that KamAZ was an association of many factories added a structural complication to Gorbachev's two key industrial reform policies. The first policy was economic decentralization, which was to be achieved primarily through *khozraschet,* or self-financing. The second policy was *demokratizatsiia,* or democratization, which in the industrial relations sphere was embodied by self-management through the council of the labor collective.[8] The policy of self-financing at KamAZ, however, raised not only the issue of the association's independence from the central ministry, but also the issue of factory self-financing within the association. Similarly, self-management at KamAZ entailed the creation of multiple councils and conferences at the association level and at the individual factory level. The organizational structure of KamAZ itself provided the setting for disputes over the distribution of authority within the association that involved both self-financing and self-management.

KamAZ faced the same problems as most other enterprises when it came to self-financing and ministerial control: while the association was expected to turn a profit, it was never given full control over funding or allowed to make final decisions regarding the disposition of even residual profits.[9] The fact that KamAZ produced heavy trucks also meant a high percentage of obligatory state orders, which gave the association little opportunity to make extra profit outside the state sector.

The problems between the center and the association were reproduced within KamAZ. One of the central goals of self-financing was to provide a mechanism for improved efficiency and higher productivity at every level. According to factory managers at KamAZ at least, this did not happen:

> Self-financing, and the economizing that was supposed to result at the shop level, has not happened because the funds are transferred to the factory level, where the shops [tsekh] have no control over them. So the shop heads and the workers don't see the benefit of working harder to economize, and the whole thing falls apart. The ministry interferes with the association, the association interferes with the factory, the factory with the shop, and the shop with the brigades.[10]

This meant that the elected self-management councils were deprived of an important mechanism for exerting control within the factory subdivisions due to the very structure of self-financing. This was an issue that was inextricably linked to the equally difficult problem of exerting control vis-à-vis management over decision-making processes at various levels within the association.

The idea that enterprise councils should share in the management of KamAZ and its factories and shops was greeted with hostility by some, elation by others, and optimistic skepticism by many. This division of opinion, however, did not fall neatly along the lines of management, technical specialists, and workers, for reasons that had to do with the size, wealth, and sectoral divisions of the KamAZ association. Opinions regarding the election of leading managerial personnel were similarly split.

The top managerial posts at KamAZ were important nomenklatura positions, and the people who held them were powerful, not only locally but regionally, and at times nationally as well. It is not surprising, therefore, that senior managers were critical of a policy that was designed to constrain their power and force them to answer to the representatives of the labor collective. KamAZ vice director Nurmukhamedov's view of "self-management reforms" was fairly typical of senior factory managers, both at KamAZ and elsewhere.

He argued that most managers "viewed the innovations sufficiently positively," but that "when everyone got involved, there was too much discussion and argument" about how to solve problems. In his opinion, "self-management . . . should mean economic independence and a normal economic system," rather than enterprise councils and elections.[11] The "positive innovations" were the decentralizing aspects of the Gorbachev leadership's industrial reform policy rather than those internal to the factory labor relations system.

No senior KamAZ official lost his post due to elections of managerial personnel or the actions of factory councils, but this did not reduce managers' dislike of the policy itself. Nurmukhamedov argued that workers began

> to elect people who were neither the most competent nor the most needed by the collective. . . . Personally, I have a very negative view of [this policy]. . . . A manager needs to be hired, on a contract basis, and must have both economic and juridical responsibility. He can't function if he can be voted out of office and someone else voted in.[12]

While there is no compelling evidence to support his claim that workers elected incompetent people, senior officials nevertheless went to some lengths to protect those managers who ran afoul of their respective councils.[13]

The president of the KamAZ association council, who was an engineer by profession and had been at the factory since the 1970s, typified the skeptical optimist in his view of self-management and of the institution of the enterprise council in particular. He argued that the entire self-management policy was an attempt by the nomenklatura (which for him included Gorbachev and his advisers) to "preserve its rights and property by improving the economy. The enterprise council was to take the heat for problems at the factories and be the focal point for workers' complaints." At the same time, he decided to get involved with the enterprise councils because, as he said, "those who were elected to it were those who were in favor of a just distribution of goods and services, and fair access for all to the decision-making process." In his view, the main role of the councils at KamAZ in the period up to 1989 was as "a forum for demands for just distribution" of bonuses, apartments, automobiles, and other scarce goods. This role began to change over time: "The enterprise councils started turning into 'councils of screamers.' This continued until early 1990, when we realized that there was less and less to distribute, that we had given it all out, and yet there was still no justice. We then turned the focus of the enterprise councils to the production of more goods so that we would have something to bargain with."[14] In other words, the main KamAZ council only began to take up issues of production and finance, which the initiators of the policy had seen as the central concern of the enterprise council, six months before a new enterprise law passed in 1990 gutted the self-management provisions of the original.

Gennadi Kirilov, who was an early organizer of workers at KamAZ and a line worker himself, agreed that the enterprise councils should have been a forum for demands for just distribution, but he held a very different view of how they had in fact developed and what had happened to them. He argued that the councils, as originally formed after 1987, were little more than another conduit for administration policy to be funneled to the workers. As a result, in early 1989 he and a group of other workers set up a temporary workers' committee, the goal of which was to alter the councils' memberships so that they could become mechanisms to provide, in Kirilov's words, "for the realization of our material interests." What Kirilov and his group wanted was a just distribution of those goods and services that were available but were under the control of the KamAZ administration.

In the view of Kirilov's group, the efforts of the temporary workers' committee were thwarted by the combined resistance of management and what Kirilov referred to as "the labor aristocracy of KamAZ." He argued that this was the case at all levels of enterprise council activity, not just at the association level. From this point of view, the councils never did become institutions that gave workers a chance to alter the existing distribution of either goods or authority at KamAZ.

The fundamental reason that management and the labor aristocracy were able to retain control was that workers did not vote for "their own," according to Kirilov. And the reason the workers failed to do so was because they knew that management controlled all the things that workers did in fact receive, little though it was. From the workers' point of view, the elections of managers and enterprise council representatives did not work, Kirilov argued, because "insofar as the ability to distribute houses, apartments, childcare, places at daycare centers, and so on rest with these people (management), workers would not dare oppose them. The workers had to decide what they would go for—freedom, or sausage? They were afraid. Afraid. They went for sausage."[15]

Kirilov's view represents an extreme assessment of the failure of the institutions of self-management to alter in any fundamental way the balance of power on the shop floor at KamAZ. His pessimistic evaluation of the policy was perhaps matched only by the distaste for the policy evinced by Nurmukhamedov. Not surprisingly, there are numerous examples of struggles concerning self-management from the various factories making up KamAZ that provide ample grist for either mill.

The dispute over the Center of Engineering and Equipment (or simply the Center, as it was called) provides a graphic illustration of the connections between control over funds, self-management, and managerial authority. In late 1989, the KamAZ machine-building shop and the machine repair shop were merged to create the Center. The creation of the new Center was seen by management as an important step toward modernizing the structure of KamAZ, while the opponents of the Center viewed it either as unnecessary or as an underhanded attempt by management to extend its control. The central issue here is not the technical merits of the Center, but rather the light that the conflict sheds on the problem of production democracy at KamAZ.

The senior managers of the KamAZ association decided to create the Center without consulting the enterprise councils of either KamAZ or the factories concerned. According to the provisions of the *LSE,* management did not have the right to make such a unilateral decision. Article 7 gave the enterprise council the right to decide questions concerning the "organizational structure of the enterprise," while article 6 only gave management the right to make "socio-economic decisions affecting the activities of the enterprise in consultation with the labor collective."[16] The very method that management used to create the Center suggests that two and a half years after the adoption of the law, managers did not feel constrained by its provisions.[17] Some of the enterprise council presidents of the factories concerned were outraged, as were the Party committee secretaries and trade union leaders. The leaders of the Party, the enterprise council, and the trade union organizations of one factory wrote an open letter to the factory newspaper: "We cannot be silent about the fact that the position of the administration and technical directors completely ignores the legal rights of the workers: structural changes cannot be carried out without the agreement of the labor collective."[18] There were other council leaders, however, who did not get involved, and one refused to discuss the issue entirely, even with other people included in the council structure.[19]

The key issue for critics of the Center was that management had taken away their independence, and therefore their ability to control the operations of their factories. The language was that of democratization and self-management; the fundamental issue was money. The setting of bonus rates was a typical case in point. The collective of the Spare Parts and Equipment Division of the central repair shop had set the bonus rate for above plan output at 0.5, meaning that workers received half again the piece rate for production over the job norm.[20] The shop head of this division, V. Makarov, explained what happened after the Center was created: "At the Center for Engineering and Equipment, to which we have now been transferred, they decided to reduce the previous coefficient to 0.15. How did this 'economizing' turn out? People see that their efforts to do more and produce better are being discouraged, and therefore concern and dissatisfaction is growing."[21] The "they" in question was the management of the Center, who again took decisions affecting the collective without consulting its representatives.

Similarly, the representatives of the labor collectives of the machine-building factory complained in an open letter to the association's director that the Center had, in effect, robbed their factory. The authors of the letter, which appeared in the factory newspaper, were particularly upset about the transfer to the Center of 141,000 rubles from the factory's social-development fund.[22] They went on to mention that the factory would lose, to the Center, in their estimation ten apartments that had been earmarked for workers at the machine-building factory that year. The point for these representatives was that while the machine-building factory would be the heart of the Center, the "resources" of the factory would be under the control of the Center's director and enterprise council rather than theirs, and that resources would be parceled out to other groups within the Center. The issue of who controlled funds was of course tied to the issue of who controlled management. For the representatives of the collectives, the creation of the Center was simply another managerial maneuver to ensure that the central directors of the KamAZ association controlled both.

The president of the main engineering factory's council, V. Khlystov, in a letter to the general director of KamAZ, N. I. Bekh, scoffed at the idea that the Center would reduce the size of management staff, as Bekh had asserted. Khlystov argued that KamAZ's chief managers were engaged in a blatant attempt to control the new Center through appointment of managers friendly to them, thereby undercutting the power of the labor collectives. "The creation of a vertical chain from the shop head to the general director signifies the formation of a multitiered structure of leadership, where the principle of election and, consequently, of subordination to the labor collective extends only to the shop head," wrote Khlystov. He went on to argue that the formation of the Center would lead to "the liquidation of the principles of self-management . . . insofar as the work of the enterprise councils and other social organizations will be reduced to a formality."[23] The main argument given by Bekh and V. Korol', the Center's new director, was that the Center would centralize and streamline the management of related aspects of enterprise production. Critics argued that this centralized management was precisely the problem.[24] The creation of the Center served to increase the size of the managerial apparat while at the same time making managers less accountable to the collectives that made up the Center, both financially and politically.

Korol' finally responded to the complaints of the collectives, but his explanation and justification were entirely technical in nature; the political issues that the factory representatives raised were never even acknowledged. Korol' argued that the Center was integral to the modernization of KamAZ, and justified this position with data that the administration had never shared with the collectives involved.[25] In the end, the decisions of the administration regarding the Center were not modified, and the organizations whose representatives had challenged management's actions did not have the leverage to force any changes.

The struggle over the Center highlights a number of the problems with the policy of self-management experienced at KamAZ and other large associations like it. Changing the organizational structure of one component of KamAZ suddenly raised questions of funding, wages, appointment of managers, the distribution of authority between the association and the factories within it, and the respective rights of management and collectives to make decisions regarding all of the above. In addition, the fact that the representatives of the factories felt compelled to resort to an open letter to Bekh as a means of fighting what they viewed as an unjust and illegal decision illustrated yet again that the enterprise law had not established any authoritative mechanisms for settling disputes such as this. The enterprise councils clearly did not have the power to stop the organizational restructuring, even if they had the legal authority to do so.

Many of the same issues arose in a case that involved a different form of "organizational restructuring"—the firing of a factory shop director by the shop's council. The shop in question was the capital repair shop, which was the part of the factory that produced spare parts. The other production unit that played a part in this story was a repair brigade, numbering about thirty workers, which at the time was a subdivision of the capital repair shop. The manager at the center of the dispute was shop head Iurii A. Astaf'ev.

According to a letter sent by seventeen workers from the capital repair shop to the factory newspaper, the general director of KamAZ, and the KamAZ party committee, ill feelings toward Astaf'ev had been building for some time. As a result of a special meeting of the enterprise council, Astaf'ev was voted out of his position on 14 January 1990. Following his dismissal, on 8 February 1990, the factory council issued a decree that stated it would find a job for Astaf'ev in a "nonleadership position" for the period of one month.

Up to this point, the collective assumed that everything was functioning according to the established provisions of the self-management policy. This assumption proved overly optimistic. On 12 March 1990, the senior management of the KamAZ association issued an order—seemingly unconnected to the ouster of Astaf'ev—concerning the repair brigade of the capital repair shop mentioned above. The order stated that the repair brigade was to be formally transferred from the factory for the production of spare parts to the Building and Works Department, which was a separate division of KamAZ. Soon afterward, the administration also announced that a shop head had been selected for the newly created repair brigade of the Building and Works Department—his name, Iurii A. Astaf'ev.

The transfer of the repair brigade and the appointment of Astaf'ev as shop head are representative examples of how management succeeded in side-stepping the mechanisms designed to ensure the participation of workers in management. The authors of the letter cited above convincingly argued that management was "protecting its own" by simply shifting Astaf'ev "from one chair to another." S. Isichko, the journalist who wrote the article about the dispute in *Rabochii Kamaza,* argued that the transfer of the brigade to the Building and Works Department was unconnected to the firing of Astaf'ev, but the sequence of events does not bear out his claim.

Astaf'ev was fired on 14 January, but the crucial issue was the enterprise council's resolution of 8 February that Astaf'ev could not hold a leadership position for a month after that date. The order transferring the brigade and appointing Astaf'ev was issued on 12 March, just four days after the expiration of the enterprise council's resolution. Technically, this was entirely proper. However, in the very same article in which the workers' letter was published, the brigadier of the repair brigade, P. A. Ermakov, stated that the brigade had held a meeting on 14 February at which it "unanimously elected Astaf'ev shop head and informed management of the decision."[26] As one worker who followed these events closely informed me, this was curious for two reasons. First, at the time the repair brigade was still under the jurisdiction of the spare parts factory, in which case the selection of Astaf'ev was in direct violation of the council's resolution. Second, since the repair brigade was still just that—a brigade within the capital repair shop—there was no reason to elect someone shop head, because brigades do not have such a post. This worker argued that the only reason for the brigade to hold such an election was that it already knew that the transfer was imminent. From this he concluded that the election was simply a means by which management could justify the appointment of Astaf'ev and charge the factory council with ignoring the democratically expressed wishes of the brigade.[27]

Transferring the repair brigade to another division was the only way to ensure that the enterprise council of either the capital repair shop or the spare parts factory would not simply vote Astaf'ev out yet again. As with the case of the Center for Engineering and Equipment discussed above, the transfer of the brigade without the approval of the labor collectives involved was a violation of the *LSE*. The transfer was also damaging to the capital repair shop, which lost thirty workers, including technical specialists and other highly skilled workers who were not easily replaced.

The workers who wrote to the factory newspaper were convinced that this was a calculated maneuver. "When we understood this, we tried to prove it to the factory leaders," they wrote in the letter. Management's response, according to the workers, was this: "The cobbler should stick to mending shoes!" The authors understood this to mean that management was afraid that "if it happens that every collective begins to evaluate its leader, then people like Astaf'ev won't be able to find a place anywhere in the factory."[28] By transferring the brigade, KamAZ's leadership killed two birds with one stone: it protected Astaf'ev and it punished the workers of the capital repair shop for challenging the power of management.

However, the self-management mechanisms did not fail entirely in this case: the ouster of Astaf'ev from the capital repair shop was not overturned, and management was forced to go through a series of contortions in order to find Astaf'ev a place in the KamAZ management hierarchy. While the council of the capital repair shop had no way to block the transfer of the repair brigade, management no longer had any way to force the shop to take back a manager that the workers of the shop found unacceptable.

The disputes described above arose primarily due to characteristic flaws in the structure of the self-management policy itself: lines of authority were not clearly specified, and preexisting standard operating procedures that conflicted with the policy of production democracy continued to function. These problems manifested themselves in a myriad of ways at KamAZ, most of which were much less dramatic than the foregoing examples.

The front page of the factory newspaper *Rabochii Kamaza* for 7 February 1990 reads like a catalogue of these less striking but equally important examples of pre-perestroika factory operations, which undercut the policy of self-management. Most of this issue of the newspaper was taken up with the text of the "collective contract" for 1990. For as many years as anyone could remember, the introduction to the contract had been virtually the same: "The collective contract [of KamAZ] for 1990 is being concluded between the administration in the person of the general director and the labor collective in the person of the trade union committee of the association with the goal of satisfying the material, social, and spiritual demands of all members of the collective from the profits received."[29] As in the past, the trade union committee represented the labor collective. According to the *LSE,* however, this was the job of the enterprise council, which was supposed to have the final say, rather than being in the position of negotiator. In more than one interview, respondents said that no one ever thought of changing the procedure. This was particularly strange because the trade unions were seen by most people as having been in the pocket of the administration from before the flood, and their very ineffectiveness was one of the driving reasons behind the creation of the enterprise council.

In addition to the continuation of the traditional role of the trade unions, two other examples of past factory practice are to be found in the paper that day. In an article entitled "The Goals for the Year Have Been Fulfilled," the newspaper announced the winners of a "socialist competition" for the fourth quarter of 1989. The institution of socialist competition dated back at least to Stalin's time, and while the competition had never been particularly effective in raising productivity, it had kept workers busy, controlled, and divided. At KamAZ, the awards were given out jointly by the administration, the trade union committee, and—the enterprise council. As happened in many other factories, the council was gradually incorporated into the existing structure and rhythms of factory life.

Another article on the first page focused on the committee of people's control, an institution also dating back decades, which was supposed to involve workers in managing the enterprise and solving social problems. In fact, this committee had always served as a mechanism for exerting social control over factory personnel—particularly workers—who were deemed insufficiently dedicated to their work. The committee was elected by the labor collective, but it was not under the control of the enterprise council or factored in to the self-management equation in any other way. This was particularly problematic, since the functions claimed by the committee of people's control overlapped with those of the new self-management institutions.[30] Serious problems arose at KamAZ and elsewhere because new institutions did not take the place of old ones but were merely grafted on to the existing system without consideration for the potential contradictions involved.

One of the central complaints about industrial reform under Gorbachev was that in spite of all the other changes taking place, the status of factories as state property remained intact. Critics argued that neither self-management nor real managerial control could develop as long as the ministries retained ultimate control over factory property. In 1990, KamAZ attempted to break this control by convincing the government to allow KamAZ to become a joint-stock company *(aktsionernoe obshchestvo)*. As with other forms of structural reorganization, the proposal to establish a joint-stock company led to conflicts between management and the labor collectives over who had the right to decide important issues concerning the transition to and control of the newly formed company.

Not surprisingly, the first question to arise was who made the decision to turn KamAZ into a joint-stock company in the first place. According to the statements of workers, council members, and in one case a locally well-known Communist Party member and former KamAZ worker who was against the joint-stock company, management made the decision unilaterally, just as it had in the other cases described above. S. Gribanov, an engineer from the foundry, in an interview with *Rabochii Kamaza,* asked "why the decision about the joint-stock company is once again being made behind our backs, once again 'up above'?"[31] And Gennadi Kirilov argued that the decision by management was "just another common, ordinary, everyday deception of the people." [32]

Management, in the person of Director for Economics and Planning Leonid Komm, argued that this was an inaccurate view of events. In response to the question of who made the decision, Komm gave a three-stage answer. There is no doubt from Komm's response that the senior management did in fact make the decision unilaterally, but he argues that (1) it was dictated by economic reality; (2) it was not the kind of decision amenable to being voted on by the workers; and (3) even so, management did consult with the enterprise council.[33] Judging from articles and letters to the editor in *Rabochii Kamaza,* Komm's multitiered explanation did not satisfy many workers at KamAZ, but the decision to create the joint-stock company stood, as had similar decisions in the past.

Next on the agenda for the joint-stock company was the issue of ownership and division of shares. The association and the government decided that KamAZ would issue approximately 4.5 billion rubles' worth of shares by the year 2000, which at that time reflected the worth of the combined components of KamAZ. According to the agreement reached between the government and the management of KamAZ, the government would retain control over 51 percent of the shares, and the remaining 49 percent would be open to purchase. The government, however, agreed that half of its shares, 25.5 percent, would be under the direct control of KamAZ. This arrangement, it was argued, would ensure that KamAZ controlled the voting at shareholders' meetings.[34] But the question was, who was "KamAZ" in this scenario?

The government would control 25.5 percent of the shares owned by the state, and "KamAZ" would control the same. But within KamAZ, the 25.5 percent would be divided three ways: the labor collective would control a third, the administration a third, and "the remaining shareholders" a third.[35] The "remaining shareholders" were not named, but they would presumably be either other factories (that is, the management of other factories) within the overarching structure of KamAZ, or those with whom KamAZ did business. In addition, the remaining 49 percent would be sold through the management of KamAZ, with priority given to KamAZ suppliers and customers.

Of course, workers at KamAZ and anyone else for that matter had the right to buy shares, but at one hundred rubles apiece, individuals would not be able to afford a sufficient quantity to have any impact on the decision-making process. The management of KamAZ certainly did not expect workers to buy shares. As Leonid Komm stated quite clearly, "at first, shares should not be purchased by members of the labor collective. Or more accurately, they should not be relied on to do so. . . . Workers, of course, will get used to the idea of being shareholders, but we really do not expect that many will want to be. This business is a bit too new for them."[36]

Workers also did not expect to be able to buy enough shares to have an impact. A. Kosenkov, a foundry worker, responding to the argument of a Communist Party member that the workers and the city should buy a controlling block of the shares, stated that "in my view, this is nonsense. By what means? The workers do not have the wherewithal to buy more than 8 to 10 percent. And to ask the government to make up the difference by giving us free of charge enough shares so that we will have the controlling block—that idea is, at the very least, naive."[37] He was correct on both counts, although other figures suggest that workers could not have purchased much more than 2 or 3 percent.[38]

When all the figures are put together, the following approximate distribution emerges. The government would control 25.5 percent; the various levels of management at KamAZ, its affiliates, and those factories that did business with KamAZ could control as much as 66 percent; and the labor collective would have 8.5 percent. The figure for management could be lower, depending on how much of the 49 percent on public sale was purchased by unaffiliated individuals or even foreign firms, but managerial control of at least 50 percent looked impossible to shake. The management of KamAZ argued that this ensured control of the joint-stock company by the "labor collective" of KamAZ,[39] but as already seen, the interests of management and those of the workers in the various factories of the association were far from coterminous.

Once the transition of KamAZ to a joint-stock company had been officially carried out, the first thing to go was management's assertion that the labor collective would control the majority of votes. In the 12 October issue of *Rabochii Kamaza*, Leonid Komm stated that the "question of who concretely will control 51 percent of the votes is still under discussion." He went on to argue that no one had come up with a logical way of dividing the labor collective's share of votes between factories, and that the issue of what rights the labor collective had in the new company should be discussed and then "included in the collective contract." And Komm finally cleared up the issue of who the "labor collective" was: he argued that the labor collective should be seen as a "single entity" distinct from the administration, which would have to settle disputes "with the management of the joint-stock company."[40]

As soon as the new KamAZ was born, disputes erupted over the relation of the constituent factories of KamAZ to the joint-stock company. The enterprise council of the foundry, which had been against the idea of a joint-stock company to begin with, immediately passed a resolution—on the recommendation of a group of specialists from the factory set up to determine the best way of ensuring the foundry's future—stating that the foundry would become a "collectively owned enterprise" outside of the new company. A referendum would also be held on the council's resolution. The administration responded by dissolving the group of specialists and banning referenda on the territory of the factory.[41] The foundry enterprise council responded that according to the law, its resolution would go into effect one month after the original decision. The administration, however, used a provision of the joint-stock company agreement to forcibly end the dispute: individual factories were not considered "juridical persons"—that is, entities with decision-making rights—until the management board of the joint-stock company conferred this status on them. The result was that the foundry stayed part of KamAZ.

A series of other factories and shops were given greater independence by means of "leasing" arrangements with the new company, and the managers of these factories were likewise given greater control over setting wage and piece rates, production norms, and hours. In some cases, leasing allowed workers to earn more if they were willing to increase the intensity of their labor.[42] Many did, for a predictable reason that also had predictable effects. A journalist for *Rabochii Kamaza* asked one worker why she no longer rested: "I decided to do extra work, and to economize on time. I really need the money, particularly now; my family's situation is such that I can rely only on myself. So I drink my tea a little faster and get back to work. It's terribly difficult, of course—but, there's the money."[43]

In other cases of leasing, serious disagreements over management's alteration of piece rates and shift schedules found their way into the factory press. In one shop, workers argued that their piece rates had been halved by management, while management responded that the previous rate had three to four hours of idle time built into it, so workers were being paid for doing nothing half the day. Besides, the shop head argued, since wage caps had been removed, workers could earn as much or more than before—provided they were willing to fulfill the daily norms of two or more machines.[44]

At the same time that these disputes were arising due to the creation of the joint-stock company, the government of Nikolai Ryzhkov passed a new *Law on the Enterprise* to supersede the 1987 legislation. The new law eliminated the self-management provisions of its predecessor. At KamAZ, however, the inadequacies of the first enterprise law and the advent of the joint-stock company had been effectively undercutting the self-management institutions for some time. From then on, the enterprise councils could no longer effectively engage in the "politics of production" or serve as mechanisms to deal with social problems. This was particularly detrimental to workers' interests because the draft of the collective contract for 1991 included none of the social obligations for which management had in the past always been responsible.[45]

In spite of such difficulties, however, the enterprise councils continued to function, and over the span of four years developed a constituency at KamAZ. The president of the USSR Union of Enterprise Councils was the president of the KamAZ council, and a large number of worker-activists at KamAZ had either begun or organized their political activities through the enterprise council system. The flaws in the self-management institutions also spurred the organization of other, independent workers' initiatives within the various factories of KamAZ, such as Kirilov's temporary workers' committee and a similar group around S. Gribanov and V. Dolgov.

The policy of self-management at KamAZ did not, in the end, give the workers of various collectives the rights and opportunities that those who wrote the *LSE* had hoped it would. By late 1990, when KamAZ became a joint-stock company, the management of the association had succeeded in turning their contingent power as nomenklatura managers into relatively permanent power as major stockholders. But factory-level perestroika at KamAZ had also raised workers' expectations, given sanction to the idea that they should be the real "masters of the enterprise," and, most important, politicized groups of workers in almost every constituent factory of KamAZ. The management of KamAZ emerged from the years of production democracy stronger than when they went in, but workers too had become more actively involved in the labor politics of KamAZ and had gained a more exact sense of who controlled what, and how. This sensibility, obtained at least in part through workers' experiences of "self-management" from 1987 to 1990, became part of the new politics of production at the joint-stock company, which still dominates Naberezhnye Chelny and the lives of its workers.

There's No Business like Your Business: Labor Relations at the Makhachkala Electric Instrument Production Factory

The Makhachkala Priboro-stroitel'nyi Zavod (Makhachkala Electronics Factory, or Makhachkala Electric), located in the capital of Dagestan, offered a very different view of the fate of perestroika on the shop floor—and the effects it had on workers and managers—than that presented by KamAZ. The structural complexities that the size of KamAZ generated for the policy of self-management did not arise at Makhachkala Electric, which is a relatively small factory, employing only about four thousand workers, technical specialists, and managers combined. This meant that everyone knew virtually everyone else, and that the actions of any individual or group quickly became known throughout the factory.

By all accounts, the factory had been in trouble even before perestroika began, but the situation became progressively worse from 1985 on. The factory's director, V. N. Istoman, stated that the factory was working very poorly, especially in technical terms, that production was disorganized and in decline, that demand for factory products had fallen, and that the consumer market did not need what the factory produced.[46] This situation led to a financial crisis that affected every aspect of life and politics both inside and outside the factory for all of those who worked at Makhachkala Electric. The financial and other problems at the factory had created a tense atmosphere at Makhachkala Electric and a corresponding deterioration in labor relations, with management, workers, and specialists all accusing each other of being the root cause of the factory's difficulties.

The problems at this factory were precisely the type of problems that the enterprise law, including its self-management provisions, was intended to solve. It is all the more curious, therefore, that at Makhachkala Electric the self-management provisions of the enterprise law had virtually no direct effect on the labor relations system or the disputes that erupted at the factory during the perestroika years. Workers and managers certainly did become more involved in politics on the shop floor during this time, but both sides used mechanisms outside the confines of the new law to press their cases. The general feeling at Makhachkala Electric seemed to be "out with the new, and in with the old," although managers and workers felt this way for different reasons.

The introduction of new policies through the enterprise law did not even slow down, much less stop, the traditional methods of management at Makhachkala Electric. The "election" of V. N. Istoman as director is a case in point. At first glance, it appears that Istoman was chosen in accordance with the procedures described by the enterprise law. He was nominated by one of the other managers at the factory, he and a second candidate gave speeches before a meeting of the labor collective describing their respective programs, and a date was set for the election. On 10 October, however, the other candidate, "during the time when the meeting was discussing and listening to the contenders' programs," withdrew his candidacy in support of Istoman. The enterprise council at that point "decided not to hold an election."[47] Istoman was confirmed as director. The entire procedure, however, was the electoral equivalent of a Potemkin village, a characteristic that the confirmation of Istoman shared with a large number of factories throughout the former Soviet Union. Istoman had been working at the factory since the fall of 1987, when he replaced the old director, who by all accounts had done nothing to improve factory operations in years. Tizutdin Adip'gereev, a worker from the factory's main assembly shop and head of the factory's informal workers' group, stated that the authorities simply "brought in a new person, like they always do. Oh yes, he was 'elected,' but he was the only candidate, after a second candidate withdrew his name. The election was a farce." The second candidate was A. Sultanov, who was the administrative head of the department on labor and wages. He was directly subordinate to Istoman both in the management hierarchy and on the factory's Party committee. The workers interviewed for this book believed Sultanov's candidacy was a ruse to give the appointment of

Istoman an air of democratic legitimacy.[48] This was not an isolated case. Workers, technical specialists, journalists, and even managers from around the Soviet Union complained about similar "false elections" throughout the years 1988 to 1990.

Like his colleagues at KamAZ, Istoman evinced a particular dislike for the policy of elections of managerial personnel, as did many of his fellow managers at Makhachkala Electric. He argued that the main problem with elections, aside from the fact that workers do not know who is qualified and who is not, is that they disrupt production. "One of the bad features of perestroika," he remarked, "is that in the course of dismantling the command-administrative system, attacks on leaders take place just because they're chic. . . . The workers have no use for demanding leaders, and they'll vote them out."[49] Interestingly, Istoman's view of elections was shared by the head of Makhachkala Electric's trade union committee.[50]

The workers disagreed fundamentally with these arguments. During a heated joint meeting with managers and workers in Istoman's office, worker representatives from shop no. 1 argued that "they say [elections] destroy the authority of the director and undermine production, but the fact is that we cannot afford not to work. It would not be in our best interests to elect an idiot, now would it? But we have to have input into the way the factory is run."[51] By all accounts, the election of managers at Makhachkala Electric was not a mechanism through which workers exerted a positive influence over factory life, but it did serve as a means of negative power. At least at the level of the shop, low-level managers did have to take the feelings of the workers into account if they wanted to keep their jobs secure and relatively untroubled. At the top, however, appointments cloaked in electoral garb remained the rule at Makhachkala Electric.

A similar problem affected the elections to the enterprise council, and the operation of the council proved little better. In response to a questionnaire on the formation and subsequent role of the enterprise council in the factory, approximately 17 percent of all those questioned indicated that they participated in the election for members of the enterprise council. Of that 17 percent, 41 percent were workers. Although precise numbers were unavailable, the percentage of workers among all employees at Makhachkala Electric was approximately 70 percent. If the workers surveyed are representative of all workers at the factory, the results of the questionnaire indicate that only between 10 and 15 percent of the workers at Makhachkala Electric took part in the enterprise council elections at all.[52]

The members of the informal workers' group who were interviewed argued that the low turnout for the elections was a reflection of the workers' view that the enterprise council was just another in a long line of institutions controlled from above. These workers argued that "there are no existing institutions to defend our interests as workers. The enterprise council is a useless institution. It could be helpful in assisting us to gain some control [in the factory], but as currently constituted, it serves the interests of the administration and the Party, not ours."[53] The majority of workers surveyed indicated their belief that most of the people elected were either "selected beforehand by the administration and agreeable to it" or "basically those whose names happened to be on the ballot."[54]

A more detailed survey, carried out by the factory's sociologists in March 1990, indicated that 46.4 percent of those surveyed "were uninformed about the work of the enterprise council," another 26.8 percent considered the institution to be "worthless," and only 5.4 percent thought that the council "was working actively."[55] As was the case in many factories, a large sector of Makhachkala Electric's workers felt that the enterprise council was powerless at best, and in the pocket of management at worst. The view was summed up by one assembly-line worker very succinctly: "People are fed up with elections and meetings because we've been doing this for years." And amid laughter and cries of "hurrah" he added, "we're used to simply voting for whatever comrades the comrade director suggests."[56] Management, for its part, shared the view of the managers of KamAZ that the enterprise council had neither the knowledge nor the authority to be effective. As V. N. Istoman put it: "The law had good intentions, but the enterprise council had no responsibility. The director answers for everything. The council could pass anything it wanted, and if it did not work out, no one would curse at the members of the council because they had no real authority."[57]

Both the management and the workers of Makhachkala Electric felt that they had good reasons for being skeptical of the enterprise council. Regardless of whose assessment was the more accurate—and I think there are merits to both—the result was that most of the workers shunned the council, and most of the managers either ignored it or simply incorporated it into their preexisting plans. The new institutions of self-management had little effect at Makhachkala Electric because they did not serve anyone's interests particularly well. A more important reason for the lackluster performance of the self-management institutions, however, was that workers and managers were engaged in shop-floor politics through other mechanisms that were already in place by the time the policy of self-management was promulgated.

One of these mechanisms was, rather surprisingly, the trade union. Soviet trade unions were best known, both to Soviet workers and to students of labor politics in the USSR, for their obsequiousness to management and their ponderous bureaucracies. Nevertheless, between 1988 and 1990 a group of workers at Makhachkala Electric tried to take control of the factory trade union committee and through the trade union apparatus negotiate what in their minds was a more equitable contract. The decision to use the trade union rather than the enterprise council was based on the fact that the enterprise council had no apparatus or membership within the factory, no funds of its own, and—most important—no regional or national committees that were independent of the factory's management. The trade union committee had all three.

The workers involved were motivated by what they saw as two interrelated issues: the failure of management to fulfill its contractual obligations concerning repair, maintenance, and other "social insurance" provisions, and the corruption of the trade union committee in the factory. The list of items that management had failed to deal with was extensive: ventilation systems in two shops did not work at all and had been awaiting repair for over a year; only one set of toilets worked in the main factory building; one entire block of dormitories owned by the factory had been without hot water for fourteen months; and in another dormitory the puddles and humidity from leaky showers located just above the communal kitchen had resulted in the hallways being inundated by swarms of mosquitos.[58] The informal workers' group accused the trade union committee of ignoring management's violations of the contracts, allowing management to use trade union funds for factory repairs and technical services, and conniving with management to distribute scarce resources to people on what was called "the first list," which not surprisingly included the officials of the trade union committee.

The first challenge made by the workers to the traditional structure and function of the trade union came in 1987 amid the "negotiations" between the administration and the trade union over the collective contract for 1988. The event that occasioned this challenge was the decision of factory trade union president Sh. N. Mishiev to step down from his position. His deputy, who was a Party member and had the approval of the administration, replaced him but soon "proved incapable of handling the job." At this point, workers from the informal workers' group decided to nominate their own candidate, but "as soon as it became known that we were doing this, the administration and the Party committee swung into action to block us."[59] The administration and the Party committee succeeded, and the new trade union president ended up being none other than Sh. N. Mishiev, who had served in the position since 1958. Mishiev said during an interview, "I was elected again in 1988, but I did not want the job."[60] To hear the members of the informal workers' group tell the story, the factory Party committee told Mishiev, who was a Party member, to stand for election again, which he was then bound to do. The president of the factory Party committee at the time was V. N. Istoman, the factory's director.

Another year and another collective contract went by, and most of the issues that had spurred the workers in 1988 remained unresolved. During the "report and ratification" cycle for the 1989 and 1990 collective contracts, therefore, the members of the informal workers' group and about fifteen other workers tried a different tactic. The workers sent a letter, bypassing the factory trade union committee altogether, to the president of the Dagestan oblast trade union committee, in which they argued that the factory trade union committee had violated the procedures for approving the report on the fulfillment of the past year's contract and for adopting a new contract.[61]

The letter argued that the trade union conference at which the old and new contracts had been approved should be declared invalid for three reasons. First, the informal workers' group, having seen that the "administration's obligations" section of the new contract was identical to that contained in the previous year's contract, had submitted an alternative draft of the contract. The trade union committee had failed to circulate the draft for discussion among the entire collective, as the trade union rules required. Second, the workers argued that there were only 128 delegates to the conference, that three shops were not represented, and that out of the 128 delegates to the factory trade union conference, only 30 were workers. And third, they argued that the rules pertaining to both quorums and voting had been violated, since there were only 80 delegates present during the vote (the workers' group had left in protest), and the vote was done by "a show of hands" *(na glaza)* rather than with the required written, secret ballot.

The response of the regional trade union committee was both long in coming and relatively vague. The original letter was dated 26 March, and the oblast trade union response was written only on 27 April, four days after the joint administration/trade union conference had met to approve the new contract. In the letter, the regional trade union committee agreed that not enough had been done to ensure the fulfillment of the 1989 contract, and that "it has been suggested to the administration, the enterprise council, and the trade union committee that a detailed report be put together on the distribution of funds during 1989 and that said report should be presented and discussed at an expanded meeting of the enterprise council." The letter did not address any of the specific violations that the workers' letter had pointed out. The last line of the letter stated simply that "we consider it unnecessary to repeat the conference." [62]

The most important aspect of the events related above about the workers' attempt to reform or bypass the factory trade union is not that it failed, but that the workers made the attempt in an open, organized, and tactically sophisticated way. The core group of about five workers went around the factory with copies of the letter asking for signatures; the worker-delegates to the trade union conference also acted in concert against the trade union, the enterprise council, and managerial groups present. And by making the letters, the complaints at the conference, and the response of the factory and regional trade union committees a subject of widespread discussion at the factory, the workers involved succeeded in undercutting the legitimacy of the entire exercise and increasing their own group's visibility. After this series of events, the group started its own one-page informational bulletin and was laying the groundwork for the formation of an independent union. The workers of the informal workers' group had, of course, wanted to win this dispute, but at least in terms of trade union politics at Makhachkala Electric, the workers' group probably gained just about as much in losing. At the same time, many of the members of the informal workers' group mentioned that the workers at the factory, themselves included, still felt "a sense of helplessness in the face of the network of institutions and rules that help to maintain and increase the power of the nomenklatura elites and keep the workers in line." [63] Two aspects of this "network" were certain articles of the labor code and the Scientific Organization of Labor office.

There were three articles in the labor code through which managers controlled their workforce: articles 29, 33, and 254. Article 254 stated that "certain categories of workers" (which are unspecified) can be fired for "a single serious violation of labor obligations."[64] According to the foreman, this translated into managerial dictatorship, because "a leader, on his own initiative, can fire someone for having one serious violation. So, say that I don't like your pretty blue eyes. I give you some idiotic order, which naturally you can't carry out, and I can have your job on the basis of this article. Everything depends on my mood. . . . Regulating workers is therefore quite simple."[65] While managers seldom used this article to fire workers, mainly due to considerations of skilled manpower shortages, the foreman's argument was that you could not have any kind of production democracy as long as such laws were on the books.

Articles 29 and 33 functioned in a similar way. They gave the administration the right to fire a worker for "systematic nonfulfillment of labor obligations without good cause," but the definitions of "systematic nonfulfillment" and "without good cause" are unspecified. In addition, article 29 stated that a worker could be fired if he or she "refused to transfer to another locality together with the enterprise, establishment, or organization."[66] The same shop foreman argued that article 29 gave him the power to "destroy [a worker] in the blink of an eye. And he has nowhere to go to appeal my decision. I can say to him, for example, 'My dear comrade, I want you to go from this workplace to that one.' This is called a change in working conditions, and if he refuses to move, I can fire him on the basis of articles 29 and 33." Such an interpretation was clearly illegal under article 29, but the foreman's interpretation of this provision was supported by "his own experience"; furthermore, it was not challenged by any of the approximately twenty people present at the meeting where the foreman spoke.[67]

Another piece in the chess match of shop-floor politics at Makhachkala Electric was the Scientific Organization of Labor office. This office had been in existence since the 1920s, founded as a means to "rationalize" production on the shop floor, but at Makhachkala Electric in the late 1980s the office also acquired a specific political role in labor/management conflicts. The workers involved in the informal group had direct experience of the office's new role.

These workers argued that, in spite of the aforementioned articles of the labor code, it was not always that easy to fire workers, especially skilled workers, because it was hard to replace them and to overcome the legal complexities involved in obtaining court approval for dismissals. It was easier for management to engage in a factory-based program of divide and rule. A worker from the main assembly shop explained, "It's troublesome to fire people, especially line workers. So the people from the Scientific Organization of Labor office come in and say that the shop is poorly organized, or that labor resources are being wasted, or that the technology is obsolete, or whatever." The administration then uses these excuses to try to get rid of "inconvenient people" in the factory. The director "is always in the know, and he uses the

Scientific Organization of Labor office as one means of breaking up groups of workers like us who have been causing him grief."[68] This is precisely what the administration tried to do to the workers who had organized the informal workers' group after the incident with the 1989–1990 collective contract negotiations. The fact that these workers were not dispersed to different shops within the factory was due to the particular shop in which they worked (main assembly and inspection) and to the relationship between these workers and the shop's head manager.

If the use of the labor code and the Scientific Organization of Labor office are illustrations of the power of management even under perestroika, the relationship between the factory's central administration, the assembly shop's head manager, and the workers of the informal group serves as an example of the limits of managerial power brought on by reform policies under Gorbachev. At the joint meeting of managers and workers on 8 January 1991, the main assembly shop's head manager was the only one of the administration people there apart from the director to speak critically and at length about the management of the factory. The workers from his shop were also the most vocal; four of them were part of the informal group. The workers from the shop later explained that their shop head had terrible relations with the rest of the administration, but that he protected the "worker-activists" in the shop and the workers protected him.

The head manager of a shop had final say over the disposition of the labor force under his authority and was in the best position to counter claims by the Scientific Organization of Labor office regarding the workforce, technology, and organization of his shop. As a result, the arguments used by Istoman and the Scientific Organization of Labor office to disperse the group were severely undermined, and because there were no technical reasons to transfer the workers, the shop head won the argument. The shop head could challenge the administration in such a way because the workers had confidence in him, and with four hundred employees their shop was "the most important in the factory. If he starts to get hassled, he knows the workers will support him. And since most of the products of the factory go through our shop, we can wreak havoc on production. It's a negative kind of power, but it's the only kind we've got."[69] There were two implied methods for exerting power in support of the shop head in this statement. The first was to slow down production or ruin products on purpose. The second involved the enterprise council. The shop head was elected by the shop council, and even if the administration tried to remove him from his job, the shop council could simply elect him again. By late 1989, the combination of a reformist manager and a politically active labor collective could not be treated lightly.

The experience of "workplace democratization" at Makhachkala Electric during the years of perestroika leaves the impression that very little changed. Unlike the self-management institutions at KamAZ, which led an active if troubled existence, those same institutions at Makhachkala Electric never took hold or enjoyed much authority. The general drive for reform, however, and the atmosphere that perestroika created during these years, led to diverse attempts by some workers to reorient older, existing mechanisms of Makhachkala Electric's organizational structure to assert their interests. The administration of the factory did much the same thing in an effort to counter these attempts and to solidify its position vis-à-vis the labor collective and the regional and central authorities. And among the workers at Makhachkala Electric, even though many of their efforts to gain some control over existing institutions proved largely unsuccessful, the drive toward greater self-organization continued.

Notes from Underground: Workers, Self-Management, and Strikes at the Gorky Mine

Among all of the workers in the former Soviet Union, the drive to create workers' organizations independent of official structures was strongest among the miners. There are a number of reasons why this was so, and they will be discussed in the following chapter. The important issue here is that the emergence of independent miners' organizations in the year following the 1989 strike had an important effect on the structure and functioning of the official institutions designed to promote production democracy in the mines and in affiliated industries. The case of the Gorky mine in Donetsk was fairly typical in this regard.[70]

The Gorky mine was simply one among many in the city of Donetsk and its environs, and the mines in this region had much in common. First, the mine was quite old: coal seams had been worked there since the nineteenth century, and consequently the shafts were very deep, the tunnels like rabbit warrens, and the coal face itself often no wider than two to three feet. As a result, working on the coal face was hazardous, due to excessive heat, flooding, and poor ventilation. Second, and not surprisingly, the mine was not profitable. Donbass coal was, according to the mine's chief engineer, "the most expensive in the Union," and the mines that produced it, like Gorky, continued to function only because of government support.[71] At the same time, however, that the government purchased the coal at artificially low prices, disputes over cost and prices played a major role in the politics of production from 1987 to 1991 in all of the major mining regions. Third, there was a distinct split among the workers at Gorky, as at most other mines, between the actual miners who worked underground and the ancillary workers and engineers who worked above ground. This split also found its way into the politics of self-management at the Gorky mine.

Like the administration of KamAZ, the management of Gorky at the time of the introduction of the enterprise law was extremely powerful when it came to the operation of the mine. The coal industry was an economically and strategically important sector in the USSR, and management was given broad scope in ensuring the steady production of coal. One of the early complaints of workers at Gorky and elsewhere was that this broad scope included ignoring both safety standards and general working conditions in the mines.[72] Their complaint was two sided: the miners criticized the official miners' trade union just as sharply for not challenging management's violations of these safety standards.

It was in this context that the self-management provisions of the enterprise law were introduced at Gorky. Many workers at the mine initially greeted the establishment of the Council of the Labor Collective "with euphoria." The reason, according to Gorky trade union chairman Valerii Miller, was that as the miners saw their situation at Gorky "there were no other organizations to which they could turn except the administration and the trade union," neither of which the workers trusted to protect their interests.[73] Many of the miners at Gorky therefore turned to the enterprise council as a lever to promote their interests, but in a way that differed from what workers in many other factories did.

The experience of managerial elections and the establishment of the enterprise council at Gorky often mirrored the experiences of the factories discussed above. Elections were not held for the majority of the managerial posts at the mine, and no administrators lost their positions as the result of those elections that were held. The election of the council was similarly uneventful and reflected the power and organization of management: "Before the [1989] strike, the administration completely controlled activities in the mine. The council members were elected at a conference dominated and controlled by the mine administration, and therefore the people elected to it were the administration's people." Most of the delegates to the conference were low-level managerial personnel, and they were also in charge of selecting nominees to the enterprise council from their shop or department, so it was no surprise that the makeup of the council reflected the administration's preferences.[74]

Even so, the workers at Gorky, particularly the miners themselves, tried to use the enterprise council, not to gain greater control over management but to light a fire under the moribund trade union committee. Trade union chairman Miller argued that the enterprise council was an "institutional threat" to the trade union:

> Originally, the council was used as a threat against the inactivity of the trade union. At trade union meetings workers threatened to transfer some of the trade union's authority over to the council. In many cases, they started to do the same things—they were two organizations with different views working on the same issues. So, a direct confrontation developed between the enterprise council and the trade union over which organization was going to do what and to which organization the collective would turn.[75]

The miners, of course, could not be sure that the council would distribute bonuses, deficit goods, or vacation passes more efficiently or justly than the trade union committee, but this was not the point. Many workers felt that the threat to undercut the union's institutional and material base would force the factory's trade union committee to focus more of its attention on protecting the rights of workers. This struggle for renewed influence over the trade union was still going on when the first miners' strike erupted in the summer of 1989.

The 1989 strike had both immediate and long-term effects on the labor movement in the Soviet Union, particularly, of course, for Soviet miners. In the aftermath of the strike, the calculus of shop-floor politics at the Gorky mine changed substantially. First, the strike introduced another player into the struggle for influence in the mine: in addition to the administration, the enterprise council, and the trade union, there was now a strike committee that had the respect of the workers and remained in operation after the strike was settled. Second, miners had gained greater confidence in their right and ability to have a substantial say in the operation of their workplaces. And third, the strike altered the relationships among workers and organizations representing workers at the mine.

The qualified success of the strike in the minds of participants—the miners did, after all, force the government to negotiate with the representatives of the workers—conferred a high level of authority on the strike committees that had organized and led the walkout. Similarly, the inaction and in some cases opposition of the enterprise councils to the strike had further undermined whatever credibility they had in the eyes of the workers. Most important, however, was the intense hostility directed at the official mine workers' unions, which had actively opposed the strike from the very beginning.

The first and most visible effect of the strike was the wave of elections that took place throughout the coal-mining regions of the USSR, the Gorky mine included. The strike committees demanded that all local and regional trade union committees face reelection; as a result, at the Gorky mine 90 percent of those who had served on the trade union committee before the strike were replaced.[76] The same was true of the enterprise councils, which were also reelected after the strike. If before the strike the administration had controlled nominations to the councils, afterward control belonged to the strike committee. "The strike committee then nominated the candidates," remarked council president S. Vasiliev, "and it acted basically the same way that the administration had before. The enterprise council was then made up of *their* people."[77]

After the trade union committee and the enterprise council had been reelected and staffed by people who had the backing of the strike committee, the newcomers took the extraordinary step of voting to ban the Party committee from the factory. Valerii Miller stated, "We can't stop workers from being in the Party—that's their personal business. But the situation before, when the Primary Party Organization (PPO) was a powerful presence here—in control of bonuses and so on—we put an end to that. The Party secretary received a bonus of 1,600 rubles one month. What for? We [the miners] paid for that. So we voted them out."[78] The "depoliticization" of the workplace was one of the demands made during the strike, but the change in the balance of power on the shop floor in the immediate wake of the strike—that made such a vote at the Gorky mine possible—was nevertheless remarkable, especially considering that most of the senior administrators were Party members.

The strike had given the miners at Gorky something they had never had before: an organization of their own creation that was not beholden to anyone or anything within the old power structure of the mine. Even more important, the strike committee, the vote against the factory Party committee, the thoroughgoing rejection of old trade union and enterprise council administrators by means of elections, and all the other changes, were examples not of what had already been achieved, but of what was now possible. The strike had given at least some of the workers at Gorky what the policy of self-management failed to provide: a real voice in the operation of their workplace.

In the months following the strike, the initial unity exhibited above gradually broke down, and a new issue came to the fore: what organization, if any, truly represented the workers at the Gorky mine? Different answers to this question provided the grounds for internecine struggles among the various union and strike committees. As was the case with all Soviet industrial unions, the miners' union at Gorky embraced everyone who worked at the mine, from underground workers to the senior managerial staff, and from workers who loaded the coal into railroad cars to those who swept the cafeteria floors. Virtually everyone agreed that this was an unworkable system, but that was where the agreement ended.

The new representatives of the official union, anxious to build their credibility after having been elected in the wake of the strike, forged a plan to restructure the union in order to bring it closer to the miners. "We wanted to revamp union membership and limit it to those who worked in mining within the enterprise. Not just miners, but those who worked in closely related jobs here at Gorky."[79] As it turned out, neither the administration nor the Donetsk city strike committee was willing to let the miners' union committee act freely: both sides saw in the proposal a chance to advance their own interests.

For the administration, the announcement of the plan provided an opportunity to sow dissension among the workers at the mine, of which there had been little since the strike. According to a number of sources at the mine and elsewhere in Donetsk, "the administration began to put out misleading information about the plan. They said that we wanted to disband the old union and start a new one just for those people [miners and workers closely associated with mining]. Well, the workers, the city strike committee, and the enterprise council were very upset."[80] The implication was that all other workers would then not have a union, which was not part of the plan: the union called for switching those workers to other unions through a coordinating committee of the All-Union Central Council of Trade Unions.

On the other hand, the Gorky strike committee and the city strike committee, membership in which was limited to underground workers, saw the plan as an invasion of their territory. By the time the Gorky trade union had come up with its program, discussions were already under way in the strike committees about setting up a new, independent mineworkers' union. As representatives of both the old union and the newly created union mentioned, a schism took place in the workers' movement at Gorky. Some were for the new union, some for the mineworkers' association (the reformed old trade union), and some stayed away from both. The dispute between the unions continued throughout 1990 and into 1991, and during this time the administration also continued its efforts to take advantage of the split and exacerbate it if possible. In the spring of 1991, the two strike committees called for another walkout; the response of the Gorky mine illustrates how divisive and fluid labor politics had become. The split had reached the point that the new Independent Union of Mineworkers (NPG) and the city strike committee supported the strike, and the old trade union—Union of Coal Industry Workers (*Profsoivz-rabotnikov ugol'noi promyshlennosti*)—and enterprise council did not. The administration then set up a third trade union committee that it could control "through bribery" to oppose the others. So by April 1991, there were three trade union committees at Gorky: one with authority derived from the first strike but little material support; one with waning authority but with a local and national infrastructure and to which most workers by default belonged; and one with no authority but plenty of resources with which to entice workers. As the head of one of the three trade union committees remarked, "The administration would like to have ten unions, if possible, in order to keep the workers divided."[81]

As the unity that followed the strike broke down and it became unclear who stood where, the enterprise council was once again reelected. The new leadership of the council assumed the role of mediator between what it saw as the conservatism of the administration and the radicalism of the Independent Union of Mineworkers and certain elements of the old trade union. The council's job was "to assist management in the running of the enterprise" while at the same time "defending the workers' interests in the economic health of the mine." This view reflected, more than anything else, the opinion and interests of the scientific and technical workers at the mine, who by this time made up the bulk of the council's members.[82] By 1990, the institution of the enterprise council had acquired a following among the mine's professional class; the development of the enterprise councils from 1987 to 1990 in many other factories in the USSR followed a similar path, which was seen in the makeup of the delegates to the 1990 Congress of Enterprise Councils in Moscow.

The key moment in the politics of production at the Gorky mine during these years was without question the strike of 1989, which fundamentally altered the balance of power on the shop floor. Among the causes of the strike, many of which concerned the deteriorating economic and working conditions in the mines, one must include the intense disillusionment that many workers felt toward perestroika and its representative institutions in the mines, namely, those intended to promote production democracy.[83] The strike itself, and the new institutions it engendered, gave the miners a sense of confidence and provided the impetus for the restructuring of these and other shop-floor organizations.

In the wake of the strike of 1989, the miners at Gorky did succeed in gaining a measure of influence over decision-making processes and labor policies at the mine. Their success was achieved as a result of the walkout and the solidarity that accompanied it, but both the solidarity and the achievements proved short-lived. The influence that the miners gained at Gorky began to slip away as the dual effects of the tight restrictions on self-management contained in the enterprise law of 1990 and the growing economic and political crises in the country as a whole made it increasingly difficult to ensure either order or equity in the mines and on the shop floor.

The Political Economy of Production Democracy

The policy of self-management legislated from above in 1987 was interpreted and used in a multitude of ways by workers and managers in Soviet industrial enterprises. In each factory, local conditions, organizational structures, and even personalities affected the implementation of what was intended to be a uniform mechanism for the enhancement of production democracy. While the preceding case studies highlight the particularities of each factory's experience of self-management, they also reveal certain commonalities in the politics of production in the factories of the former USSR. Based on these case studies, and on data gathered from a number of other Soviet industrial plants, one can evaluate the policy of workplace democratization, its short-term effects, and—most important—the lasting, perhaps unintended, changes that the policy of production democracy set in motion.

Of "the two main pillars of the policy of self-management," as Professor Evgenii Torkanovskii characterized managerial elections and the enterprise councils,[84] the election of leading managerial personnel was by all accounts the more controversial and, at least in terms of its intended effects, the less successful. There were a number of reasons for this, including ambiguities in the law, ministerial interference, and a dearth of qualified candidates to replace managers who were voted out of office. Within the factories, however, there were two overriding obstacles to the successful implementation of the electoral provisions of the enterprise law, both of which stemmed from the prevailing power structure of the Soviet labor relations system.

The first obstacle was that managers were categorically and vehemently opposed to the policy from the very outset, all the more so the higher up one went on the managerial ladder. Every senior manager who granted an interview, including those whose comments are included in the preceding case studies, considered the policy "absurd," "destructive," or at best "inappropriate for our country at the present time."[85] Most senior managers were willing to tolerate elections of shop-floor personnel such as brigadiers or foremen, and in some cases shop heads, but they drew the line at managerial positions that they viewed as requiring "particular qualifications." If this line is seen in terms of factory politics, managers drew it just below the point where the real nomenklatura positions began. From the level of shop head on up, managerial positions provided people with access to important information and economic resources. In the factory this meant power, and managers opposed any policy that gave workers access to it.

The policy of managerial elections struck at the security and privilege of the factory nomenklatura, which managers viewed as their right, not only by virtue of their connections but also due to their qualifications and achievements. Therefore, managerial concern about the effects of this policy was as genuine as concern for their jobs. One participant in the debates over elections stated that by late 1988

> directors were beginning to feel the complexity of their new situation, of having to take the concerns of the labor collectives into account. As a result, a great deal of force was being used on the government and the CPSU organizations to compel them to change the policy, particularly regarding the election of directors. There was simply a massive amount of pressure—on the Central Committee, the Council of Ministers, all the highest levels.

Torkanovskii goes on to state that within a year the issue had reached the Politburo: Leonid Abalkin, a professional economist and adviser to Gorbachev, asked Torkanovskii to draft a resolution for the Politburo "stating that the election of directors should be stopped."[86] Some directors, such as Valentin Landik of the Nord Association, simply refused to take part in elections; this type of opposition did not bode well for either democracy or production.

At the same time that managers were pressuring the government to stop the policy of elections, they were using their positions within the factory either to preempt elections or to control elections when they were held. The methods employed ran the gamut from the consensual to the coercive. At the Sibselmash Association in Novosibirsk, for example, the enterprise council and administration set up elections at all levels, but with an interesting twist: all those who occupied managerial positions were subjected to a "confidence" vote, and new elections were held only if the manager in question lost the vote.[87] Such examples of cooperation between independently minded enterprise councils and administrations, however, were few and far between.

In the majority of cases, elections of senior managerial personnel were purely formal affairs. The managers who occupied senior posts would be duly nominated; a second candidate, almost always a lower-ranking manager from the same enterprise, would also be nominated. Immediately before the election was held, the second candidate would withdraw his or her name from nomination in favor of the incumbent, and the current manager would win. The cases of Istoman at Makhachkala Electric and Nurmukhamedov at KamAZ (described above) fit this pattern; according to Torkanovskii, almost 90 percent of the elections held in 1987–1988 (which did not embrace all enterprises by any means) were conducted in this way.[88]

Regardless of the number of candidates, the single most important factor ensuring the election of managers to the posts that they already occupied was their power to reward and sanction those who worked beneath them. Workers and technical specialists in every factory included in this study echoed the opinion of Gennadi Kirilov from KamAZ: "There was no democracy in the elections, because the leaders and workers both knew that the workers got everything through the administration, and so they dared not oppose it."[89] "Everything" included job assignments, bonuses, housing, deficit goods, rooms at vacation resorts, spots on delegations to foreign firms, and, as the shop head at Makhachkala Electric argued, job security. Workers had a great deal to lose by voting against managers: those workers who were already beneficiaries of the patronage system—the labor aristocracy—could lose their perks, and those who were not stood to lose things much more basic.

For all the purely formal elections that were held, however, there were instances, such as the dismissal of the KamAZ shop head, in which elections did matter for the collectives involved. A number of other cases, usually involving directors of large enterprises, that were widely reported in the Soviet press[90] also demonstrate that the experience of elections was not uniformly negative. Nor should one conclude that only those cases in which managers were replaced represent legitimate elections: in many shops, workers voted for managers because they had confidence in them.

Over 90 percent of managers retained their positions in Soviet industry throughout the process of elections. In spite of this, managerial opposition to the policy grew steadily after 1987. Managers had two basic grounds for objecting to elections. First, senior managers felt that just as one would not elect just anyone to be a welder or lathe operator, so too managers could not be selected at random. While this is a sound argument, there is little evidence to support the contention that labor collectives in fact elected unqualified people to these posts or made unrealistic demands concerning wages, labor schedules, or work rules.[91] Second, many senior managers opposed the policy because it denied them tenure and denied the factory stable leadership. What troubled managers the most, however, was not the fact of elections, but the idea of elections. Soviet managers as a group did not accept the idea that they could be removed from their posts by the workers and technical specialists, that there should be "control from below," as Nikolai Shmelev put it. Even though as a rule managers successfully controlled the process of elections, the very fact that they increasingly had to spend time justifying their work, or more often finding ways to circumvent or manipulate the electoral provisions of the *LSE,* intensified their opposition.

The record of the enterprise councils—and the reactions of managers and workers to the councils—was much more mixed than that of elections. The enterprise councils of the factories discussed above are representative of the variations: the virtually inactive council of Makhachkala Electric was at one extreme, the council controlled by the strike committee at the Gorky mine was at the other, and the many KamAZ councils ran the gamut between them.

But for all the variations, the enterprise council as an institution in all these factories suffered from similar problems. The fundamental dilemma of the enterprise council, which proponents of self-management had predicted in their critiques of the *LSE,* was that its role and authority were unclear. Who did it represent, and what powers did it really have?

The answer to the first question was, of course, that the enterprise council represented the "labor collective," but no one knew exactly what that term included. As a result, the overwhelming number of councils elected immediately after the enterprise law came into effect were controlled by the factories' administrations. In 1987 and early 1988, it was relatively easy to create what was termed "a pocket council." In large part, this was a result of the majority of workers never having read or even seen the final version of the enterprise law. As one worker put it, "The law came down from on high and the ordinary workers didn't understand what the hell it was supposed to be."[92] Administrations often simply selected the members of the enterprise council and then presented a list of the names to a factory meeting. More often than not, the name at the top of the list was that of the director himself. It was estimated that in early 1988, over 80 percent of all council presidents nationwide were factory directors.[93]

As long as this was the case, the enterprise councils did not represent a particular threat to managerial control of enterprise operations or labor policy at the factory. This became particularly obvious during the 1989 strike, at Gorky and other mines. As Mikhail Kisliuk, the vice president of the Kemerovo regional council executive committee, put it: "The director and administrators were elected to the enterprise councils, and during the strike, no one heard from or saw the councils at all."[94] The issue of the propriety of having directors leading enterprise councils led to heated exchanges in the press;[95] eventually, the question had to be resolved by the Politburo, which published a "normative act" that recommended directors not be elected to head councils. As a result, the percentage of council presidents who were directors dropped to approximately a third by the middle of 1988; this coincided with the increased activity of the enterprise councils at KamAZ and other factories.[96]

Even when the councils began to achieve a modicum of institutional identity apart from the administrations, by more consistently representing the interests of workers and technical specialists in enterprises, it was still unclear what the councils had the authority to do. The constant disputes between the enterprise councils and the management of KamAZ over bonus rates and the reorganization or transferral of particular shops or factories within KamAZ are cases in point. In a different way, the arguments between the enterprise council and the trade union at the Gorky mine reflected the same problem. At Sibselmash, as at many other factories, the councils focused on devising long-range plans for the development of the enterprise, but the council presidents did not know if these plans could be made binding on the administration.

By 1990, the enterprise councils in many factories had found a niche for themselves in the structure of Soviet industry and labor relations, but they had never become the "second pillar of self-management" that the advocates of this new institution had hoped they would be. In part, this resulted from a poorly written law, but even more from the tenacity of existing power structures and shop-floor culture. The former made it possible for the administration to manipulate the enterprise councils, but failing that to either circumvent or ignore them. Self-management also had to fight against two "truths" that were deeply ingrained, at least among workers: first, that orders and initiative came from above, and decisions were made "on high"; and second, that all officially sponsored attempts to draw the workers into the management of production were by their very nature suspect. Overcoming these attitudes proved singularly difficult, particularly because the ways in which enterprise councils were elected and used by management at the factory level in 1987–1988 seemed to confirm these "truths" rather than debunk them.

The problems that emerged from the policy of self-management inside the factories were compounded by constant interference in managerial elections and enterprise council decision making by institutions outside the factories. Both the industrial ministries, which had the right to confirm or reject managers elected by labor collectives, and Party committees, which did not, tried to block candidates they did not like or otherwise influence elections, particularly where directors were concerned.[97] Torkanovskii estimates that only about one in ten elections in 1987–1988 was free from manipulation by the administration, the ministry, the Party, or some combination thereof.

The concept of self-management ran afoul of the ministries in other ways as well. In spite of the provisions of the enterprise law pertaining to the independence of factories and associations, ministries continued to unilaterally reorganize, restructure, or close enterprises, to ignore enterprise council and administration decisions on plan targets, and to violate regulations regarding limitations on state orders.[98] There were two separate but related issues here. The first was whether the enterprises would be independent from the center; the second was who would control the enterprise if it became independent. Disputes with the center pitted ministries against both administrations and enterprise councils, and continual ministerial interference undermined economic reform, the idea of economic reform, the institutions of self-management, and the idea of production democracy all at the same time. It was difficult for workers to focus on the issue of internal factory democracy while enterprises still suffered from a lack of external democracy—that is, remained under the control of the ministry. What good was electing managers or controlling the enterprise council if the ministry still decided all major questions anyway? So managers and workers often worked together to free the enterprise from the ministry before going after each other.

It was in this context, perhaps inevitably, that the question of changing the forms of state property arose with increasing frequency after 1988. More and more, workers, managers, and the Gorbachev leadership came to the conclusion that gaining any level of firm control over their lives at the workplace depended on obtaining complete control over planning, budgets, and the physical plants themselves. As enterprises such as KamAZ, Nord, Makhachkala Electric, and others began leasing and joint-stock programs, struggles over the makeup of leasing councils and the distribution of stocks added a new component to the already complex issue of self-management and control over industrial property.

In a formal sense, the disputes and struggles engendered by the elections of managerial personnel and the existence of councils of the labor collectives were resolved with the stroke of a pen when the 1990 *Law on the Enterprise* came into force. The provisions of the original law for the election of managers were eliminated entirely. The Council of the Labor Collective was replaced by a new Council of the Enterprise, which was to be made up of an even split between managers and "representatives of the labor collective." The rights of this new council were also severely circumscribed. In effect, the policy of self-management was officially abandoned. The government, facing an increasingly serious economic crisis, wanted to eliminate any factors that complicated production; by 1990, Ryzhkov and the rest of the leadership had become convinced that self-management was such a factor.

The reasons they came to this conclusion are not entirely clear. Although Ryzhkov, Ligachev, Abalkin—and apparently Gorbachev, who said nothing against the resolution banning elections—all argued that elections proved damaging to production, there is no statistical or other data to confirm this position. Since over 90 percent of the managers who stood for election retained their posts throughout the perestroika years, it is difficult to imagine the correlation between managerial election and disruptions in production. There is at least arguable evidence—some of which is presented above—that the factory councils caused managers consternation and delayed or altered decisions that managers deemed wise. But here too, there is no direct evidence to support the claim that the councils exacerbated the economic crisis.

The most likely reason for the decision, based on the comments of labor specialists and indirectly on Ryzhkov's statements, is that managers did not like the policy, and felt that standing for elections and arguing with the factory councils was beneath them and a waste of time. Managers considered the policy to have been ill conceived, they lobbied furiously against it, and they welcomed the change when it came. What Nikolai Shmelev termed the administrators' "caste arrogance" seems, in the final analysis, to have won the day.

Workers responded to the elimination of the self-management provisions of the enterprise law in a variety of ways, just as they had to the provisions themselves. Many workers also believed that the policy was ill-conceived and never took part in the self-management mechanisms. For others, however, the factory councils were "schools of democratization," and the gutting of the enterprise law undermined an important mechanism for involving workers in politics at the shop-floor level.

While it was relatively easy to rewrite the *Law on the Enterprise,* it proved impossible to reverse the effects of the original legislation. The policy of self-management had shaken up Soviet industry and life on the shop floor, and it had changed the face of labor politics in some important ways. Although ministerial interference in the operation of enterprises continued unabated throughout this period, the policy of self-management had made ministerial control a reality to be challenged rather than a fait accompli to be accepted. And such control was increasingly rejected by enterprises after 1987, both rhetorically and in fact. In this sense, at least, democratization in industry shook both the ideological legitimacy and the control mechanisms of the neo-Stalinist system. The reduction of such control was central to any form of self-management, particularly one predicated on giving workers enhanced opportunities for involvement. Before 1987, there was no question of who made decisions about factory plans and development: it was the ministry, either in consultation with the management of the enterprise or not. To workers, it made little difference, because in either case they had no say in such decisions.

The transfer of a measure of power away from the ministries to the enterprises, limited though it might have been, altered the nature of factory politics by suddenly making the question of who controlled factory decision making an important issue. All of those issues previously decided by the ministries alone—wage rates, bonuses, expenditure of funds for social development, plan targets, and so on—became, in the period from 1987 to 1990, the fodder for struggles between the enterprise councils, the unions, and the factory administrations. The change in center-periphery relations brought on by the enterprise law gave workers an opportunity for influence that they had never before possessed.

The greater latitude given to factories by the enterprise law was, however, a double-edged sword, at least for workers. Although workers obtained the structural space to exert greater influence, so too did management, and management was better placed to take advantage of it. Given the intent of the enterprise law, it is ironic that managers in many factories—according to workers at both KamAZ and Makhachkala Electric—became even more capricious after 1987 than they had been before, because neither the central ministries nor the central trade union apparatus exercised sufficient control. One of the striking features of this period of perestroika was seen in the large issues of labor politics formerly resolved by the ministry/Party/trade union apparatus in Moscow or regional centers being decided at the factory level, where so much more depended on the outcome of shop-floor struggles than had ever been the case in the past.

Managers as a group won most of these shop-floor struggles, benefiting more than either the workers or the ministries from the industrial reform policies of the late 1980s, and thus were in a better position economically and politically to take control of the privatization process that began after 1990. For the administrators of most factories in the Soviet Union, the industrial legislation of 1990 that formally abandoned any pretense of self-management was epiphenomenal. The important victories of management were those that allowed it to gain control over the new institutions in the factories and to direct the development of industrial relations policy in this period. As examined above, managers at the factories included in this chapter achieved their goals in a myriad of ways, acquiring more power at the factory level when central ministerial and Party control eased.

This was not always a bad thing from the point of view of the labor collectives these managers controlled. In many cases, managers in the localities had a much better sense of what the workers and technical specialists of a given factory wanted, and of what the needs of a region were, than did ministerial or Party representatives. Relations between managers and workers were by no means uniformly adversarial: managers were not always "authoritarian types," and workers as a rule respected capable and influential administrators. Most managers interviewed here were more than happy to maintain cordial and cooperative relationships with workers and technical specialists as long as those workers and specialists "knew their place" and stayed in it. This, of course, was the problem. The ideology of Soviet socialism always maintained that direct self-management by a politically conscious populace was legitimate, necessary, and the ultimate goal of socialist construction. This tenet of Soviet ideology was inculcated into Soviet workers for decades, and was part of workers' political culture. Communist or not, Soviet workers believed in their right to participate in the management of their lives at work and of the lives of their enterprises. Gorbachev's policy of democratization appealed to this belief, and managerial opposition to labor's participation in enterprise management exacerbated relations between managers and workers that were often already seriously strained. Self-management inside the factory was all about adding more chairs at the head table. On this question, management drew the line, in most cases successfully.

The rhetoric of perestroika—like that of Soviet socialist ideology in general—promised that in the area of labor relations the workers would become the "masters of their enterprises," but the reality fell far short of the words, partly because no one knew how to translate the idea of self-management into viable institutions. It happened even more, however, because managers struggled against the idea, and the institutions and the workers became disillusioned with the process of and prospects for restructuring Soviet socialism in a democratic direction. The old system of industrial relations began to disintegrate in the years after 1987, and with it the security that came with familiarity. Although workers were told there was going to be a new system in which they would have greater say, they continually had to fight for the rights ostensibly given them in the enterprise law. Workers were told they could elect managers, but management seemed more powerful than ever. Perestroika was supposed to reinvigorate the economy, but after 1988 Soviet living standards and working conditions began to deteriorate noticeably. Self-management had failed in so many ways that it bred cynicism, frustration, and anger among workers, rather than producing an economically and politically empowered constituency to reform the Soviet system into a democratic socialist state. Gorbachev and his allies had staked a great deal on workers' enthusiastically embracing perestroika and democratization on the shop floor. These leaders were disappointed—but no more so than the workers, who although promised much had gained little of concrete value from Gorbachev's reforms of the labor relations system.

If the self-management policy of the 1987–1990 period failed to provide workers the tools and the impetus to assist the Gorbachev leadership in carrying out its "programmatic goals," it nevertheless played an important role in the reemergence of workers as political actors in the Soviet (and now post-Soviet) system. The role this policy played in the process was both positive and negative. In spite of all the problems with managerial elections and the enterprise councils, both elements of the self-management policy affected the organizational politics of factory life. In many cases, enterprise councils became centers for opposition to managerial abuses of power or trade union inactivity, as occurred at KamAZ and Gorky. Although the councils seldom succeeded in achieving their goals, they provided workers and technical specialists with organizational and political experience. Just as some enterprise councils were "absorbed" into the existing structure of labor-management relations, there were cases in which the councils became institutions for workers and specialists to express their interests outside of the traditional institutional "triangle" of management, party, and trade union committees. And even though "pocket councils" could be found, there were councils that helped to reinvigorate, and came to represent, "factory civil society."

The very fact that there were extensive struggles in some factories to gain control over the enterprise councils, or to gain enough votes among council members to adopt policies favored by workers, also provided workers with important lessons in organizational politics. Hundreds of informal workers' groups sprang up in factories throughout the Soviet Union in these years. Some were short-lived, others continued to function well after the self-management policies of the 1987–1990 period were eliminated, and some even served as a basis for future independent union organizing. The issues these councils were concerned with varied enormously, from wages to working conditions to the distribution of deficit goods. The ability of workers to form such groups was not only the result of the atmosphere bred by the general policies of glasnost and perestroika. It was also the result of having an institution in the factory to which workers could address their concerns—an institution that in principle they were supposed to control. The frustration that many workers felt because they did not control the enterprise council was the original impetus for forming these groups in the first place.

The inadequacies of the self-management institutions were made all the more apparent by the increasing freedom of management to make decisions independently of the center, which often manifested itself as managerial capriciousness from the workers' point of view. This "managerial authoritarianism," as a Dagestani lathe operator termed it, fueled worker resentment against perestroika, against Gorbachev, and eventually against the Soviet political order as a whole. It also contributed to the emergence, among certain elements of the Soviet working population, of what used to be called "working-class consciousness," although this is perhaps too grandiose a term for what was developing by 1990. As the Soviet command-administrative system began to break down, the party/state-enforced elements of coercive corporatism that typified industrial relations began to founder as well. Factory administrations, for example at KamAZ, began to distinguish themselves from "the labor collectives" that they managed; workers, most visibly the miners, began to do likewise by separating themselves from the factory nomenklatura, the Party committees, the unions, and in some cases other groups of workers.

Political and economic reform in the industrial realm gave workers an opportunity to participate in factory-level decision making; it gave them a forum for presenting their views and interests, and a reason to organize in support of those interests. The limitations, contradictions, and ultimate failure of the policy of self-management, however, drove workers away from participation in the system and then on toward a rejection of the fundamental bases of Gorbachev's reform program. But the failure of the policy of self-management to significantly empower workers did not drive workers out of politics; rather, it prompted them to seek new, independent mechanisms through which they could articulate and struggle for their interests. Gorbachev's program did not create a constituency for his brand of reform socialism, but it did trigger the creation of a number of different constituencies among workers for other types of political and socioeconomic change. Some groups were socialist but not Soviet; some were liberal democratic, some nationalist and authoritarian, and some nationalist and democratic. Perestroika in industry revealed the structural imperatives that led workers to embrace or resist democratization in the Soviet Union, and that continue to function in Russia today. For all of the failings of the policy of self-management, this is an enduring legacy.

CHAPTER FOUR

Class Power and Power Politics

Workers' Responses to a System in Crisis, 1989–1991

Given the perspective of most theories on the transition from authoritarianism, Gorbachev's policy of workplace democratization was a mistake because it challenged the existing form of control over property. In the Soviet case it turned out differently: workplace democracy advanced the reform program by bringing workers back into politics through engagement with their economic lives. The same was true in the case of labor protest and radicalism. Excessive demands by workers are believed by most transition theorists to be at the very least unhelpful and at the most dangerous to the transition process. In the Soviet case, however, labor radicalism from 1989 to 1991 advanced the transition process in three ways. First, it drew workers further into the process initiated by Gorbachev's policy of workplace democracy. Second, the strikes of 1989–1991 helped to undermine the cohesiveness of the central ruling apparatus. While this may have increased the likelihood of a conservative reaction to reform on the one hand, it also emboldened reformers and made a coherent response by the Soviet party/state less likely. Third, labor radicalism initiated a process of institution building (and rebuilding) among workers—an essential step (but by no means a conclusive one) in the emergence of civil society.

It may seem counterintuitive to argue that labor radicalism advanced the transition from authoritarianism in the Soviet Union since the Soviet system was a thing of the past by 1992. The end of the Soviet system, however, was caused by the political machinations of three republican leaders, not by the inexorable forces of history or even by the forces unleashed by Gorbachev's perestroika. There is little doubt that the Soviet Union would have looked very different after a new Union treaty, a coup in August 1991, and the rise of Yeltsin in Russia, but the reform of the Soviet Union as a unique social formation might well have continued. It was in reforming *this particular social system* that the labor movement played its positive role. What happened after the abolition of the Soviet Union in terms of democratization and labor politics is the subject of the following chapters. When viewed from the perspective of politics, the economy, society, and culture at the grassroots level, the effects of labor radicalism on the Soviet Union's transition were important and progressive.

Compared to other crucial issues in early 1989—national separatism, the problems associated with democratizing the political system, and the overall economic situation—the conflicts arising out of the industrial relations reforms seemed manageable and under control. It was true that Gorbachev's program for restructuring industrial relations had proven controversial and divisive. However, all of the arguments and political maneuvering had taken place within the parameters of industrial reform measures legislated from the center. Workers, when they organized, did so in an effort to elect managers in whom they had confidence, to gain control of factory labor councils, or to force their trade unions to take a more active role in defense of workers' interests. Unlike nationalists in the Caucasus and the Baltic republics, workers as a group were not in the streets.

Yet beneath the relative calm, another storm was gathering force, driven by two interrelated problems that industrial perestroika had engendered. The first was the failure of the policy of production democracy. While the promise of greater control over the workplace contained in the *LSE* had mobilized a great many workers in support of shop-floor restructuring, that promise had proved to be illusory. The second was the growing perception of the crisis and the drift in the economy. This was manifested concretely for many workers by the decreasing buying power of their pay packets, increasing shortages of consumer goods, supply problems and deteriorating job conditions at the workplace.

The storm broke in the summer of 1989, when over five hundred thousand miners from across the Soviet Union went on strike, changing the complexion of Soviet labor relations and Soviet officialdom's perception of the working class in the process. The labor movement in the Soviet Union was not in fact one movement, but several. These movements were from their inception deeply divided over goals and tactics, and within these movements goals and tactics changed over time. They all emerged, however, as the result of the progressive disintegration of the Soviet labor relations system after 1987 and the politicization of workers that the growing contradiction between the stated policies of perestroika and the realities of shop-floor life helped to foster.

The Long Hot Summer: The Miners' Strike of July 1989

In his 1989 New Year's address to the Soviet people, Mikhail Gorbachev noted that the upcoming year "did not promise to be and will not be without its problems."[1] In the sphere of industrial relations, the list of unresolved issues and problems was long and growing longer. In addition to the continued lack of effectiveness of the self-management institutions and related economic difficulties, the self-financing and decentralization policies contained in the enterprise law continued to be blocked by opponents at the center and subverted by either the avarice or the incompetence of managers and privileged workers at the periphery. As the situation worsened, center and periphery were often abetted by the official trade union apparatus. From local committees in factories to the highest officials of the All-Union Central Council of Trade Unions, the official Soviet unions evinced little interest in reforming the labor relations system, and more often than not proved an impediment to those attempting to do so.[2] Added to this were an increasing level of unemployment, the absence of new laws on trade unions, the settling of labor disputes, and unemployment compensation.

All of these issues had been fodder for the debates surrounding the future of the labor relations system in the context of perestroika. For industrial workers, the questions were not solely related to legislation or distant issues of large-scale structural reform. At the workplace, Gorbachev's statement of 31 December 1988 that "economic reform has not yet begun to work at full strength"[3] translated into a lack of supplies, a disruption of work schedules necessitating longer hours or extra workdays, and a decrease in safety procedures due to excess haste. What looked like long-term structural problems on the level of the national economy appeared as day-to-day problems of labor relations on the shop floor.

These problems had been building up long before the miners of the Kuzbass began their strike in July 1989. Although many of the difficulties faced by mines and other industrial enterprises had their roots in the pre-Gorbachev era, workers' grievances focused on the failure of Gorbachev's policies to solve them, and more particularly on the inability or unwillingness of enterprise managers to address them.[4] The scale of the July strike took most analysts, officials, and even workers by surprise, but the early months of 1989 had witnessed a number of small-scale strikes in mining regions and other industrial plants throughout the Soviet Union.[5] The workers' demands during these strikes, and the reaction of officials and commentators to the strikes, demonstrated not only the workers' state of mind, but also the misapprehension by officials and analysts of the realities of industrial relations as they stood in 1989.

Three years of glasnost, much of it in the industrial regions directed against the corruption, waste, and poor working and living conditions in and around Soviet factories, had created an atmosphere of protest and expectation. At the same time, however, a long list of unresolved economic and social problems festered, while the self-management institutions at the factory level seemed incapable of forcing managers to respond to the grievances of workers. At the same time, the political leadership, at the local, regional, and national levels—believing the new perestroika-era institutions did work or at least claiming to believe so—continued to view strike action as the result of either ignorance, hotheadedness, or irresponsibility on the part of the Soviet industrial worker.

The July strike was not well planned or organized ahead of time. It began in the Sheviakov mine with 80 workers from the night shift, soon joined by 260 miners on their way to work. The strike spread quickly to other mines in the city as well as to cities throughout the Kuzbass; from there it spread to the Donbass basin in Ukraine, to Karaganda, Vorkuta, Komi, and elsewhere.[6] The most important aspects of the strike for understanding the transition process in the Soviet Union were the responses of the major institutional players in the system, the nature of the demands made by the miners, the organization of the strike, and the effects of the walkout on industrial relations and politics.

The organizations that operated at the level closest to the mine workers, the trade unions, and the councils of the labor collectives were conspicuous by their absence from the ranks of the strikers. Although individual leaders of union locals and enterprise councils of the mines did play a significant role in the strike on the side of the striking miners, the unions and councils as organizations not only did not lead the strikes but in most cases ended up on the opposite side of the table in negotiations with the miners. The All-Union Central Council of Trade Unions, in fact, signed the protocol ending the strike on the same side as the government, with the strike committees signing it on the other.[7]

The reaction of the Communist Party to the strike was notable only in that it evidenced the growing schism and lack of coordination between the central Party leadership and the leadership in the provinces. Although clearly concerned by the implications of the strike, Gorbachev saw it as "evidence of grassroots worker support for reform."[8] Local Party officials, on the other hand, saw it as "lack of discipline, illegality, and permissiveness." Not surprisingly, the appearance of Aleksandr G. Mel'nikov, the First Secretary of the Party's regional committee, along with the USSR's coal minister Mikhail Shchadov, at a strike meeting on 11 July was greeted with "noise, shouting, and hissing from the square."[9] The local and regional Party apparatus took an oppositional stand not only toward the strike and later toward the workers' committees, but also toward Gorbachev and his stated position on the strike and on the importance of glasnost and democratization. The position of the local and regional party apparat was to prove highly detrimental to Gorbachev's standing in the region as time wore on and went a long way toward radicalizing the workers in the years ahead.

The administrative hierarchy of the coal industry—from the scientific and technical workers to the coal minister Shchadov—was seriously divided about the strike. In general, the technical workers, engineers, and shop-level managers were supportive.[10] Working as they did in close proximity to the mines, these groups were affected by the same increasing supply and safety problems as faced the workers and were equally frustrated by the pace of reform. The attitude of the local and regional administrators of the mines, namely, mine directors and the bureaucracy of the mine associations, ran the gamut from support to vitriolic opposition. Many mine directors sympathized with the demands of the miners and said nothing against the strike, even though most were uncomfortable with the miners' methods. A few managers took an active role in the strike. M.I. Naidov, the former general director of the Lenin mine in Prokop'evsk and head of a mining research association in the Kuzbass at the time, was asked by a journalist if he had read the strikers' demands. The journalist reported, "Naidov smiled, lowered his voice, and said: 'I haven't read them, I wrote them.'"[11] Many other directors, however, sided with the association-level bureaucracies, which were uniformly hostile to the strike.[12]

This bifurcation of the elite reached the highest levels of government. As noted above, Gorbachev was concerned about the effect of strike action, but he believed the miners' demands were just and said so on more than one occasion during the strike. The attitude of the government's point man—the coal minister M.I. Shchadov—was quite different. Shchadov was known as an "apparatchik's apparatchik," one who knew the coal industry well and tolerated no challenge to the system of administrative hierarchy or his own authority. Prior to the strike, a number of people's deputies from the Kuzbass came to him to discuss the problems facing their mining region. Their recollection of the end of the meeting was that "Shchadov responded: '*I* will solve these problems—here,' and he pounded his fist on the floor of his office."[13] Although he was the person sent to the Kuzbass to negotiate an end to the strike, Shchadov exhibited no sympathy whatsoever with the strikers.[14] The miners, for their part, had no time for Shchadov either, which only added to the problems of negotiation.

The divergent responses of the various elites to the strike had two effects on the nature and conduct of the action. First, lack of unanimity among the elite made it easier for the strikers to organize and coordinate the initially disparate and locally organized strike committees. Second, the clash between different sectors of the elites over the strike as a method of protest was quickly translated by the miners into a clash between pro- and anti-perestroika forces, which led to the ratcheting up of demands directed against the perceived (and often real) opponents of reform. This process in turn hardened the positions of both sides, exacerbating existing tensions and serving as a foundation for the further radicalization of opinions in the months and years to come.

One cause of the fissures within elite opinion was the nature of the demands and appeals made by the miners during the strike. Although the list of requirements varied from region to region, reflecting the particular problems facing each one, the core demands in all of the mining areas were the same. The miners wanted to receive what the enterprise law had in theory given them: economic independence from the ministry and the association structure, and greater control over the internal operations of their places of work. To be sure there were also wage appeals, including increases to offset inflation and supplemental pay for dangerous jobs and night work,[15] but the essence of the demands was a call to implement Gorbachev's policy of industrial perestroika. Gorbachev acknowledged this, and the miners proclaimed it at every opportunity.[16] Gorbachev's reforms, and the vitriolic debates that surrounded those reforms by 1989, convinced the miners that they had the freedom to protest, for Gorbachev himself had even encouraged Soviet citizens on numerous occasions to oppose those who stood in the way of reform. The decision to strike was the result of long pent-up grievances and the politicization of the miners due to the failures of perestroika both inside and outside the factory gates. At base, however, it was still a strike in support of the system and those attempting to reform it.

The way in which the strike was organized and conducted reflected the miners' concern that they not be seen as enemies of the reform process. There were three elements of the strike in particular that were important in this regard. The first concerned the scope of the strike. The regional councils of the strike committees wanted to avoid causing undue economic disruption in order to counter any claims that the miners were motivated solely by self-interest. Regional representatives of Party, state, and trade union institutions made such claims early on in the strike. An address from a number of "official organizations" dated 13 July stated that "the closing of enterprises in Mezhdurechensk has led to economic shortfalls. The further development of the strike . . . may lead to accidents, not to mention huge losses [in production]. Therefore these questions need to be resolved not so much through stopping work, but through established committees by means of negotiation and consolidation."[17] In response, the strike committees pointed out that (a) there was a two-month coal reserve already mined by the Kuzbass pits, and (b) selected mines producing coal for the region's immediate use had been instructed to remain in operation. In addition, workers from other sectors of industry were requested by the regional council of the strike committees not to go on strike for fear of putting undue strain on the economy or causing excessive inconvenience for those living in the mining cities.[18]

The second element involved the formation and functioning of the strike committees. Originally, these committees had been formed at the individual mines without any coordinating body guiding their activities or helping to formulate their demands. On 16 July, a regional committee was elected from the members of the city strike committees, which had already been formed out of the committees elected at the individual mines. Thus, by the sixth day of the strike a pyramid of strike committees was in place, providing the miners with a set of organizations parallel and analogous to those of the Party, state, and trade union apparatuses. This development facilitated coordination and negotiation, which proved crucial for the miners' labor movement in the long term.

The third element concerned the relationship between the strike committees and the local governments. Two aspects of this relationship were crucial in lending legitimacy to the strike. First, the miners and the strike committees went out of their way to maintain social order in the cities affected by the strike. Measures taken by the committees for this purpose included suspending the sale of all hard alcohol in the cities concerned, organizing joint patrols with the local militia, sending anyone who showed up drunk at a meeting to a "sobering-up center,"[19] organizing food deliveries, transport, and so on. This was done in order to deny the opponents of the strike any claim that the strike would lead to social chaos and rampant crime.

Such actions were also necessary because in many of the cities affected by the strike, the local power structures had simply ceased to function as local officials became paralyzed by the scope and intensity of the walkout. Mikhail Kisliuk, strike-committee member in 1989 and by 1991 deputy president of the Kemerovo regional government, recalled that "from the very first hours of the strike, the leaders of the command-administrative system virtually disappeared. The party committee, the local government organizations, everyone. And here, practically all power went over to the strike committees. Everything. Trade, the police, transport, communications—completely to the workers' committees."[20] It was not until well after the arrival of Shchadov and the government commission that local Party and state organizations, including the trade unions, began to function more or less "normally." The failure of local elites to respond to the strike quickly and maintain the operation of city services undermined the standing of these groups, but increased the prestige of the strike committees and laid the foundation for the evolution of competing authorities in the mining regions, a development that profoundly affected the politics of these regions during the next three years.

The emergence of such rival power centers in the mining regions reflected and encouraged a similar process that was taking place in the country as a whole in 1989. As the unity of the party/state system cracked in response to fundamental disputes within the ruling elites over the course of reform, other social and political groups seized the opportunity to establish themselves as important players in the political process. The strike committees composed one such group. In the mining regions, the strike committees put up slates of candidates for local, regional, and national elections in opposition to those nominated by the local and regional Party and state organizations.

In the midst of these events, and after a week of negotiations, the strike committees of the Kuzbass reached an agreement with the government commission and signed a forty-seven-point protocol; some of the miners' demands were met fully, and the government promised to negotiate the rest.[21] The strike wave continued, however, to spread to other regions, and it was not until the end of the month that the government secured the agreement of strike committees in most regions to cease striking on the basis of the protocol signed in the Kuzbass. The protocol, agreed to by the Supreme Soviet, became Resolution 608 of the USSR Council of Ministers. It was the first time since the mid-1920s that industrial action had forced concessions from the Soviet government.

The majority of the demands in the protocol dealt with long-term issues of economic restructuring, but the effects of the strike were felt immediately throughout the mines and mining communities in a number of ways. As with the negotiations and settlement of the strike overall, the organizational strength of the strike committees proved crucial in changing the power relations among organizations in the mines and within the mining regions in general. In the mines, the strike committees continued to function after the strike was concluded. The official reason was to ensure the enactment of the strike protocol, and the maintenance of the committees had been written into the agreement. The committees also provided the impetus for an extensive series of new elections within the power structures of the mines. The trade unions, enterprise councils, and Party committees were the most seriously affected. By September, miners in the Kuzbass had voted in new presidents for twenty-five trade union committees, and had elected entirely new trade union committees in eighteen mines.[22] In the Donbass, elections were held in all of the mines that had been on strike, and in some mines over 90 percent of those elected were new to the trade union committees.[23] The behavior of the trade unions during the strike and the pounding that the local and regional trade union apparatuses took after the strike also set in motion a debate about the future of the entire Soviet trade union system.[24]

Much the same occurred with the staffs of the Councils of the Labor Collectives, which were controlled by the strike committees to a greater extent than the local trade union committees, because the latter still were subordinate to the regional and central organizations of the official trade union structure.[25] In both the Kuzbass and the Donbass, the newly elected enterprise councils in some cases voted to expel the factory committee of the CPSU from their mines, and in the Donbass, the local strike committees passed votes of no confidence on forty-two mine and association directors.[26]

The opposition of Party committees located in the mining regions did a good deal of damage to the credibility of the Party. The most lasting effect of the conflicting positions taken by the local, regional, and central party organizations was that workers' organizations stopped viewing the Party as a unified organization that was willing (or able) to carry out the policies of the leadership. In terms of industrial relations policy, and to a lesser extent in terms of economic policy, the July strike and the signing of Resolution 608 forced the government into a reactive position and took some control out of its hands.

The wave of strikes that occurred in 1989, the miners' strike first among them, sent a shock through the Soviet system and generated great soul-searching in many quarters. The miners' strike alone affected over one thousand enterprises, decreased coal output for the year by 7.6 million tons, and cost the coal industry over 200 million rubles in profits, according to official statistics.[27] The money these strikes cost the economy spurred calls for the restoration of order and labor discipline throughout the system.

On 21 September 1989, when Gorbachev met with workers who were also elected Party officials, they made it clear to him that in their opinion further industrial action would cripple perestroika. K. N. Panov from Gorky stated that "disorder, brought on by strikes, leads to crime." V. M. Malykin argued that "only someone with a grudge or who wants to force his way into power calls for a strike. Such 'agents' should be decisively repulsed." And V. S. Kostin from Prokop'evsk—the birthplace of the July strike—warned that "some sort of social-political organization" had been created in the Kuzbass and was sending couriers to other regions to disturb the workers. "In my view," he added, "these issues demand the attention of the central authorities."[28] The "social-political organization" to which he referred was the Union of Workers of the Kuzbass, founded on 6 September 1989. As a means of defending perestroika, regional Party workers were asking Gorbachev to turn the Party apparatus against groups that Gorbachev, only two months before, had called genuine examples of perestroika from below. In industrial centers, particularly, the fissures in the Party were widening.

The strike also highlighted the fragility of the Soviet planned economy and the consequent vulnerability of the central government to large-scale strike action. The economist P. Slezko, writing in *Nedelia,* argued that "our economic system, with its strict central links, is many times more vulnerable to strikes than any other system. And their destructive effects are absolutely incomparably greater than any achievements that the strikers might hope to gain." In Slezko's view, this was ample reason for severe limitations on strikes and strict enforcement of laws governing labor disputes, all the more so because the government had nothing to give the miners by way of monetary or other concessions. The argument that strikes were both pointless and dangerous was made by many, and Slezko delivered it with a note of venom: "What's the use of putting a knife to someone's throat if his pockets are empty?"[29]

The miners maintained that they were not putting a knife to the throat of perestroika but rather trying to break the chokehold of those who were strangling it. For this reason the strike focused on economic demands designed to bring to fruition the very policies upon which Gorbachev's perestroika was based. But while the demands were economic, the essence of the strike was political. As the late Len Karpinskii, editor of *Moscow News,* argued:

> They struck "for" and they struck "against." . . . They struck for perestroika in fact, and against the attempts of conservative forces to block its development, to reduce it to nothingness. . . . [T]he miners stopped their work because administrative functionaries, to the contrary, show up to their jobs every day in an orderly fashion, sabotaging, in essence, the course of history. The miners' strike was an answer to the "sit-down strike" of the bosses.[30]

The accumulated economic problems and perestroika's failure to solve them were only part of the reason the miners struck. The successes and failures of democratization made up the rest.

Democratization and glasnost as general policies had provided political space and sanction for groups and individuals outside the official sphere to function and speak out. These policies also encouraged the idea that people had a right to participate in social, economic, and political affairs. At the shop-floor level, however, the specific forms of the policies had failed to empower workers sufficiently to enable them to address effectively their social and economic problems. The strike was seen as a remedy for unsolved problems and dysfunctional institutions. It appeared, therefore, inherently political as well as economic, since fulfilling the economic demands required changing the balance of political power from the center to the periphery and from the bureaucracies to the collectives. Of course, in the Soviet Union of 1989 any large-scale strike by industrial workers would have constituted by its very nature a political act. Self-organization by workers called into question the hegemony and the adequacy of the Communist Party and the Soviet trade unions—indeed, of the entire party/state system—as guardians of working-class interests.

Evolution from Below: Miners' Organizations, 1989–1991

In the early spring of 1991, Soviet miners went on strike again, but the goals of this strike were different. In 1989, the miners had supported Gorbachev and his reforms; in 1991, they demanded his resignation and the abandonment of the Soviet political system and the centrally planned economy. The reasons for such a massive reorientation of this wing of the labor movement were the failure of the central and regional government and Party institutions to implement the economic points contained in Resolution 608 and the increasingly bitter power struggle between the workers' organizations and the party/state apparatus. The struggle over economic reform and political power influenced even the politics of the Union treaty and the election of Boris Yeltsin as president of Russia. The struggle also intensified the divisions among the various labor movements in the Soviet Union.

The conflicts that arose after the strike cannot be explained, however, without considering the changing role of the strike committees. At the end of the July strike, the committees were reorganized into smaller, but permanently functioning, workers' committees. As foreseen in the strike protocol, these committees were to monitor the implementation of Resolution 608, but also "took it upon themselves to guarantee social order and the necessities of daily life. They enjoyed great authority among the people. It was to them, much more than to the *ispolkomi* (executive committees of the local Soviets), that people went with their troubles, requests, and suggestions."[31] The workers' committees thus became the second locus of a system of dual power in the coal regions after the strike.

Developing the organizational structure of the workers' committees was central to the workers' movement in three ways. First, the committees provided an alternative base for political organization independent of existing structures. Second, they served as an alternative conduit for information, through an affiliated independent newspaper called *Nasha gazeta*. Third, the committees in each region provided core groups that facilitated interregional organization of the movement.

The organizational structure of the committees reflected the growing "anti-centralist" mood in the country as a whole. Aleksandr Aslanidi of the Council of Workers' Committees of the Kuzbass described this structure as "the opposite of democratic centralism." Each mine-level committee elected representatives to the city committee, which in turn elected members to the regional committee. Only the decisions of the mine committee were obligatory for the mine; the decisions of each higher committee carried the status of recommendations. According to Aslanidi, there were two reasons for this: "first, local demands or circumstances might dictate some other course; and second, we view it as a much more democratic way to control the movement."[32] This loose arrangement worked well in keeping the rather volatile committees together while maintaining a constant organizational presence in the major regional centers. In the Kuzbass, the committees' presence was nicely symbolized by their offices being located in the Supreme Soviet building in Kemerovo—just down the hall from the oblast president's office, and across the square from the Communist Party's headquarters.

As important as the organizational structure of the committees in keeping the workers' movement alive was the committees' struggle to gain access to the media. Such access was not easy to attain; the workers' committees and the journalists allied with them fought a long battle for glasnost in the Kuzbass. The problem was finally solved by the founding of independent newspapers, first in the Kuzbass in December 1989 and later in 1990 in other regional mining centers.[33] The example of *Nasha gazeta* is particularly important because the struggle to found the paper contributed to the radicalization of the workers' movement in the Kuzbass. The issue of media access first arose during the strike, when inaccurate information about the development of the strike was published in the Party-controlled press in the Kuzbass and Donbass.[34] A number of reform-minded journalists from the regional Party paper set out, with the agreement of the regional strike committee, to publish an independent paper. The local Party apparatus, however, which controlled all the major printing presses, refused access to the presses and blocked the registration of the paper at the regional level. The paper finally received permission to publish after a four-month struggle, but opposition from Party and local government officials became something of a cause célèbre among the workers' committees. Such opposition simply reinforced the impression, formed during the strike, that the party/state apparat was determined to sabotage the labor movement.[35]

Equally important, opposition to the paper by regional Party and government institutions helped draw workers from other industries into the labor movement. Before receiving permission to go to print, the paper's editors and the regional workers' committee arranged to have it published under the auspices of various factory newspapers controlled by sympathetic labor collectives. In this way, the official papers of the construction workers, the chemical workers, the metalworkers, and the railroad workers became closely tied to the miners' committees. The image of outmaneuvering hostile local elites gave credence to the power of the labor movement and helped politicize workers in other important industries.[36]

Finally, the restructuring of the strike committees into permanent workers' committees provided a foundation for building intra- and interregional links between sections of the labor movement. On the initiative of the workers' committees, the Union of Workers of the Kuzbass was formed on 6 September 1989. By its fourth conference, it brought together not only miners' committees but also representatives of other industries in the Kuzbass and delegates from the coal-mining regions of the Donbass, Inta, Vorkuta, and Karaganda. The continuation of the workers' committees was also instrumental in organizing the Confederation of Labor (Konfederatsiia Truda) and the miners' congresses in 1990.

The official reaction to the formation of the Union of Workers of the Kuzbass and to the plan to publish a newspaper of the workers' movement had already worsened relations between the workers' movement and the government by the fall and early winter of 1989. As the deadline (1 January) to fulfill Resolution 608 approached and the government failed to act, reaction in the mining regions was swift. On 20 December, Mikhail Kisliuk reminded readers in the newspaper *Stroitel'* that the government's declaration on self-management and self-financing for the Kuzbass had "been returned to the USSR Council of Ministers, where it was already reviewed and signed." This, he argued, was "a maneuver that signified the practical burial of self-financing for the Kuzbass."[37] Another article of the same day called the process "a series of small deceptions" and concluded: "All of these manipulations bear out what we have already said: today the regional association is *the* brake on perestroika."[38] Dissatisfaction in the mining regions increased when Prime Minister Ryzhkov turned the draft resolutions on regional self-financing over to the republics' councils of ministers. This was viewed as a delaying tactic and prompted even more strident responses.[39]

As tense as the situation was, neither side was willing to force the other's hand. In January 1990, a government commission led by Lev Riabev arrived in Prokop'evsk to conduct further negotiations with the council of workers' committees over the implementation of the strike protocol. The result was a new draft agreement for implementing Resolution 608 in 1990.[40] A major conflict had been averted, but the underlying feeling within the workers' movement had shifted from one of expecting the government to fulfill the protocol to one of having to force the government to do so. When asked what would happen if the government did not accept the draft, one of the leaders of the Kuzbass workers' committee responded in a way that reflected the new mood: "There are a number of options. Which will we pick? We will consult with the people. In any case, we have a rich arsenal of ways to exert influence. Which ones we deploy will depend on the strength of the opposition."[41] The opposition from this point on was no longer limited to just ministerial apparatchiks and Party conservatives. After January 1990, everyone was suspect.

Most of 1990 was taken up with an endless series of meetings, congresses, conferences, and elections, all of which in various ways fueled existing disagreements and disputes. The events of the year intensified the spiral of radicalization of the labor movement and the increasingly hostile attitude of the party/state apparatus toward it. The process of radicalization was pushed along by conflicts at both the national level and the local level; the year 1990 also saw the labor movement becoming involved for the first time in power struggles at the highest echelon of the Soviet system.

In April, a congress of the official state trade union representing miners—the Union of Coal Miners—was held in Moscow. The congress seriously undermined the confidence of most miners that the union could be restructured. One delegate to the congress from Vorkuta, V. Kopasov, noted that "actual miners were in a minority at the congress." Among the delegates to this trade union congress were 1 minister, 4 ministerial assistants, 24 general directors of associations, 19 mine directors, 232 trade union committee chairmen, 67 regional trade union chairmen, and 11 trade union central committee secretaries. Only 161 delegates were workers.[42]

The majority of the miners left the congress to draft a document in favor of convening a congress of miners independent of the trade union, and the rest of the congress proceeded to elect new leaders and a new central committee, which was dominated by trade union and former Communist Party apparatchiks.[43] The reorganization of the official trade union system had been one of the demands of the miners in 1989, and the All-Union Central Council of Trade Unions had agreed to hold a congress that was representative of the structure of the industry. The miners felt that they had been deceived once again and that the existing trade unions were unsalvageable.[44]

Reports on the trade union congress were given at the first Congress of the Independent Workers Movement held in Novokuznetsk from 29 April to 2 May 1990. Although the months since the strike in July 1989 had already seen the radicalization of the workers' movement, the Declaration of the Confederation of Labor, which was founded at the congress, went further in its denunciation of the system than any previous statement of the labor movement. In one year, the miners and other workers supporting them had gone from "purely economic demands" to the statement in the Declaration that "the Confederation of Labor must participate in political struggle, because without the active participation of independent movements and workers' organizations democratization and economic reform are impossible to achieve."[45] These congresses were a watershed for the workers' movement. Previously, the workers' movement had used its independent organizations as a lever to gain either influence or control over existing institutions that they felt could be altered to serve workers' interests. After the official union's congress and the congress of the Confederation of Labor, at least one wing of the labor movement irrevocably broke with the institutions that the party/state deemed acceptable mechanisms for reforming the Soviet system.

The confederation called for the "end of the *diktat* of the CPSU," the "depoliticization of the MVD, KGB, the army, the courts, the procurator, and other state organizations, and the liquidation of Party committees from enterprises." Once the miners had proclaimed no confidence in the coal minister Shchadov, the confederation demanded the "complete resignation of the existing government." The confederation expanded its critique of the CPSU and demanded the nationalization of all Party property.[46] First Secretary Mel'nikov responded that "the movement of the union to politicization under radical slogans is dangerous," and accused the confederation's membership of being "deproletarianized elements and people who are trying to make political capital. That is why the leaders of the union often use incorrect methods in relation to the Party."[47] The tone of this and other pronouncements from the regional Party and government once again highlighted the split within the Party.

Mel'nikov's remarks led journalist Victor Kostiukovskii to remark that "the summer promises to be hot once again."[48] This judgment was reinforced and all of the events leading to the radicalization of the workers' movement were brought together at the first Congress of Miners, held in Donetsk during the second week of June. The resolution of the congress denounced the government for its failure to implement the strike agreement and demanded that the government resign in favor of a government "enjoying the people's trust." The congress declared its intent to create an independent union of miners, noting the failure of the existing unions to reform themselves and defend workers' rights. And finally, the miners' congress did not stop at denouncing the Communist Party's "monopoly on power" or its failure to reform; a separate resolution stated: "We do not consider the Communist Party of the Soviet Union our party. We call for a mass exit from the party."[49]

At the end of June 1990, a meeting took place that proved crucial in changing the dynamic of the labor movement. On 23 June, a delegation from the workers' committees of the Kuzbass met with Boris Yeltsin, who had been elected chairman of the Russian Supreme Soviet less than a month before. The dispute between the workers' movement and the central government now became embroiled in the power struggle between the republics and the Union (that is, the USSR), and most particularly between Gorbachev and Yeltsin. The increasing radicalization of the workers' movement was only one manifestation of the growing conflicts within the Soviet Union; since 1989, nationalist movements and ethnic conflicts had also been gathering force. The drive for republican "sovereignty" began later in the Russian Republic than elsewhere in the Union, but by the spring of 1990 it had gained considerable momentum. Yeltsin's program, presented in his campaign for the speaker's chair, reflected this drive and included demands for "ownership of all the republic's natural resources, an independent foreign policy, and the primacy of republican legislation over that of the USSR."[50]

Yeltsin's proposal for transferring ownership of Russia's natural resources to the Russian Republic provided an opportunity for the workers' movement to adopt a new tactic in its struggle to obtain the implementation of Resolution 608. The Council of Workers of the Kuzbass and the Confederation of Labor agreed to support Yeltsin in his struggle to wrest power from Gorbachev in exchange for a promise from Yeltsin to enact Resolution 608. Yeltsin was all too willing to accede to this arrangement. At the 23 June meeting, Yeltsin stated that "as far as the agreement that the Union government has refused to sign—hand it over to us. . . . We are prepared to take the most radical steps."[51] With this declaration, a new triangular conflict began to develop, gathering strength in the coming months.

Increasing divisions within the Party during the summer led the strike committees and workers' organizations of hundreds of mines and factories across the country to call for a one-day political strike to be held on 11 July. In all, an estimated three hundred thousand workers throughout the Soviet Union took part in work stoppages.[52] The strikers' demands included the resignation of the government, the nationalization of the property of the Communist Party and the official Soviet trade unions, and the "depoliticization" of all major non-Party institutions. In addition, the strike was a show of support, in the various republics, for the claims of republican leadership to sovereignty and regional economic autonomy, which the workers' committees had come to view as the best guarantor of their rights to enterprise self-management. The strike hardened the positions of all concerned. Virtually everyone in the central government, including Gorbachev, denounced it.

The Yeltsin government supported the strike, and in so doing drew the miners' organizations closer to the Confederation of Labor's representatives both in Moscow and the provinces. Between the strike in July and the end of 1990, while the Union and republican governments were concentrating on the issue of the Union treaty and the distribution of powers it contained, the focus of activity in the workers' movement shifted to organizational questions. The fifth conference of the Council of Workers' Committees of the Kuzbass in September indicated that there was a growing feeling within the workers' movement that the committees were becoming too involved in politics, to the detriment of factory-level organization and economic concerns. In order to rectify this problem, the conference resolved to delineate more clearly the sphere of activity of the various groups that had emerged since the 1989 strike. The Council of Workers' Committees of the Kuzbass was to focus on economic concerns and building independent trade union structures, while the Union of Workers of the Kuzbass would concern itself mainly with "political struggle" at the regional and national level.[53]

The second Congress of Miners opened in Donetsk on 23 October, after months of preparation marked by haggling over the agenda, disputes about who could be delegates, and arguments over who would pay for the meeting. The main goal of the congress was to create an independent union of mineworkers; while the union was finally created, the discussion leading up to the vote revealed deep divisions among the miners regarding the future of the movement. Many delegates were against the creation of an independent union, arguing that the old union could be reformed and had the material base to be effective, which a new union would lack. Proponents pointed to the mineworkers' union congress earlier in the year as evidence that the old unions enjoyed no confidence among the workers. Although the resolution creating the union passed, the vote revealed splits among the delegates that continued to exert an influence on labor politics in the coal industry beyond the abolition of the Soviet Union in 1991.

In the eighteen months after the July 1989 strike, the workers' committees based in the mines and the labor organizations of workers in other industries, loosely linked through the Confederation of Labor, had changed dramatically. They had evolved from spontaneously generated and ill-organized strike committees and workers' groups into a well-organized political and politicized force of substantial importance. While it is true that by late 1990 this workers' movement embraced only a small fraction of all Soviet workers, the unprecedented nature of their actions in the context of the Soviet system gave these workers' groups an influence vastly in excess of their numbers. By the end of 1990, the attitude of the labor movement toward the Union government, the Communist Party, and the issue of republican sovereignty was a liability for Gorbachev and an important asset for Yeltsin and other republican elites. But for all the vitriolic language that the various sides in these disputes had exchanged since the first strike, negotiations were still under way as the new year began.

Strike Three, We're Out: Politics, Economics, Sovereignty, and Soviet Workers, 1991

By 1991, the Soviet Union was in the grip of an unprecedented political and economic crisis. Since at least May of the preceding year, a "war of laws" between the Union government and the republics had deepened the country's economic problems. After months of debate surrounding the Shatalin plan, the Union government had finally adopted a new program of economic reform that was a significantly watered-down version of the five-hundred-day program. As part of the government's plan, a series of stabilization measures was adopted, designed to reassert the central government's control over the entire economy and polity.[54] These measures were taken without the agreement of the republics, and they came into direct conflict with the economic programs that had been adopted by the Supreme Soviet of the Russian Republic under Yeltsin and by other republican legislatures. The stabilization plan also restricted the right to strike, which heightened worker resentment against the government. The question of economic control was central to the negotiations over a new Union treaty.[55] While Gorbachev appealed for strong republics and a strong center, and warned against the "Lebanonization" of the Soviet Union, the republican elites demanded extensive economic and political rights, with a very limited role for the central government.

This war of laws affected labor collectives directly, insofar as the different economic programs gave the republics, regions, and enterprises vastly different rights, yet it was unclear which laws were authoritative. The labor movement centered around the miners' committees had already sided with Yeltsin and the other republican elites on the question of sovereignty. The workers' committees viewed the central government's economic program and position on the Union treaty as evidence of "a growing reactionary wave," with the "center strengthening the union structures, which are blocking radical reform." This view was compounded by the appointment of people like Gennadi Yanaev as vice president and Boris Pugo as minister of internal affairs, appointments seen by the workers' committees as further evidence of Gorbachev's growing authoritarianism.[56]

In the wake of the regime's use of violence in Vilnius in January 1991, the workers' movement shifted the focus of its activities away from a concentration on organizational matters back toward politics; at the same time, the movement started to show some signs of strain. The major organizations of the workers' movement called for a political strike to protest the government's use of force and began to reemphasize their relationship with Yeltsin and other republican elites. After January 1991, this wing of the Soviet labor movement lined up directly against Gorbachev.

Although unified in their opposition to the government's actions in Lithuania, the call of the workers' committees for a political strike in response brought to the surface the strains that had emerged in the movement since 1989. To the surprise of the leaders of the workers' committees, the political strike they had appealed for did not materialize, and there was a great deal of recrimination within the labor movement as a result. A panoply of opinions explained why the strike failed to occur,[57] but two factors seemed central. First, a year and a half of conflict and strikes had not brought improvement in either the economic or the political situation, and people in the movement were simply tired. They were also skeptical of the utility of further demonstrations of opposition that did not address specific issues concerning the well-being of local populations. Second, the workers' movement had not entirely succeeded in carrying out the organizational work that it had begun in September 1990. The council of the workers' committees worked throughout the late winter and early spring to rectify this situation, but political concerns deflected their attention.

By the beginning of March 1991, several factors leading to increased calls for strike action by workers' committees had coalesced in a number of republics. From the middle of February on, Yeltsin's opposition to Gorbachev had become more uncompromising and the drive within the Russian Parliament for full sovereignty ever more insistent. Yeltsin's statements encouraged the workers' committees, which had been strongly favoring such sovereignty for some time. All of this occurred in the context of the upcoming referendum on the future of the Soviet Union, and the workers' committees saw a strike as a means to counter the pro-Union appeals of the Party and state institutions. The political demands, and the workers' committees' justifications for them, were similar to those raised at the time of the unsuccessful strike in January, but by March an additional set of problems had arisen in the economic sphere that added an entirely new set of demands and a much more local and regional dimension to the strike call. Because of the generally deteriorating economic conditions and, more immediately, the recent innovations in currency and pricing policy of the government of Valentin Pavlov, supply problems and inflation had increased throughout the country. In the run-up to the strike, wage demands reappeared near the top of the initial manifestos of individual mines.[58]

For the labor movement as a whole, the reemergence of economic issues was represented by the General Standard Wage-Rate Agreement, a document designed to redefine and codify wages, pensions, health and social insurance, and workplace safety regulations.[59] The enactment of new regulations regarding these matters had been one of the central demands of the 1989 strike, but little progress had been made in the interim. The government and the miners' union had been negotiating over the General Agreement for months, particularly over changes in pension rates, the length of employment needed to attain them, and the issue of wage indexing. Although an agreement was reached, the version announced by Pavlov did not match the one that the Independent Union of Mineworkers had agreed to. As a result, the miners' union set a 12 March deadline for the government to sign the original; if it did not, the miners would strike.[60]

The crucial difference between the strike call in March and the one in January was that by March the miners' organizations had reestablished a strong link between the political and economic demands that most affected the future of the mining regions. Wages, pensions, and social insurance were bread-and-butter issues for miners, and the leaders of their workers' committees had become effective in linking these issues to the broader political situation. Although basic economic issues could not be solved, so the argument went, by negotiating with the Union government, the Russian government had said it stood behind the miners' demands. Gorbachev had been promising action since 1989, but had not delivered. Therefore Gorbachev must go, the Union government must resign, and the Russian Federation must be given greater authority to make economic decisions. In the referendum, miners should vote against the Union and for sovereignty. Thus, by 1991 it was clear that the workers' committees and the miners no longer had faith in Gorbachev or the Union government, but their unhappiness was only translated into effective action when the bread-and-butter issues of economic security were tied to the great issues of the day.[61]

The strike of 1991 began in earnest on 4 March and was confrontational from the outset. By this time, none of the sides involved—the Union government, the Russian government, or the miners—was in any mood to compromise, and it was unclear that they could have done so had they wanted to. The strike continued for over two months as each side tried to outmaneuver the other. The workers' committees, the national and regional apparatus of the Communist Party, and the Union government engaged in an ongoing propaganda war over how the strike was represented in the country as a whole, and particularly in the mining regions. The Union government had a dual strategy: first, it refused to engage in any negotiations with the workers' committees whatsoever and ignored their demands entirely. Second, through the Party and central press and television, the government tried to create the impression that the miners were attempting to improve their own positions at the expense of everyone else and that the strike was threatening the very existence of the nation's economy.[62] On the regional level, authorities attempted to set workers against each other, particularly the metalworkers and electricians, for whom regular coal supplies were vital.[63]

The workers' committees responded quickly. Newspapers affiliated with these committees kept a running account throughout the strike of the number of workers involved, the different industrial sectors from which they were drawn, and the letters, telegrams, and donations in support of the strike that came in from workers and workers' committees throughout the country.[64] The strike committees in individual cities and the regional workers' committees sent delegations to all of the major factories in their areas to explain their version of the strikers' demands and to respond to the statements of Party and government spokesmen.[65] Finally, the workers' committees were careful to keep the strike limited. From the outset, the regional council decided to continue coal production and delivery to those factories that worked on a "constant production cycle," which included both metallurgical and electrical plants, and to ask workers from other industries not to join the strike, but rather to support the miners in financial and other ways.[66]

In spite of the best efforts of each side to undermine the position of the other, the impasse that had existed since the beginning of the strike continued throughout April. Neither side had the ability to force a solution to the problem. The government could not compel the miners to return to work, and the strikers could not force the government to resign. The government appeared weak because it could not stop the strike, but the length of the strike was taking a serious toll on the miners and the coal regions.

Yeltsin and the Russian government found themselves in the middle of this dispute from the start, and it was Yeltsin who finally broke the impasse. On 1 May, Yeltsin arrived in Kemerovo and proposed to the workers' committee that it end the strike if the Gorbachev government transferred all of the mines in Russia from the jurisdiction of the USSR Ministry of Coal to the jurisdiction of the Russian Federation.[67] The workers' committees agreed, and on 6 May 1991, the Council of Ministers of the USSR (Sovet ministrov SSSR) and the Council of Ministers of the Russian Republic (Sovet ministrov Rossiiskoi Federatsii) signed an agreement transferring control of the mines to Russia.

As strongly as they had claimed that the 1989 strike was economic in nature, the miners and their representatives asserted that the 1991 strike was political in nature. While it is true that the demands made in the first strike dealt with "economic" issues and those of the 1991 strike with "political" ones, the two strikes were equally economic and political in character. In the Soviet system, it could not be otherwise. Demands for greater control over the economy by regions or by a particular social group required the diminution of the nomenklatura's control over economic resources, and this was a direct attack on its base of political power.

In the 1991 strike, attention focused on the demands of miners that Gorbachev and the government resign, but the rationale behind those demands was fundamentally economic. The story of the radicalization of the labor movement from 1989 to 1991 was the story of a movement reaching the conclusion that its economic demands could not be fulfilled as long as the centralized Soviet economic system existed and as long as those who ran that system were in charge of dismantling it. The compromise that ended the strike—the transfer of jurisdiction—signified a shift of political power from the centralized Union government to that of the Russian republic. The miners accepted the compromise because Yeltsin promised to cede greater control over the coal industry to the localities. The central government's failure to cede this control in the two years since the first strike was the reason the miners demanded Gorbachev's resignation; in this sense, the 1991 strike was an economic act as much as a political one.

The strike of 1991 completed the reorientation of the labor movement from a group dissatisfied with the results of restructuring but still pro-perestroika to one that saw perestroika and those supporting it as irredeemable and irrelevant to the concerns of labor. The attention of the workers' movement shifted to the governments of the republics—which now bore responsibility for fulfilling workers' demands—as well as to the continuing disputes with local and regional governments and Party institutions that the workers' movement still considered attached to the center, and to questions of reorganizing the structures and policies of the trade unions, still viewed by many as bastions of the old order.

Reinventing Trade Unionism in the USSR, 1989–1991

For independent organizations and activists in the workers' movement, the All-Union Central Council of Trade Unions and its constituent official unions stood as a symbol of everything that was wrong with the labor relations system in the Soviet Union. The official unions were seen as unreformable, conservative, an appendage of the Communist Party, a place where time-serving apparatchiks could feel at home. In large measure, this view of the official Soviet unions was accurate and the appellations well deserved. When change did come to the unions beginning in late 1989, it was only under the pressure of events beyond their control.

The response of the official trade unions to the advent of perestroika was most notable by its absence. The opposition of the trade unions to self-management provisions in the enterprise law was particularly significant because Gorbachev had severely criticized the unions for just this type of behavior in late 1986, when he had accused trade union leaders of "walking around arm in arm with the bosses."[68] It was not until the Sixth Plenum of the All-Union Central Council of Trade Unions (Central Council) in September 1989 that the unions seemed to conclude that radical changes were in order if unions were to weather the storms created by perestroika. The catalyst that forced the trade unions to review their position was the miners' strike of 1989. The official Union of Mineworkers and the Central Council sided with the government during the strike, and this helped destroy the credibility of the official union structures.

In response, the unions adopted what was for them a new position: that the primary task of the trade unions should be defending workers' rights. To do this, the Central Council drafted a new law on trade unions that gave the unions broad powers in economic and social policy making; the unions also became advocates of a consumer price freeze, wage indexing, and a crackdown on cooperatives, which they (and many workers) viewed as a haven for speculators. Changing specific trade union policies, however, only solved half the problem; policy changes could not alter the unions' image as an integral part of the command-administrative system. Throughout 1990, the official unions tried to change that image by taking advantage of the emergence of independent workers' groups and the rising tide of sovereignty sentiment that was sweeping the Soviet Union.

In the early months of 1990, the official unions and the government engaged in a cold war over planned price increases, which the unions eventually succeeded in reversing.[69] With this "evidence" of their new commitment to workers' interests, the official union structures began to distance themselves from the party/state system. In May, the Central Council published a new trade union charter that declared trade unions independent from any political party or organization, including the Communist Party. The Central Council also decentralized the union structure in the hope of making local unions more responsive to their constituencies.[70]

These changes were "codified" at the nineteenth Congress of the official unions in October. The leadership of the Central Council of the congress was also changed, with Gennadi Yanaev, a longtime party apparatchik who would soon become famous as the titular head of the failed August coup, replacing Stepan Shalaev as head of the unions in April. The nineteenth Congress marked the end of the All-Union Central Council of Trade Unions, which became the scapegoat for everything that was wrong with the Soviet trade union system. In the best *Casablanca* tradition, delegates announced that they were shocked, *shocked,* by the "8 billion rubles a year spent on maintaining the apparatus of the Central Council" and complained that the central unions had taken on extraneous activities like the Society for Sobriety.[71] The congress officially abolished the Central Council and replaced it with the General Conference of Trade Unions of the USSR. The transformation of the Central Council into the General Conference of Trade Unions did little to obscure the fact that nothing had changed except the name. With the exception of the highest leadership, the trade union apparat remained the same, all trade union functions remained firmly under its control, and the unions' connections to the Party and its policy line remained as strong as ever.

The General Conference of Trade Unions ended up being primarily a coordinating organization, due to a reorganization of the official unions within the Russian Republic. In March 1990, the Central Council set up a Russian trade union center, which was directed to create a new organization of specifically Russian trade unions. The timing was not coincidental. That same month, elections to the Russian Socialist Federated Soviet Republic (RSFSR) Congress of People's Deputies sent a large number of radical deputies to Moscow ready to press for greater sovereignty for Russia.[72] Also, at this time the CPSU was developing a plan to establish a specifically Russian Communist Party. The trade unions merely followed suit, as everyone became aware that the strength of sovereignty sentiment was making representation on the republican level crucial to political survival.

The resulting new institution was the Federation of Independent Trade Unions of Russia (FNPR). At its founding congress in April 1990, the FNPR declared itself "a voluntary association of equal and independent republican, *krai,* oblast, and city trade union organizations . . . independent from state, national-economic, political, and other social organizations."[73] Although this formulation reflected the spirit of the time, it could not obscure the fact that the FNPR was simply a scaled-down version of the old Central Council. The FNPR retained both the apparatus and the organizational principles of the old Central Council. The leadership of the FNPR, including its president I. E. Klochkov, consisted entirely of Central Council functionaries; the same applied throughout the FNPR's bureaucracy.[74] The structure of the FNPR's unions remained based on the territorial/branch system, which meant that everyone in an enterprise from the director on down was a union member. Finally, the relationship between the FNPR and workers remained as it had been. When the FNPR was formed, all of the workers in the branch unions were automatically reenrolled in the old unions, and union dues continued to be deducted automatically from workers' paychecks and sent to the FNPR.

The most important element of continuity between the Central Council and the FNPR was the existence of the state-funded social insurance fund. Through this fund, the FNPR controlled the distribution of health benefits, vacations, daycare, and deficit goods. The independent unions had made the nationalization of this fund a priority: it was the most powerful incentive available to get workers to join or remain in a trade union.[75] The FNPR had a severe credibility problem among workers, but its control over this fund made workers wary of leaving.

Keeping workers in the FNPR unions was not a particular problem as long as the Soviet central government and the CPSU remained in control of the political and economic situation, for neither had any interest in stripping the FNPR of its resources or its privileged position as the representative of Russia's workers in negotiations with the state.[76] As 1991 wore on, however, the

Russian Federation under Boris Yeltsin increasingly became the focal point of political and economic decision making. The Russian government saw the FNPR as an ally of the "center," while the FNPR was sure that Yeltsin would be only too happy to take control of the FNPR's resources, particularly since Yeltsin had good relations with the independent unions that were out to destroy the FNPR's power base. Without the emergence of the independent trade unions, the FNPR would not have felt so much pressure from Yeltsin and the democrats, because there would not have been any other institutional structures representing workers in Russia to which the democrats could have turned. By 1990, however, the independent unions were constantly reminding anyone who would listen about how unsatisfactory the old trade unions' performance had been since perestroika began in 1985.

The best known of the independent unions was the Independent Union of Mineworkers (NPG), founded at the second Congress of Miners in October 1990. The first major issue facing delegates was the question of membership. The sectoral organizational structure of the official union meant that everyone who worked in the coal industry in any capacity—from a janitor in a mine office to the minister of coal—was a member of the same union, a fact that made miners a minority within it. Such an organizational structure was constitutive of the union's ineffectiveness, but there remained the question of whom to allow into the new union. In the dispute between the "inclusivists" and the "exclusivists," both sides agreed that management would be excluded, but the inclusivists wanted to allow ancillary workers into the union. The exclusivists argued that membership should be limited to underground workers because their interests diverged from those of others who worked in the industry.

The miners' relatively high wages and their occupation in a crucial industrial sector gave them resources and the leverage to go on strike that other workers in their old union lacked. The miners insisted that their actions be legal, so as "not to give the government any advantages,"[77] but the only way to ensure that they could achieve the required two-thirds vote for a strike was to limit the new union exclusively to miners. The exclusivists won the argument, and their victory set an example that other emerging trade unions followed.

The Independent Union of Mineworkers focused its attention on economic matters. Although supporting the "political" demands of the strikers in 1991, the union was responsible for making the standard wage rate agreement a central point of the strike. After the strike, the Council of Workers' Committees of the Kuzbass and the Confederation of Labor devoted their attention to the election of Yeltsin as president of Russia and to the continuing struggle to oust pro-communist local and regional officials. The Independent Union of Mineworkers concentrated on negotiating new collective contracts between mine administrations and labor collectives, on challenging the official trade union's control of social insurance and benefit funds, and on giving workers a free choice of unions by halting the practice of automatically deducting trade union dues from workers' paychecks.[78]

The three bedrock principles of the Independent Union of Mineworkers—complete independence from any political party or movement, a profession-based organizational structure, and an economistic program—were adopted by a number of other new, independent trade unions. These new unions embraced workers in an odd collection of professions, but in each case the particular location in the national economy of the workers involved provided an opening to break with the official trade union system.

Three independent transport unions emerged in 1990–1991: the Association of Airline Employees, the Air-Traffic Controllers' Union, and the Union of Locomotive Engineers. These independent unions were relatively small, but they enjoyed institutional strength due to the close connection between their trade union officials and the rank-and-file members, their profession-based membership, and their lack of entrenched bureaucracy.[79] The strength of these unions, and the main reason that they emerged in these sectors, derived from the fact that their potential members were workers employed in a single sector who occupied key jobs in the economic infrastructure. In May 1991, the air-traffic controllers threatened a one-day strike over wages, vacations, and working conditions that would have cost the government an estimated 150 million dollars. Similar tactics used by railroad engineers brought the rail administration of their district to the table within a week.[80] Like the miners, workers in these other unions had a specific kind of control over a resource and were not easily replaceable—at least not in the time it would take for a strike by such groups to cause considerable economic turmoil.

Unlike the profession-based unions, the trade union association Sotsprof (Sotsialisticheskie Profsoiuzy, later renamed Sotsial'nye Profsoiuzy) was originally formed by a small group of intellectuals and workers to serve as an organizing force and umbrella organization for a growing number of independent unions.[81] By its own count, by February 1991, Sotsprof consisted of 142 trade union organizations active in 119 enterprises across the Soviet Union;[82] independent sources put its membership at approximately 200,000 by the time of the coup, making Sotsprof the largest independent trade union in the country.[83] Like other emerging independents, Sotsprof adopted a profession-based organizational structure but combined it with a territorial overlay. Members of the same profession would organize their locals on the basis of the smallest available administrative unit in the area, be it a section of a city, a town, or a region.[84] This was done in order to avoid single-enterprise unions, which the leaders of Sotsprof thought were too easily controlled by management, and to prevent a coalescence of power in a trade union bureaucracy, which they felt was the cardinal evil of the FNPR.[85]

Sotsprof was perhaps most adamant in its "economistic world" view. Sotsprof president Sergei Khramov described his organization as "a trade union of the classical type, meaning we have two concerns: signing contracts with management . . . and defending those who are unemployed." Sotsprof leaders dismissed any talk of "worker self-management," "co-determination," "labor politics," or "the working class," as "Bolshevik terminology."[86] Up to the time that the Soviet Union was officially abolished, the union's involvement in politics was limited to cooperation with other independent unions in the attempt to strip the official unions of their control over social insurance funds and other benefits.

The independent unions, however, found it difficult to adhere to the principles they enunciated. They had to establish themselves in factories and enterprises in order to be effective, and this meant convincing workers that the new union could better serve their interests. All of this had to be done within the confines of an existing labor relations system in which the unions played a political role. The new unions had to take on in practice the role that they had condemned in theory, while at the same time embroiling themselves in regional and national politics in order to advance the transformation of the Soviet Union's political and economic system into one in which they could more faithfully adhere to their theoretical positions.[87]

The Changing Calculus: Trade Unions, Labor Politics, and Political Power after the August Coup

The new trade unions and their allies in the workers' committees were gearing up to renew their battle with the old unions over control of trade union property when the attempted coup was launched on 19 August 1991. The reactions of the various trade unions and labor organizations to the coup were predictable. The old, official trade unions responded by doing nothing. They did not come out openly in support of the coup, but neither did they respond to Boris Yeltsin's call for a general strike; few work stoppages occurred where the old trade unions held sway.

The new unions immediately sided with Yeltsin, and representatives of most of the independent unions were present in the Russian White House throughout the coup. The leader of the Independent Union of Mineworkers, Viktor Utkin, whose office was in the White House, contacted the workers' committees in all of the major coal regions of the country. By the end of the first day of the coup, one-third of the mines in the Soviet Union were shut down. The other unions asked their members to support Yeltsin's call for a general strike, and most of their members responded positively.

The behavior of the old trade unions during the coup weakened their already flagging credibility, and in order to counter the threat of being stripped of its property and resources, the FNPR adopted a two-pronged strategy. Taking advantage of the increasingly dire economic situation in Russia in 1991, the FNPR leadership voiced increasingly harsh criticism of Yeltsin's reform program and its negative effects on the population's living standards.[88] This criticism became particularly strident after the dissolution of the Soviet Union in December, as the FNPR made ever more populist appeals in an effort to "create an image [of itself] as a champion of social justice"[89] in order to garner greater support from hard-pressed Russian workers.

At the same time, the FNPR pressed the Russian government to enact programs guaranteeing a minimum social safety net, an expanded list of products to be sold at fixed prices, and wage indexing, and also to set up an economic arbitration commission to resolve disputes over the course of economic reform.[90] The unions threatened to call a general strike if the demands were not met, even though just one year before the leadership of the old unions declared that they "were against strikes on principle."[91] In late 1991, the government agreed to set up the arbitration commission, despite little evidence to suggest that the FNPR had the power to actually bring workers out on strike.

The establishment of the commission was a major victory for the old unions. Not only did its formation seemingly vindicate the FNPR's tactics, but the makeup of the commission made certain that the old unions would remain, for the foreseeable future, the main institution representing Russian workers at the national level. Out of fourteen seats allotted to trade union delegates on the commission, the FNPR was given nine; three of the independent unions split the rest. Commenting on the commission, one Russian analyst argued that "it·seems very much that under a new facade, there exists a great desire to continue the same old games. It will be very sad if our young government travels down this ruinous path."[92] In fact, negotiations between the government and the FNPR broke down by midyear, but the FNPR's domination of the commission secured the power of the old unions that had seemed so threatened only six months before. By the middle of 1992, the FNPR had become an important component of Civic Union, and the major advocate among labor groups of gradual reform toward a market economy.

In the course of the transition from authoritarianism started by Gorbachev in 1985, events seemed to conspire at different times either to unify workers, drive them apart, or compel them to reassess their views toward the Communist Party, socialism, democratization, trade unions, and the market. In terms of the ultimate success of the transition, the results of these events were less important than the processes themselves, because through them workers began to develop a sense of themselves as an independent force in society, having interests that could only be realized by conscious action on their part. While the events of 1989 to 1992 were instrumental in forming this consciousness, they also demonstrated that building a consensus in favor of any particular vision of democratization and economic reform would be a far greater challenge.

The lack of consensus also testified to how far Gorbachev's perestroika had brought Soviet society. While Western Sovietologists probably overestimated the "atomization" of this population in the pre-Gorbachev years, under Gorbachev societal opinion evolved quickly from unarticulated to organized and divergent, even if among a minority of citizens. It was the dialectic between reform from above and reform from below that pushed the transition forward, and it was precisely the willingness of certain sectors of society—in this case elements of the working class, as strikers and union organizers—to strain the limits of elite-sponsored reform that drove the process onward.

Even if it is true, as Jerry Hough and others have argued, that Gorbachev and his allies were more radical than their early policies suggested, it is difficult to understand the evolution of the program they started without taking into account the social pressure that resulted from those initial policies.

At the very least, the experience of workers during perestroika should serve as a caution to transitologists against making claims about the inherent dangers of social activism during transitions from authoritarianism in state-socialist systems. In formerly communist states, including Russia, where this transition is still under way (or is in limbo), Western analysts and advisers have been quick to offer assistance to governments on issues such as privatization and the building of market mechanisms. With few exceptions, these same analysts and advisers have been wary of doing the same for social groups wishing to defend their own interests. Insofar as this is the result of preconceptions about the effects of social mobilization, the evidence presented here suggests that a reassessment is in order. Specifically, and in contrast to much democratization literature, the experience of Soviet workers during perestroika shows that the best way to build a democratic society is to support those social groups that are attempting to develop one.

Apart from prescriptive questions, the experience of Soviet workers under Gorbachev also points to the importance of examining microprocesses during transitions. Understanding the extent of democratization necessitates going beyond the narrow confines of crafting new government institutions, writing constitutions, or freeing up means of communication and the media. Many analysts seem too ready to equate change with progress, but scholars must look past regime change to understand what the building blocks of the post-Soviet social formations in Russia, the Commonwealth of Independent States (CIS), and Eastern Europe are likely to be. Indeed, it was the reforms of the Gorbachev period and the changes that they set in motion that provided the institutional and social context for what was to come under the Yeltsin regime.

CHAPTER FIVE

Disempowering Labor

Workers and Trade Unions under Yeltsin

From early in the Gorbachev period, it was clear that the nature of democratization and therefore of Soviet and later Russian democracy would depend on the disposition of state-owned property that made up the economic infrastructure. It was not a question of *if* control over the means of production would have to change for a transition to occur, but rather *how and in whose favor* that control would change. This issue established the political and economic agenda of the Gorbachev and Yeltsin periods. Gorbachev set out to democratize the Soviet system so that a grateful and empowered population would use its power to support him and his concept of reformed socialism. In a limited but nonetheless very real way, the working class was meant to be the vehicle of Gorbachev's democratization program. The self-management initiatives of the perestroika years reflected the particular nature of the Soviet social system and were designed to democratize it in keeping with Gorbachev's understanding of socialism and democracy. For workers, Gorbachev's reforms succeeded even as they failed. Workplace democracy Soviet-style was never realized, but perestroika did manage to politicize and empower workers in other ways. The strikes of 1989–1991 and the actions of the enterprise councils demonstrated that the structure of the Soviet political economy gave workers in particular sectors power beyond their numbers. The ideological justifications of the Soviet system, tattered as they were by the late 1980s, added to workers' opportunities. The passage of time has brought to light one of those ironies for which history is famous: the system that workers helped to destroy in 1991 was by its very nature the one that gave workers greater opportunities for political and economic empowerment than the system they helped to create under Yeltsin and Gaidar and their Western advisers.

As ideologically predisposed to "socialist democratization" as Gorbachev was, Yeltsin was no less driven by ideological imperatives. Partly to differentiate himself from Gorbachev, and partly because his advisers were true believers in capitalist democracy, Yeltsin by 1991 argued for a clean break from the Soviet past. This included the abolition of the USSR along with radical reform of the economy, the polity, and society. Yeltsin spoke of constructing a "people's capitalism," building democracy, and making Russia a "normal, civilized country." Like Gorbachev, Yeltsin recognized the need for sweeping change.

The difference between them was not the *extent* but the *intent* of the changes involved. The heart of the matter was who would be empowered by Yeltsin's policy changes. The changes hung on two issues: access to the state, and the structure and speed of economic reform. The failed coup and the dissolution of the Soviet Union gave the state to Yeltsin and his allies. Their idea was to establish political democracy in Russia, in exchange for which a grateful population would use its power to support Yeltsin and his radical economic reform policies. Democracy would be the compensation for the economic difficulties of transition.[1] In the economic sphere, the plan was to create a capitalist market system that would stop Russia's economic crisis, integrate Russia into the world economy, and ultimately improve living standards. Unlike the policies of the Gorbachev period, however, political and economic reforms were presented as separate and distinct. This too was part of the jettisoning of communist ideological baggage, which had always insisted on the inseparability of politics and economics. Western governments and economic advisers encouraged Russia to sever these two spheres—with predictably disastrous results. The separation became one of the key factors in Russia's subsequent economic collapse and political turmoil.

Yeltsin's policies were highly detrimental to the interests of Russian workers, who lost access to the political system, economic security, and the economic leverage that the Soviet political economy had afforded them. By defining politics narrowly as the building of democratic institutions and economics as the creation of market structures, the Yeltsin government attempted to break the connection between them rhetorically and practically. Whatever influence labor had derived from its position in the economy, Yeltsin's policies led rapidly to the collapse of working-class power in postcommunist Russia.

It was not only the government and its advisers, however, that advocated severing the connection between the economic and the political. Some leaders of the labor movement, along with large numbers of workers, did so as well, partly in reaction against the old system. This was due to the complicated relationship between workers and the idea of "class," "class struggle, "the working class," and "labor organization" in the Soviet period. Because the working class had been for decades the justification for the communist system, class was deeply compromised as an organizing principle and as a legitimate means of understanding among workers and among the new elite. For workers, class was the condition and principle of their servitude. The history of the Soviet Union, particularly its labor history, tells the story of workers whose living standards were poor, who were politically controlled, and whose lives on the shop floor were by turns monotonous, dangerous, and frenetic, but rarely empowering. The idea of class struggle was used to justify repression at home and adventurism abroad, but victory in that struggle always seemed elusive.

Given this history, it is not surprising that the argument for separating politics and economics resonated with Russian workers. The majority of workers, however, also realized that they needed some mechanism to protect their interests in the face of economic and social crisis. The question was what such a mechanism should be and what it should do. This issue continues to divide workers and trade unions against themselves, and workers against political groups that in other countries would be their natural allies. The view that politics and economics should be separate carries a particular cost in Russia: it may have been imaginary workers who ruled in the "workers' state" that was the USSR, but it is very real workers who are paying the price for dismantling the structures and iconography of communism.

Russian Workers and Yeltsin's Reforms: Shock Therapy as Policy and Worldview

Shock therapy is presented in the literature on postcommunist transitions as a series of economic policies designed to quickly and completely dismantle the economic structures of communism and replace them with the structural and institutional foundations of a capitalist market economy.[2] While shock therapy is certainly this, it is also a worldview that is elitist, suspicious and dismissive of democracy, and extremely wary of any kind of popular involvement in the elaboration and implementation of economic policy. Furthermore, shock therapy has serious social and political implications that cannot be divorced from its economic effects.[3]

The essential features of shock therapy in Russia consisted of a series of macroeconomic stabilization policies that included price liberalization, attempts to balance the federal budget by eliminating subsidies, and alteration of the tax system to increase revenues. Shock therapy was designed to control inflation and put the economy on a sound footing by imposing hard budget constraints on industrial enterprises and other economic units. This would encourage foreign investment and loans from foreign banks and the International Monetary Fund (IMF).

The results of shock therapy were mixed and controversial. Evaluations of the policy's success depended on what people expected shock therapy to accomplish. Anders Aslund, one of the architects of the program, argued that "[d]espite the profound economic crisis at the end of 1991, the stabilization policy got off to a decent start. Gross shortages disappeared, and inflation fell month by month." While acknowledging that inflation remained too high in

Russia, Aslund pointed out that the inflation rate continued to fall through the summer of 1992, until the Russian government abandoned Gaidar's strict monetarism in the face of rising opposition. Supporters of shock therapy also argued that the fall in industrial production triggered by the policy was a good thing, since it was weeding out economically harmful production.[4] Others examined the same data and saw a catastrophe in the making. Lynn Nelson and Irina Kuzes offer an indictment of shock therapy as blistering as Aslund's is optimistic, citing massive inflation, falling real wages, plummeting industrial production, in addition to increasing income inequality, homelessness, death rates, infant mortality, and crime as the main results of the policy.[5]

There was little debate about the immediate economic effects of shock therapy—although the extent of the industrial collapse has been disputed—but there was fundamental disagreement about what these effects meant. Some analysts saw them as the necessary price of extricating Russia from the economic death grip of a failed centralized economy. Others saw these effects as the predictable result of irresponsible policy making. Still others argued that they were the result of not pushing shock therapy far enough. For good or ill, what most analysts seem to agree on is that shock therapy quickly ran afoul of Russian political, economic, and social realities.[6]

The second element of shock therapy broadly defined was the privatization program, which began in 1992 and continued through 1998. The goal of the program was to reduce the size of the state sector, to cut subsidies to remaining state and quasi-state firms, and to force enterprises to sink or swim in response to their ability to restructure. As in other postcommunist states, there were heated debates about how to privatize, how quickly to do so, and how much to sell off. Most of the countries in question adopted a form of voucher privatization in which all adult citizens received vouchers that they could either sell or use to buy shares in the companies of their choice. In Russia, everyone received a voucher worth 10,000 rubles—approximately eighty-four U.S. dollars at the June 1992 exchange rate. The intricacies of the privatization program are exhaustively described in the literature;[7] for the purposes of this argument, the key factors in the program were the options for privatization, how they were implemented, and the effect of these two factors on workers and trade unions.

There were three forms of privatization available to Russian enterprises; 73 percent of those enterprises chose the second option, which allowed for 51 percent of the shares to be purchased by "members of the enterprise collective."[8] On the surface, this seemed a relatively democratic way to privatize state property, but the process and outcomes were as controversial as other aspects of shock therapy. Like the macroeconomic stabilization policies that came before it, privatization did not solve Russia's economic crisis, but it did alter the political economy of labor relations at the enterprise level and beyond.

By 1998, Yeltsin's policies had failed to put Russia's economy on a sound footing. The macroeconomic stabilization policies succeeded in eliminating some distortions in the economy, but also wiped out people's savings, caused a serious decline in most people's real income, led to massive capital flight, accelerated the criminalization of the economy, and wreaked havoc on the social infrastructure. Every year since 1993, the Russian government has declared that the collapse of the Russian economy has ended, that wage arrears will be paid, and that industrial production has begun to increase. Each year it has proven otherwise. By July 1996, over 60 percent of Russians rated the economic situation as bad or very bad, over half rated their own material situation as bad or very bad, and a plurality expected worse to come.[9]

Russia's economic crisis and the population's pessimism, however, did not immediately undermine shock therapy as worldview. As worldview, it became the hegemonic discourse of Russian political and economic debate after 1991. This discourse consisted of little more than a restatement of the classic positions of pre-Keynesian economics: the free market should drive the economy with minimal state involvement, and the role of politics is to create the conditions for the market to properly function. While lip service was paid to the idea of a "social market economy," the discourse of shock therapy did not articulate any role for society in the establishment or operation of that economy.

The role of the hegemonic discourse was to preempt any alternative view from getting a serious hearing before shock therapy was adopted. Judging by working-class responses to Yeltsin's policies for the crucial period between 1992 and 1994, this discourse played its role extremely well. As was true in the region as a whole, liberal norms emerged as central and "the hegemony of liberal norms exclude[d] Socialist claims for distributive justice in settling the issue of property rights" and other issues.[10] This is not to argue that there was no debate over economic and political issues, but rather that the parameters of this debate ruled some possible options out of court, privileging capital over labor and the market over the state and civil society at every turn. This hegemony was only strengthened by the consolidation of power in Yeltsin's hands after the destruction of the Russian Parliament and the adoption of an executive-centered constitution. By 1993 Russia had become a "delegative democracy" that was more delegative than democratic.[11] For labor, this political structure only exacerbated the results of shock therapy. As worldview, shock therapy excluded labor from the determination of policy as a matter of principle; as policy, shock therapy severely undermined the position of workers and the labor movement after 1992, and complicated the issue of redefining the interests and role of workers in the political economy of Yeltsinism.

Which Side Are You On?
Labor Organizations in Conflict, 1992–1998

The conflicts among labor organizations that began during the Gorbachev period have continued under Yeltsin, but they have been altered by the emerging political economy of postcommunist Russia. On one side still stands the FNPR, on the other the cluster of new unions that emerged as a result of perestroika and glasnost. In addition to the conflict between these two large camps, disputes within each of these groups have further undermined any sense of unity in the labor movement. The issues that divide the labor movement range from the material to the ideological. The most serious conflicts still center on the disposition of the property the FNPR inherited from its Soviet holdings, the administration of the pension fund, the issue of union membership and dues, and the rules for union registration. The socioeconomic well-being and the organizational and political power of millions of people are at stake in these conflicts, and changing one element in the mix has follow-up effects on the others.

The struggles of the labor movement—involving the state, managerial personnel, and other actors—are emblematic of the larger issue of the nature of democratization in postcommunist states. It has proven impossible to change the political power structure of labor relations without changing the economic and social foundations on which those relations are based. Recognition that changing these foundations is a necessary condition of any meaningful political change in Russia requires changing the analytical definition of the term "democratization" from what has become standard usage in the literature. The regime could not simply restore the right of labor unions to be politically active, to strike, or to serve as intermediaries between state and society, as is often the case with transitions in states where capitalism already exists. Rather, workers, managers, and the state have been forced to engage in a process of redefining what trade unionism and labor politics mean in a postcommunist system. The conflicts within the labor movement are part of this process. The internal evolution of the labor movement since 1992 has been a cause and a consequence of these conflicts; who the players are and who they perceive themselves to be have direct implications for what democratization means in Russia.

The Players

The FNPR was the immediate successor to the old Soviet trade unions and as such brought with it all the advantages and disadvantages of the old unions. It was structurally, organizationally, and financially better placed than the independents, but it carried the stigma of its association with the old order. The FNPR faced two major challenges in the post-Soviet period. The first was to retain the property, resources, and positional advantage it inherited. The second was to remake itself in the eyes of workers and prove that it was the workers' best defense in the world of emergent Russian capitalism.

By the end of 1997, the FNPR had met the first challenge fairly well. While it appeared in the early postcommunist period that the FNPR was going to be stripped of its vast property holdings, neither the state nor the independent unions made good on their early threats to do so. The FNPR still controls vast assets in land, banks, hotels, holiday camps and spas, trade union buildings across Russia, and substantial financial resources.[12] The FNPR has also retained the majority of its membership, by far its most valuable resource. According to FNPR president Mikhail Shmakov, at the end of 1996 the federation consisted of 122 member organizations with a membership of forty-five million workers.[13] This constitutes a drop in membership of approximately five million in four years, most of which seems to be accounted for by workers quitting unions altogether rather than transferring membership to other trade unions. Membership numbers of the independent unions do not indicate a substantial influx of workers since 1993. The evidence suggests that Shmakov is correct in his assessment that the drop in union membership is mainly due to "the growth in unemployment, migration of the population, and transfer of workers to new enterprises where trade union organizations do not exist."[14]

The structure of the FNPR has changed little since 1992. The federation still consists of unions built on either a regional or a sectoral principle rather than on a craft-based conception of membership. These unions represent all workers in a sector of the economy or in related industries within a region, therefore clouding the issue of whose interests the unions represent. The FNPR structure also leads to odd problems of overlapping union membership, where a worker can be a member of sectoral and regional unions simultaneously. An official of the Iron, Steel, and Mineworkers Union (PGMPR) noted that the situation can lead to conflicts "when a decision is taken by the FNPR. The leader of the regional organization may vote in favor, while the leader of the sectoral union may vote no; so the worker for whom this decision was ostensibly made is between a rock and a hard place."[15] The arrangement is little better for the upper echelons of the FNPR. As Shmakov argued at the 1996 congress, the organization is not really a federation, but "a confederation, in the worst sense of the term. Our coordinating bodies practically cannot make even one necessary decision, with the exception of the acceptance of mutual trade union membership . . . and dues, which unfortunately are not paid on time or in the allotted quantities."[16]

The problems with the FNPR stem in large part from a lack of fit between the federation's structure and the new context in which it has to operate. As long as all decision making was centralized in the Central Council, the issue of structure remained purely an administrative one. With the partial breakdown of the central state apparatus and the shifting of a substantial amount of power to the regions after 1991, this was no longer the case. Regional unions became more assertive and more apt to address their economic and social problems to regional governments and managers than to the center. As the political economy of Russia has changed due to the effects of shock therapy and privatization, so too have the strategies of the unions that make up the FNPR. The ongoing tensions between the central FNPR apparatus and the regional/sectoral unions is partly responsible for the FNPR's lackluster performance since 1991.

The FNPR is also suffering from an ideological identity crisis brought on by Yeltsin's policies. The crisis is reflected in the leadership's statements about the role of unions in a postcommunist system. Like most of the other trade unions in Russia today, the FNPR claims to be an "apolitical organization." Shmakov remarked at the 1996 congress that the FNPR was "not fighting for our place in the higher echelons of governmental power, and does not desire to establish or overthrow any concrete sociopolitical structure; we do not see our ideology as a universal one in accordance with which all society should live." The role of the unions is to serve the needs of workers, which he said "makes us opponents of any owner of the means of production, whether it be the state, a private owner, joint-stock company or collective, or any government, be it bourgeois, socialist, or any other type." As if the contradictions in this passage are not enough, the problems arising from the claim to be non-political become even clearer in his remarks about "economic democracy." Shmakov states that the term has "a very deep and important meaning. Economic democracy is not a synonym for freedom of ownership, as the term is understood by some, but rather is a method through which *labor's right to participate in the management of production and to receive its share of the profits is realized.*"[17] This issue has been at the center of labor's social democratic agenda in a host of countries for decades, and it is exactly the opposite position to that taken by Gaidar, Anatolii Chubais, and other advocates of free-market capitalism in Russia and the West.

The FNPR's position on economic democracy and its attitude toward the owners of the means of production have put the federation, by association if not by choice, on the left in Russian politics. More than this, however, the FNPR's ideological pronouncements illustrate the bind that the federation is in. It does not want to be "political" because of the association between politicized unions and the Soviet past—a problem that the independent unions do not have. On the other hand, because Yeltsin's policies have made the economic directly political (and most of the time vice versa), the FNPR has little choice but to be political. Attempts by the FNPR leadership to limit the notion of the political to running in elections or holding public office have not resolved the ideological contradictions, but they have constrained the FNPR's ability to forge alliances with political forces that would be logical associates.[18]

The independent unions experienced as difficult an evolution from 1992 to 1998 as the FNPR. The number of independents has increased dramatically since the dissolution of the Soviet Union, and their organizational structures and ideological dispositions are for the most part very similar. Even by 1998, however, there were still only a handful of independent unions that could reasonably be called influential, and these found that life in Russia's new political economy was vastly different from what they had expected in the early period of Russia's transition.

The Independent Union of Mineworkers of Russia (NPGR) remains arguably the most important of the newer trade unions. Its membership stands at approximately one hundred thousand, although its influence among miners is greater than its membership would suggest. Among delegates to the third NPGR congress, only 14.6 percent indicated that a majority of miners were NPGR members in their respective mines, but 60 percent indicated that the NPGR was the most trusted organization among miners.[19] The NPGR altered its membership structure in 1994, providing that all workers and employees in the mining sector could join the union with the exception of those involved in the "hiring, firing, or command of the workforce."[20]

The power of the NPGR has been undercut by two sets of interrelated events: the virtual collapse of the Russian coal industry and internecine conflicts. While it was common knowledge that a large number of Russian coal mines were unprofitable and probably unsalvageable, many members and supporters of the NPGR did not take the prospect of closures seriously in the early days of the movement. After 1991, however, the situation in the coal industry became increasingly desperate. Demand for coal fell as the industries that used coal curtailed production or closed outright. Many industries that remained operational continued to receive coal, but often were unable or unwilling to pay for it. Lack of funds led to shutdowns, layoffs, and nonpayment of wages. As government subsidies were slashed and the income of the mines fell, investment in the industry's infrastructure diminished. Consequently, safety standards that were never high in the first place were increasingly neglected. The scale of these problems overwhelmed the organizational capacity of the union.

While the miners were buffeted by the changes in their industry in the 1990s, tensions over how to respond began to rise within the union. The miners' union had been one of the staunchest supporters of Yeltsin and his policies since 1991, but as the economic and social conditions of miners worsened this support was challenged from within the union. The workers' committees of the NPGR in Vorkuta and other regions began to oppose the NPGR leadership on issues ranging from support for Yeltsin to strike activity.

Of the remaining profession-based unions, five stand out as important actors in the labor movement as of 1998: the pilots' union, the air-traffic controllers' union, the sailors' union, the longshoremen's union, and the locomotive engineers' union. These unions differ substantially in terms of resources, percentage of eligible workers who are union members, and tactics, but they share an organizational and ideological outlook. One sees in the founding documents of all these unions a primary concern for organizational democracy. Some go so far as to include constitutional provisions that make decisions by higher-level union bodies provisional, pending approval by union locals.[21] These unions make a point of delineating in very specific terms the rights and obligations of the organizational subdivisions at all levels.

Sotsprof, the oldest of the independents, continues to function on the basis of its original charter and form of organization as an umbrella for a varied collection of trade unions across Russia. The leaders of the union claim membership of over 400,000, although this number is disputed. The claim made by Sotsprof leaders that 42 percent of Russian workers consider themselves Sotsprof members seems to have no basis in fact.[22] This is not to argue that Sotsprof does not have support beyond its membership; like the other independents, such support seems to be out there. The union proved a significant force at the AZLK auto plant in Moscow in 1993, in spite of having a membership of only three hundred out of a workforce of 37,000. Like the other independents, Sotsprof's organizational structure attempts to be very democratic, with all central decisions provisional except for those pertaining to strikes and other forms of protest.

One final union that deserves mention due to its recent evolution is the Iron, Steel, and Mineworkers Union (PGMPR). With a membership of approximately 2.2 million, the PGMPR was a member of the FNPR until 1992. At that time, the union broke with the federation over issues of membership and the FNPR's attitude toward Yeltsin's economic policies, becoming instantly the largest "independent" union in Russia. The question of just how independent the PGMPR really is has been the subject of debate within the labor movement. In terms of its operations and the nature of its charter the union occupies a position between the FNPR and the smaller independents.

Apart from the individual trade unions that have emerged during the 1990s, a number of labor associations of varying stripe continue to play a role in the labor politics of Russia today. The two that have had the greatest impact are the Association of Independent Unions of Workers "Defense," or "Zashchita," and the National Association of Russian Trade Unions, or NORP.[23] These associations are hybrids—not really trade unions but not political parties either—that have been appropriately described by Leonid Gordon and his colleagues as "trade unions in the making, whose nature is not finally determined."[24] The organizations that make up these associations are diverse, ranging from groups of workers who consider themselves trade unionists to political groups that fancy themselves to be anything from communist revolutionaries to anarcho-syndicalists to neo-fascist corporatists. All of these groups have played a generally divisive role in the labor movement in the 1990s.

This collection of labor organizations is certainly not exhaustive: thousands of trade unions, strike committees, protest committees, labor associations and confederations, and groups with the term "labor" in their titles emerged and disappeared during the 1990s in Russia. In one publication of the Russian-American Fund for Trade Union Research, the listing for new labor organizations in the Saint Petersburg region alone runs almost fifty pages. The mushrooming of such organizations is testimony to the chaotic conditions brought on by Russia's transition, as well as to the democratic opening that this transition has provided. At the same time, the intense and ultimately unsuccessful struggles that these organizations have waged speaks to the peculiar and ultimately restricted nature of that democratic opening.

The Conflicts

The first set of struggles involves conflicts among labor organizations. In some ways, these disputes are examples of what Freud called "the narcissism of minor difference," but they also involve serious issues of power and ideology that directly affect the lives of workers. For much of the period between 1992 and 1994, the most salient feature of labor politics in Russia was the bitter fight between the FNPR and the independent unions—a fight that began under Gorbachev. The conflict centered on four issues: control over property and the insurance fund; membership, dues, and factory-based union representation; ideological orientation to the "reform" process; and structural relations with the state. The disputes have not really been resolved; they simply do not seem as consuming as they were up to 1994, mainly because the unions have decided that the continuing economic and social crisis in which most workers find themselves demands more of the unions' attention, if the low esteem in which unions are held by workers is any indication.[25]

The question of the disposition of trade union property first arose in 1990, but did not take on central economic and political importance until after the Soviet Union was abolished. Until then, no political pressure emanated from the state to divest the FNPR of its property, and little pressure came from the independent unions since Sotsprof had only been in existence one year and the NPG was in its infancy. Yeltsin's victory over Gorbachev and then over those who attempted the coup in 1991—added to the independent unions' support of Yeltsin—fundamentally changed the political dynamic. The FNPR did not support Yeltsin during the coup, and the federation's situation worsened in 1993 when the FNPR sided with Ruslan Khasbulatov and the Congress of People's Deputies during the constitutional crisis. Once Yeltsin had destroyed the parliament, the FNPR's last reliable institutional defender was gone.

As the constitutional crisis mounted, so too did calls for a redistribution of FNPR property. In October 1993, PGMPR president Boris Misnik wrote a broadside in the now pro-Yeltsin newspaper *Izvestiia* in which he outlined in graphic detail the financial and material resources of the FNPR. These resources supposedly included secret hard-currency bank accounts, part ownership of Inturist, as well as "[c]ompletely unknown income from commercial activities, created under the aegis of the FNPR." Misnik went on to enumerate the FNPR's other assets and the underhanded ways in which the federation sought to keep them. "Taking advantage of this 'time of troubles,' the FNPR leadership has been busy creating joint-stock companies or privatizing sanatoria and health centers, taking large proportions of trade union stock, and selling, leasing or distributing property of all of its member as if it were its own."[26] Not surprisingly, Misnik called for the fundamental restructuring of the organization and the division of its assets, as did most of the leaders of the independent unions.

The central issue in the dispute over union resources between the FNPR and the independents was control over the social insurance fund, which up to 1993 was administered exclusively by the FNPR (with the exception of the NPGR, which had its own fund). The fund is worth billions of rubles and provides workers with medical treatment, pensions, summer vacations for workers' children, and a host of other services. Prior to 1993, the FNPR also received millions of rubles a month to administer the fund, so it was able to maintain the membership and support of the FNPR bureaucracy. The FNPR knew that, as long as it controlled the fund, workers would be loath to leave their unions if it meant the loss of access to benefits. The independent unions knew this as well.

The FNPR's support for the losing side in the 1993 constitutional crisis seemed to spell the end of its control over the fund. As part of the government's attempt to punish the FNPR, Yeltsin issued a decree that essentially put the fund under the control of the state.[27] This was not, however, the end of the matter. The state had neither the will nor the capacity to administer the fund, and shifting its administration to the central state or even to regional or local government agencies would require the construction of a massive bureaucracy and the training of thousands of new personnel. The government did create the Fund for Social Insurance of the Russian Federation, and provided that this fund be handled by enterprise administrations with the government agency acting as a watchdog. Yeltsin also announced, however, that the fund would be administered by the state with the participation of "all-Russian associations of trade unions." Since most of the knowledgeable administrators were FNPR members, the federation retained substantial influence. Yeltsin's decrees left ample room for conflict among union organizations, managers, and state representatives, as well as for confusion among workers as to who controlled their benefits.

In a series of cases, these disputes involved the disposition of insurance benefits to workers who belonged to different unions within the same enterprise—a situation that became increasingly frequent after 1992. Typically, a group of workers, either on their own or with the help of outside organizers from one of the independent unions, would organize an "alternative" union in a factory dominated by the FNPR union. As a means of either breaking up the new union or discouraging others from joining, local FNPR officials would often try to withhold benefits from members of the new union. This was made easier by the FNPR union's structural relationship with the administration of most enterprises: the trade union leaders, accountants, medical officers, and managers had often worked together for years. Such was the case in a Novosibirsk chemical plant where the FNPR union leader ordered the head of the medical center not to transfer the insurance premiums of members of the Sotsprof union to the proper account. The absence of those premiums made it impossible for the workers to receive benefits. It mattered little that this was illegal. Workers and union activists had neither the expertise nor the resources to fight a legal battle, and the legal basis for such a case did not exist because of the unreformed state of the laws pertaining to insurance, union rights, and the labor code.[28]

The issue of social insurance caused a different kind of conflict between competing miners' unions. As noted above, the NPGR had been allowed to keep control of its own insurance fund at the time that the FNPR, and more specifically the FNPR miners' union, was stripped of its control over the general fund. Not only was this deemed unfair by the FNPR, it also created inequality among miners, since NPGR members had access to both the general fund and the NPGR fund. It also created an organizational nightmare in multi- union factories. There was a general sum of money that was distributed by the state to a factory; the factory administration then had to divide it and channel it through two—and sometimes three or four—different unions, and then the unions had to get the money to workers. This made it difficult for workers to find where their benefits were coming from if the workers were unsure of which union they belonged to, if they belonged to more than one union, or worse if they were not union members at all.[29]

The unions' battle over social insurance related as much to organizational survival and growth as to principle. The independent unions felt that the FNPR did not enjoy the confidence of its own members, and that it was using the fund as a lever both to keep workers in the FNPR and to maintain the FNPR at the top of the trade union hierarchy. The FNPR claimed that as the representative of most of Russia's workers, and as an experienced organization in this regard, it had a right to keep control of the fund. The original problem derived from the peculiar structure of the Soviet system and the role of the trade unions within it. The problems subsequent to the state's "nationalization" of the social insurance fund derive from the government's failure to design, plan, and institute a new system and a new legal foundation for it before dismantling the old one. This was shock therapy as worldview in action.

Another financial weapon in the battle for membership was trade union dues. Like social insurance premiums, trade union dues during the Soviet period were deducted automatically from a worker's paycheck. This practice continued after 1991, to the benefit of the FNPR. From the perspective of the independents, such a practice was not only illogical but harmful to their interests. If workers had to pay two sets of union dues as the result of joining a new union, they were less likely to leave the FNPR. In addition, dues paid to the FNPR were not going to the independents, depriving them of resources with which to organize. While it is true that this practice has been deemed illegal, it continues in a great many factories where the FNPR is dominant.[30]

The final element of this conflict involves plant-level union representation and the complexities that arise when there are multiple unions in one factory, mine, or other enterprise. At times the conflict manifests itself as direct disputes among unions; at others, the problem is one of coordination among these unions. While a number of specific issues have led to conflicts among the unions, disputes over contract negotiations can serve as an example. Technically, all of the officially recognized unions have the right to sign contracts; in practice the process is much more complicated.

At the Moscow auto factory AZLK in March 1994, the administration decided that, due to a financial crisis, it would shorten the workweek and reduce pay. This decision required the agreement of the trade unions because it constituted a change in the collective contract. In the words of Mikhail Voroshilov, head of the Sotsprof union at the plant, the administration "cut a shady deal" with the FNPR union without consulting Sotsprof, and this led to weeks of haggling, which only worsened conditions at the plant.[31]

A similar situation arose in January 1994 between the management of the Moscow-2 and Pushkino railroad depots and the two unions represented at these depots, one an FNPR union and the other an independent union of locomotive engineers (RPLBZh). In December 1993, the newly formed RPLBZh locals demanded that the management negotiate a new contract, which management was legally bound to do within a week. The director of the depots ignored the new union, went to the leader of the FNPR union and "on the first workday after the new year's holiday [the director and the FNPR union] signed their own contract, and there it was written in black and white: 'The leadership of the railroad division recognizes the [FNPR] trade union organization as the *sole authoritative* representative of the labor collectives in contract negotiations.'"[32] While clearly illegal, the actions of the management and the FNPR union undermined the authority of the RPLBZh and strengthened the relationship between management and the old union. The RPLBZh had the right to challenge the outcome, which it did in this case, but its limited resources make using the laws and fighting every instance of this common practice prohibitively expensive.

In these conflicts between trade unions, workers are caught in the middle. The competing trade unions often do not talk to one another, so any kind of solidarity or joint action is difficult to achieve. When one union negotiates a contract, it often negotiates wage rates, hours, and conditions only for its own members without regard to the effect it will have on the other union's members or on nonunion workers. With the collapse of the FNPR's monopoly in 1991, new unions emerged, as the Russian saying goes, like mushrooms after a rainstorm. In the Vorgashovskaia mine in Vorkuta there were four unions by early 1994, "each with its own interests, each with its own demands of the director," and each pulling workers from one side to the other as the unions vied for membership.[33] This pattern of union multiplication and conflict was repeated throughout the country and remains one of the most divisive features of the Russian labor movement.[34]

Underlying these conflicts is a broader political schism between the FNPR and the independents. The independent unions continue to view the FNPR as at best a collection of pseudo-unions, more interested in commercial activities and in maintaining a close relationship with state bureaucracies and management than in defending workers' rights. In the view of the independents, this has caused the FNPR to oppose Yeltsin's economic politics so as to limit the effects of market-oriented changes that undermine the privileged position of the large industrial sectors in which the FNPR is strongest. The FNPR, for its part, sees the independent unions as representatives of the neo-liberal reformers in the government and among the workers, and seems to find them only among the labor aristocracy at that.[35]

Trade Unions, Conflict, and "Democratization" in Russia

There is some truth in both contentions, but the years between 1992 and 1998 saw a gradual erosion of the differences in the actual political stands of the two sets of unions, even though the political descriptions of one set of unions by the other remained as critical and one-sided as they had been six years before. The erosion of differences occurred as the result of changes on both sides. The FNPR, while still critical of the Yeltsin government, has been more willing to work with the regime since the events of 1993, because it really has nowhere else to turn. The government, for its part, was more willing to work with the FNPR after Viktor Chernomyrdin emerged as the dominant force in the cabinet. Until his ouster in the spring of 1998, Chernomyrdin's connections to the old industrial infrastructure and his conservative approach to economic reform—in comparison to the likes of Chubais, Gaidar, and Boris Nemtsov—created a more congenial atmosphere for relations between the FNPR and the government. The independent unions began to move away from their staunch support of Yeltsin when the effects of shock therapy and the privatization program began to be felt more intensely among workers, and as the government proved uninterested in including the trade unions in the policy-making process. In short, the ideological and political conflicts that still manifest themselves between the two sets of unions have lost much of their programmatic ideological and political content. They now serve primarily as a way of justifying and elevating the continuing and very real conflicts over organization and resources that occupy so much of the unions' energy, time, and attention.

In spite of the disputes among the unions, the course of economic change in Russia has provided grounds for some cooperation, particularly since 1994. The growing problem of wage arrears has led to joint action by usually rival union organizations such as the NPGR and the FNPR miners' union.[36] In a statement of principles, Sotsprof leaders conveyed a good sense of the grudging level of cooperation that now exists between the old and new unions:

> It is well known that the president of a FNPR local union committee has close ties with management, participating in the division of unreported profits, receiving premiums and so on. However, it happens from time to time that a union local president does defend the rights of workers and conflicts with management and the trade union bosses. In such a situation, the regional committee of Sotsprof will support the FNPR union local president and actively participate in the trade union conferences.[37]

Seven years into the post-Soviet era, the competing trade union structures have found at one level a commonality of interests, but they have yet to build any kind of trust, without which solidarity within the labor movement in Russia is unlikely to occur.

Quite apart from the effects of these conflicts on Russian workers, the nature of trade union disputes is important because of what it illustrates about Russia's transition from communism. On the one hand, these conflicts can be seen as examples of Russia's success in democratizing its political and social life. The existence of hundreds of trade unions, operating freely and openly in a social space once reserved for a single organization controlled by the Communist Party, is certainly evidence that Russia is more democratic today than it was, for instance, under Leonid Brezhnev. What the presence of these unions and the conflicts among them do not tell us, however, is whether Russia is more democratic now than the Soviet Union was in 1989 or 1990, when the union movement and these conflicts first arose. One cannot cite the multiplicity of unions and their conflict as evidence of democratization in Russia before examining the larger structural context in which the unions operate. Since the political resources of the unions and their ability to influence policy at all levels are structurally weaker now than they were in 1990–1991, it is difficult to argue that democratization has advanced, in spite of the number of unions and the conflicts among them. Indeed, since shock therapy was introduced, most of these conflicts have become more intense as the unions have become structurally weaker.

What the nature of the union movement and the conflicts within it do demonstrate is the difference between the Russian transition and transitions occurring outside the postcommunist world. The conflict between the FNPR and the independent unions could not exist outside a country that was based on the Soviet model. While there are of course certain types of corporatism in which state-run unions have existed, in no other case have the official union structures been so deeply embedded, not only in the realm of production relations, narrowly construed, but in the socioeconomic and political structures that governed workers' lives more generally. It may be true that the FNPR, as the independent unions contend, does not so much defend workers' interests as define and administer them; it is also true that most workers are tied to the FNPR for precisely this reason. Since the state's transition policies after 1991 did little to help or incorporate labor, the old unions were left with a role to play, and in playing it the FNPR survived.

This being the case, it is not surprising that the initial target of the new unions would be the FNPR. The independents had emerged in the first place due to dissatisfaction with the old unions. When the FNPR refused to wither away, the independent unions had to attack it for reasons of organizational survival, if not of principle. These conflicts among unions are at base archetypical examples of the Leninist legacy at work. This legacy has made it more difficult than it might have been for workers to negotiate the emerging political economy of Yeltsinism, because it deflected the attention and resources of workers' organizations away from defending workers' interests vis-à-vis managers and the state during the introduction of shock therapy and privatization. This is not to argue that conflicts among labor organizations do not take place in other countries or contexts, but rather that the particular Soviet/Russian setting and context are analytically decisive in explaining the content of these struggles.

Laboring under Illusions?

Russian Workers and the
Political Economy of Yeltsinism

While the Soviet Union existed, relations among workers, unions, managers, and the state were determined by the structure of the statist system inherited from the Stalin period. The Party controlled the state ministries that regulated the factories and their workforce, and the trade unions primarily served as transmission belts conveying Party policy to the workers. In exchange for the workers' lack of autonomy, the state privileged them materially in comparison to other sectors of society, for ideological reasons, while repressing any sign of labor unrest, also for ideological reasons. Under Gorbachev, democratization meant giving society more power in relation to the state, but still keeping it within the confines of a statist socialist system.

In theory, Russia's transition from communism to a market-oriented, Western-style democracy would mean a severe restriction of state involvement in labor relations and economic management, for this is what shock therapy as worldview and policy entailed. Workers, trade unions, and managers would be forced to redefine their relationship to the state, while the state also defined its role in the new system. The ideology of shock therapy aside, the Russian state would not be able, as Leon Trotsky once remarked about his job as commissar of foreign affairs, "to issue a few revolutionary decrees and close up shop."[1] The ongoing process of defining the relationship among workers, managers, and the state, with its discussions of rights, obligations, powers, and proper roles, is a mirror of the larger transition, its successes, and its failures.

"Social Partnership" and the Tripartite Commission

The idea of social partnership and its embodiment in the Tripartite Commission (Rossiiskaia trekhstoronnaia komissiia, or RTK) was predicated on the rapid withdrawal of the state from the direct management of the economy and labor relations. The combination of shock therapy and privatization would create a new class of Russian capitalists, transform workers into independent wage laborers, and make the state the referee of last resort between the two groups, through the legal system and social legislation. The concept was vaguely western European in origin, a type of societal corporatism reminiscent of Germany or Sweden. The goal was to regulate labor relations, to move them away from a model based on confrontation toward a more "peaceful, law-based system, based on a relative equality of forces and a corresponding understanding by both sides of the destructiveness of further confrontation. This model is based on a system of negotiations and a developed set of procedures defining the joint obligations and responsibility of the parties, and a sufficiently effective mechanism for maintaining a balance of interests between employers and workers."[2] In theory, this was shock therapy with a human face.

The Tripartite Commission was to be made up of representatives from the trade unions, a Russian association of entrepreneurs, and the Russian government. The goal of the Commission was to negotiate a "General Agreement" on issues including economic policy, employment, income and living standards, social welfare, labor standards, and regional development. The agreement was to be binding for all sides for one year, whereupon it would be renegotiated. Other agreements could also be entered into by the three sides at the regional and local levels, as long as they did not contradict the General Agreement.

The Commission was founded in 1992 and continues to function, but all indications are that social partnership in Yeltsin's Russia has been a failure. Viewed from the perspective of workers and trade unions, the reasons for this failure are found equally in the design and in the implementation of the concept. The initial difficulty was that the Russian government tried to do by fiat what it had taken the labor relations system in Europe decades to accomplish. The achievement by European workers of various types of corporatist arrangements was the result of long periods of organization, struggle, strikes, electoral campaigns, and negotiations by strong, independent, and legitimate trade unions. In 1992, the Russian trade union movement was in chaos, with some unions lacking legitimacy, others lacking resources, and most unable to agree on much of anything. The same problem existed on the entrepreneurial side. There was no private capitalist class in Russia, and the managers who ran state enterprises were powerful *government* employees. The only clearly defined actor was the state. As Russian labor specialist Viktor Komarovskii noted, the Commission was ineffective because the sides were unformed, the tactics were wrong, and the participants were unprepared.[3] It was yet another example of the Yeltsin government adopting a policy designed for a different context and trying to make it fit Russian conditions.

The second problem was a more specific version of the first. Each side on the Commission had to be represented by specific organizations and people; on the trade union side, this meant another venue for conflict between the FNPR and the independent unions. Of the fourteen seats allotted to the unions, the FNPR received nine, Sotsprof three, and the NPG and the Airline Pilots' Union one each. The independents argued that this arrangement not only legitimized the FNPR as a union organization and thus its claim to represent workers, which they argued was untrue, but also made their own participation meaningless. The FNPR argued with equal force that its membership gave it the right to hold the majority of seats, and that the independents were in fact overrepresented on the Commission. In the end, the representatives on the Commission consisted of state officials, industrial managers who were mostly from the state sector, and trade union officials who until 1991 were part of the Soviet state bureaucracy.

Even after two years of economic "reform," which included privatization, the emergence of new private businesses, and the further differentiation of the labor movement, the composition of the Commission did not change. The deputy minister of labor, Vladimir Varov, argued in 1994 that "in civilized countries, the side of the entrepreneurs is represented by owners, or more generally by private capital. And here? More than 100,000 enterprises are now private. Nevertheless, the representatives of industry on the RTK are mainly from the state sector. So you have a curious situation: on one side, you have the government, and on the other the industrialists who are in fact—the government." He pointed out that even though there were at the time over seventy trade unions, the FNPR still held 90 percent of the seats, and that the FNPR often "defends the corporate interests of the power structures."[4] While Varov's analysis of the FNPR was less accurate in 1998 than it was in 1994, the composition of the Commission did over time become increasingly unrepresentative of its ostensible constituencies.

A third problem that has plagued the RTK and analogous institutions at the regional and local levels is the lack of any effective enforcement mechanisms. The General Agreement declares itself to be binding, but it does not seem to have legal force. The text states that the agreement is controlled by the Russian federal law, *On Collective Negotiations and Agreements,* which does have penalties for violations, but the first two articles of that law clearly state that it only applies to employers and workers, not the state, and further only applies in enterprises.[5]

Quite apart from the legal status of the agreement, its substantive sections over the years have covered areas so broad that violations are inevitable. The agreement calls on the government, for example, to take concrete measures to support the production of domestic goods for internal and external markets. As industrial production fell throughout the 1990s, the unions viewed the collapse as a violation.[6] This meant that the unions were not bound by the agreement, although there was nothing they could do to enforce its pro-visions. The leader of the trade union Unity, Vladimir Grishchenko, sug-gested only half-jokingly that if the government failed to live up to the agreement "either the representative who signed the agreement, or the per-son who directed him to sign it, or maybe the entire cabinet should be forced to resign."[7] The agreements clearly create the expectation of account-ability, and this has fueled the fire of worker discontent as the economic sit-uation in Russia has worsened. Without enforcement mechanisms, the RTK agreements have actually hurt the prospect for social partnership since 1992.

The final and perhaps most important problem with the Tripartite Commis-sion and the concept of social partnership in Russia in general is the assump-tion of "relatively equal power" among the participating sides. The workers and their trade unions are by any measure in a disadvantaged position relative to the state and the representatives of capital. To be successful in defending its interests, any group needs organization and resources. In the case of Russ-ian unions, the FNPR has resources, but its relationship to workers is such that it cannot make a credible threat of coordinated industrial action; the inde-pendents have a strong organizational base, but in most cases lack the size and resources to make their threats believable. The disparity in power among the groups has only increased over time, particularly as a result of privatiza-tion, the emergence of a wealthy entrepreneurial class, increasing unemploy-ment, and the expansion of private-sector businesses where trade unions do not exist.

On the problems with social partnership in contemporary Russia, Vladimir Grishchenko raised the key issue in March 1994: "At the time that the President published the directive creating [the RTK], neither he nor any-one else asked a very simple question. Do the sides really want to come to an agreement? To me, for example, this was not at all obvious."[8] The failure of most attempts at social partnership since 1992 is perhaps the best answer to that question. The presidential administration held the levers of political power, particularly after 1993, and there were no social forces in the coun-try that had the resources to exert sustained pressure on the state. In a 1994 statement remarkable for its candor, the deputy minister for social security Evgenii Gontmakher remarked that "in 1992–93 there was no social policy as such. There was a fire brigade on the staff of the government's social ad-ministration, which in the conditions of price liberalization, the growth of the strike movement, and social unrest tried in various ways to patch holes, put out fires, and give people some kind of extra help or compensation."[9] The government policies that caused the problems were enacted unilater-ally, and the rest was prevention, not partnership. At the same time, entre-preneurs were virtually unhindered by the state or by law in their pursuit of wealth, so there was little incentive for them to embrace a social partnership that would restrict their activities. The trade unions seemed to be the one side that would have benefited, but even the unions appeared more interested in using crises and threats of strikes to maintain their influence than in making sure that agreements to help workers were enacted.

Labor Legislation and Its Discontents

The laws governing labor relations changed numerous times from 1985 to 1998, most often in response to changes in state policy but also as the result of developments in the labor movement. There was no sea change in policy after the Soviet Union was abolished. The 1990 law on trade unions remained in effect until 1996, and the Soviet labor code still serves as the basis for regulating labor issues. In addition to the labor code, there are three laws that in theory govern labor relations in the Russian Federation: *On Professional Unions, Their Rights and Guarantees of Their Activities; On Collective Contracts and Agreements;* and *On the Procedure for Resolving Collective Labor Disputes.* These laws were designed with the concept of social partnership in mind: the rights and obligations of unions, management, and the state are enumerated in detail, and the rights of workers are well protected.

There are two major factors, however, that obviate the force of these laws. First, they are extremely complicated and allow for differing interpretations on many points. Such nebulousness is extremely dangerous in the context of Russian labor politics, because workers are often on their own in trying to defend their rights. Even when help is available, the time and expense of adjudicating claims is often prohibitive for workers and trade unions. Second, the condition of the economy and the realities of power relations on the ground often make the existence of laws completely beside the point.

The law on trade unions provides workers with the basic rights of association and the authority to undertake industrial action that one would expect in a democratic system, but it goes well beyond this in order to address a number of legacies of the Soviet system. In the process of addressing those legacies, however, the drafters created new problems for workers attempting to organize unions. In the union law, there are provisions that are designed to put all unions on an equal footing. The most important articles state that management cannot refuse to recognize or negotiate with any legally formed union; this often happened in the past when both an FNPR and an independent union had locals in the same enterprises. In two other changes from Soviet-era practice, the law forbids managers from being union members and it delineates, although not clearly, the relationship of the trade unions to the insurance fund. All of these provisions are designed to limit the advantages and power that the FNPR inherited from the Soviet period.

In the context of the changing political economy of Russia, the issue of trade union formation has become a key arena of labor politics. The process of transferring managerial authority from the centrally run ministries of the Soviet state either to the directors of state-run enterprises and joint-stock companies or to private capitalists has also transferred the question of union representation from the center to individual enterprises outside that axis. In addition, the emergence of new businesses has raised for the first time in decades the issue of forming unions in enterprises where no unions exist. The trade union law spells out in detail the procedures for forming a union and registering it with the government. This is intended to make the process transparent, thereby helping workers exercise their right to association. In practice, the law is complicated enough to allow labor's opponents to delay, discourage, or avoid trade union formation altogether.

While unions have to be established in a legally acceptable way, what constitutes legal acceptability is not in the hands of workers, but ultimately in the hands of the courts if a dispute about a union's charter arises. The trade union law does not provide workers with a charter on which the organizer can simply fill in the blanks—although some of the independent unions have now done just that.[10] Depending on how it is written, there are any number of points on which a new union charter can be challenged as violating the new union law.

The case of the workers who attempted to form an independent union at the Kopeiskoe Avtotransportnoe Predpriiatiia, or Kopeisk Auto, is not atypical. The union organizers, who were ordinary drivers at the enterprise, began by holding a meeting, electing a local committee, and writing a charter. They named their organization The Union of Auto-Transport Workers of the City of Kopeisk, and sent off the documents to the local branch of the Justice Ministry in Cheliabinsk for official registration. The workers then sent a message to management informing the director of the formation of a new union and requesting that management provide the union with an office, a telephone, and the office equipment necessary for the union to do its work, all of which the administration is legally bound to do.[11] The union then asked that the administration begin negotiations on a new contract.

A commission was set up according to the law on collective bargaining, and the union began making demands for changes in the draft contract that the administration put forward (which was the same contract that the FNPR union had always agreed to). The management rejected the demands, forcing the creation of an arbitration committee. At this point, management took a different tack, beginning what are colloquially called in the labor movement "bureaucratic capers." As a labor lawyer familiar with the case described events, "the management suddenly asked: 'And who are you?' To which the workers responded, 'What do you mean who are we? We are members of the union.' To which management replied, 'Which union?'" This approached the crux of management's strategy. The workers replied that they were members of the auto-transport workers' union. Management then asked them *where* the union was created, and the workers replied, "Here, in our enterprise." Management then produced a copy of the charter, and showed that it was written in the charter that the union was a *citywide* organization. When the workers denied this, management responded, "It is written right here: The Union of Auto-Transport Workers of the City of Kopeisk; but we are the Kopeisk Auto-

Transport Enterprise. So what have you created, a citywide union or a union in an enterprise in Kopeisk?"[12]

The difference hung on the provisions in the union law on writing the charter, which has to include the name of the union and the territory on which it functions. Management argued that the two were in contradiction, and that if it was a citywide union the administration was not obliged to negotiate with the new union because it could contain workers who were not under the jurisdiction of that enterprise. The union went to court, which agreed with the management, and the union had to start again from scratch. The members wrote a new charter, chose a new name, and went back to the administration, which still refused to negotiate, saying, "First you were this, now you are that. We will not recognize either one until we know what's what." So the workers took the case to the regional court in Cheliabinsk. This court too supported management, saying, "If you had been formed this way, it would have been fine, but since it was this way it is unacceptable: therefore, you do not exist." The union was not recognized by the administration on the basis of the regional court's decision.[13]

In the wake of these events, the management began to use its powers to punish and harass the workers who had tried to form the union. The director instituted fines for "violations of labor discipline" against the workers' wages. In one case, the fine amounted to 25 percent of a worker's monthly salary for being five minutes late for work. In another case, the administration changed the workers' driving schedules without informing them directly or posting the changes at the plant. As a result, the workers did not show up for work on the correct days and were fined again. This went on for months, until some of the workers finally went out on a wildcat strike. Since the strike did not conform to the procedures for the resolution of labor disputes, it was declared illegal and the leaders of the new trade union were promptly fired. One year and a trip to the Russian Supreme Court later, the decisions of the regional court were overturned and the workers reinstated. By that time, however, some of the organizers had quit or left for health reasons. The administration had achieved its objective.

Although the intent of the administration was clearly to disrupt the formation of an independent union at Kopeisk Auto, it is not clear that in a narrow, technically legal sense the management was wrong. What managers did to workers later in terms of fines and dismissal was certainly illegal, but the initial issue had as much to do with the workers' lack of experience as it did with managerial duplicity. The case is emblematic of one of the major problems with the political economy of Yeltsin's Russia. The central controls of the old system have been torn down, and shock therapy and privatization have left enterprises to their own devices while allowing the power structures that strongly favor management to remain intact, but no resources have been provided to help society cope with the new realities of postcommunism beyond a problematic legal framework.

There are two other laws in this legal framework that apply to labor and that are equally problematic. The law on collective contracts and the law on the resolution of labor disputes are part of a continuum that is designed to minimize labor unrest. There is much in these laws that could serve to defend workers' rights as well as to protect the interests of managers and the state, but there are also aspects of the laws that restrict labor's rights. The authoritative sides in a negotiation under these two laws are the employer and the trade union or, in a way that complicates matters, trade unions. The law applies to "all organizations, factories, and enterprises regardless of the form of property, departmental subordination, or number of workers."[14] Either side can call for negotiations, and the other is obliged to respond. Most of the remaining sections of the laws deal with the procedures for carrying out the negotiations, which are detailed and specific.

The complexity of the negotiation procedures provides ample opportunity to drag the process out. Since in the vast majority of cases it is workers who want a new contract and employers who lose nothing by keeping the workers without one, this works to the advantage of the employer in most cases. In many cases in Russia today, these disputes are about the nonpayment of wages, which are often withheld by employers even when they have the money to pay them. The implied threat of further delays if workers do not agree to a contract is powerful, and this also works to the employer's advantage.

The issue of negotiating contracts in enterprises with multiple trade unions is a difficult one for labor as well. The law recommends that the unions work together on a joint draft contract to present to management, but it does not mandate that they do so. The individual unions have the right to negotiate singly with the employer, and any contract the union signs is binding only for members of the union in question.[15] The problem with the law's recommendation of joint negotiation is that multiple unions in enterprises have been founded precisely because some workers are dissatisfied with the existing FNPR union. In the vast majority of cases, therefore, the two unions in the plant despise each other and find it extremely difficult to cooperate. With the unions divided, employers can use the contract negotiations to play the unions off against each other, thereby working out a better deal for management with the added benefit of further estranging the unions. In addition, the two unions usually represent workers in the same professions, many of whom work side by side. Differentiation among workers in the same profession as an outcome of contract negotiations cannot but have serious effects on the prospect for labor solidarity.

The ultimate sign of labor solidarity has always been the strike, and Russia's labor laws put serious restrictions on its use. For a strike to be considered legal, a meeting of union members must be held at which no less than two-thirds of all members are present, and of these at least half must vote in favor. After the strike vote is taken, the union or unions involved must give the employer written notice of the strike ten days in advance. Finally, the union must produce a written statement prior to the strike that indicates the sources of disagreement that justify the strike, the date and time of the strike's initiation, its projected duration and number of participants, the name of the organization leading it and a list of authorized negotiators, plus suggestions regarding the minimal amount of work the union thinks is necessary if the strike affects certain protected industries. Beyond these requirements, there are limitations on the right to strike for workers in particular sectors of the economy. The law states that "strikes are illegal for members of the armed forces of the Russian Federation, for law enforcement agencies, and for the Federal Security Service—if this creates a threat to the defense of the country or the security of the government."[16] The qualification is meaningless, since it is the state that determines what constitutes a threat.

In all other sectors of the economy and society, the limitations on strikes are couched in terms of public safety, but there is much room for interpretation within the relevant articles as to what this means. The unions involved in a strike must agree to allow workers to go to work and provide the minimum level of service necessary to keep certain sectors of the economy functioning. These sectors are defined as those in which workers' jobs are "connected with the security of the people, the provision of health care, or the vital interests of society." Moreover, strikes are illegal altogether if they constitute "a real threat to the basic constitutional structure and the health of others."[17]

There are no specific definitions of what "the vital interests of society" are or what constitutes a "real threat to the constitutional structure and the health of others." This determination is made by the state through the court system. There is a further provision that in cases of particular importance to the vital interests of the Russian Federation or its constituent territories, the president or the government has the right to declare a strike illegal before the court has made its ruling. Note that the legislature has no rights in this regard.

If taken to their logical conclusions, the provisions of the law would allow the state to declare illegal any strike that it deemed to be against the national interest. Prior to the passage of this law in 1995, the same basic arguments were made in declaring the strike by the Airline Pilots' Union illegal in May 1994.[18] One could easily see how the same criteria could be applied to unions in the transport and energy sectors, particularly the coal miners' unions, since much of Russian industry and many homes and apartments depend on coal for power and heat. Given the language of the law and the institutional structures of the Russian state, the government's discretion on outlawing strikes is extremely broad.

Viewed in its entirety, the cluster of laws that make up the new labor relations system puts a much greater burden on workers and their organizations than it does on either employers or the state. In part this is the inevitable result of the nature of the protagonists: there is only one employer in a given case, who can make a decision as he or she sees fit; unions need the authority of hundreds if not thousands of workers, and organizing is difficult. More serious still is that for labor at least these laws are contingent in a way that they are not for employers. The fact that the state can declare any strike illegal vitiates the entire process of negotiation, conciliation, and arbitration. The laws *appear* to be examples of the balanced, and even somewhat liberal, democratic proceduralism dear to transition theorists, but they are so only as long as the state permits, and there is no procedure for challenging the judgment of the state, in this law or elsewhere in the legal code. These laws do not represent democratization in labor relations; rather, they represent a shift in the focus of labor relations that reflects the privatization of the economy while leaving the state the final arbiter.

The ideas of "social partnership" and "relative equality" of the parties involved are written into these laws as guiding assumptions. There is nothing that better represents the belief of the Russian government and its Western defenders in the fiction that democracy equals the establishment of "the rules of the game." The resources of workers and trade unions, be they strike funds, access to information, means of communication, legal expertise, or access to the political system are extremely limited in comparison to those of employers, be they state functionaries or private capitalists. The laws were written this way, according to the deputy minister of labor Viktor Kalashnikov, because "that is the way they do things in countries with developed market relations."[19] The labor laws of the Yeltsin period put into sharp relief the disjuncture between the worldview of those charged with democratizing Russia and the socioeconomic realities of the society they govern.

Russian Workers, Economic Collapse, and the Politics of Reaction

All of the conflicts and policy innovations discussed above have been overshadowed by the unprecedented collapse of the Russian economy, and in particular the industrial economy on which most workers depend. In the context of this rapid collapse, it is not surprising that labor's responses to the emerging political economy of Yeltsinism have been for the most part reactive: angry, at times militant but uncoordinated, sporadic, and dictated by policies and events beyond the control of workers and their unions. It was unavoidable that workers would be the social group most profoundly affected, for good or ill, by the economic, social, and political strategies that the Russian state has adopted since 1992. The Russian working class is the largest single group in the country, accounting for 62 percent of the population in the mid-1980s.[20] By 1994, skilled and unskilled workers were the main income-earners for 53 percent of all working families in Russia.[21] Workers held a privileged place in the social and political mythology of the Soviet Union, and this made them vulnerable when that mythology was rejected and transformed into heresy.

At the beginning of the post-Soviet period, workers were for the most part supportive of democracy and free-market capitalism, as the intended program of the Yeltsin government was always presented to them. This was not surprising, given that the regime promised them the transition would be relatively short and painless. More than this, however, workers supported the reform program for the same reasons that they had initially supported pere-stroika: it promised to give them what they believed they had earned, namely, the right to a good living and some control over their lives at home and in the workplace. "Control" for workers did not necessarily mean "factories to the workers" in the Bolshevik sense, but it did mean at least the kind of social partnership that the regime promised in the wake of the Soviet Union's demise.

When the collapse of the Russian economy accelerated after the introduction of shock therapy, therefore, the angry response of workers was generated not only by the economic hardships that the collapse entailed, but also by a deep sense of betrayal that reverberated throughout the country, particularly among activists in the independent union movement. Workers have demonstrated, picketed, walked off the job, and even gone on hunger strikes. Miners have protested by refusing to emerge from mine shafts and by blocking the Trans-Siberian Railroad. Unions and workers have lobbied Yeltsin and his government, the parliament, regional and local political leaders, and on occasion even banks and venture capitalists to try to improve their situations.

For all this, however, the situation for workers in the political economy of Yeltsin's Russia remains desperate for some, precarious for most, and uncertain for almost everyone. The labor movement is fragmented, and strikes and other forms of protest have not led to any lasting improvement for workers. According to the Russian Center for the Study of Societal Opinion, by 1995 only 12 percent of workers believed that trade unions played any kind of positive role in society, 9 percent believed they played a negative role, and 64 percent felt they played no essential role whatsoever.[22] In spite of this, the vast majority of workers remain trade union members, so it is difficult to read these statistics as anything but a reflection of the frustration felt by workers and unions over their lack of power.

Economic Collapse and Labor's Options

While there is some dispute in the literature about the extent of the collapse of the Russian industrial sector, the statistical and anecdotal evidence is overwhelming that for workers the socioeconomic effects of Yeltsin's policies from 1992 to 1998 have been devastating. Using the least dire estimates, by March 1996 one-quarter of the Russian population was living below the minimum established poverty line. In November 1993, 61 percent of unskilled workers and 52 percent of skilled workers qualified as "poor" or "very poor." By conservative estimates, the percentage of people living below the poverty line was five times higher in 1996 than it had been prior to the introduction of shock therapy four years earlier.[23]

The issue of wages, specifically the nonpayment of wages, remains the most explosive problem in the sphere of labor relations. The real wages of Russia's workers have fallen dramatically since shock therapy began. Taking 1985 as a baseline (1985=100), the average real wage fell from a high of 132 in 1990 to 55 in 1995;[24] that is, the value of a worker's pay packet fell almost two and a half times in the space of five years. In addition, the distribution of income became more and more skewed between rich and poor in the same period.[25] Wage arrears have mounted rapidly since the winter of 1992. As of September 1998, Russia's workers were owed more than nine billion dollars in unpaid wages, most of which is owed by firms in the private sector. While the Russian government has at times paid the wages of workers in certain sectors, the overall scope of the problem continues to increase. To make matters worse from labor's perspective, in January 1998 the Russian Supreme Court overturned the part of the Russian Civil Code that required enterprises to use monetary resources to pay wages before using it for any other purpose, such as paying taxes.[26]

The wage issue has complicated the unemployment and underemployment situation, which has also been worsening since 1992. By the fall of 1996, the International Labor Organization (ILO) estimated unemployment at 9.2 percent of the working population, in a country that had not known structural unemployment for sixty years. These figures do not include workers who are officially employed but who either receive no wages or are on "administrative leave," meaning they are on the books as working at a plant but neither report to work nor receive wages. Estimates of the number of workers in this situation vary, but recent studies suggest that approximately one-third of all workers fall into these two categories.[27] This puts the overall actual unemployment rate at around 40 percent.

There is little incentive for either enterprises or workers to change the administrative leave situation. For enterprises, keeping workers nominally employed carries no cost, because the firm neither pays them nor provides the social services offered during the Soviet period. If, on the other hand, the firm were to fire employees, the workers affected would be eligible for severance pay, which is theoretically the responsibility of the enterprise. The immediate reasons why workers choose to remain nominally employed are that staying on means they retain their right to severance pay (which they lose if they quit) and are positioned to go back to work should the enterprise expand production.

The phenomenon of nominal employment is also connected to the nature of the labor market. By some accounts, the labor market has been the most flexible of all the markets in Russia over the past seven years. Unemployment is relatively high, wages have fallen dramatically, and wage differentiation has increased, all of which makes the labor market a buyer's market. In theory, this should vastly increase labor mobility as workers are forced to search farther afield for jobs, which is all the more possible now that residency requirements for most areas of Russia have been removed.

While labor mobility has increased,[28] the flexibility of the labor market remains restricted due to the difficulty workers face finding jobs and then attempting to relocate. Recent studies indicate that the majority of workers find jobs either through personal contacts, friends, and relatives, or through direct contact with an employer; thus, it seems their sources of job placement are by and large local. Employment agency offices also do not tend to have Russia-wide employment lists.[29] For most workers, the pool of jobs is quite limited practically. Even if workers do find jobs in other cities or regions, it is often impossible to take those jobs because of the expense and difficulty of moving and finding housing, and even more because it is difficult to live without the support of the informal social and economic ties that workers have in their home cities.

From the workers' perspective, all these reasons make remaining on the books of an enterprise as an employee on administrative leave in one's hometown distinctly preferable to chancing a move. At the same time, nominal employment ties a worker down and limits her or his ability to earn a living and advance in a profession that requires new skills. According to recent data, the economic collapse of Russia and the particularities of the labor market are leading to a deskilling of the labor force and a downward pressure on the professional makeup of Russia's workers.[30] Thus there is little incentive to give up even nominal employment when the chances of finding another job at the same or higher level of employment are virtually nonexistent.

Viewed in the aggregate, the picture that emerges is one in which labor has few options and little power. The collapse of the industrial economy has taken away from workers the limited amount of economic power they had during the Soviet period. By removing the artificially taut labor market that gave Soviet workers some measure of control over the shop floor, Yeltsin's economic policies shifted the balance of power at the factory decisively in favor of management. Falling real wages and wage arrears have eaten away at the economic resources of workers and their unions. Workers who do not get paid do not in turn have their union dues deducted from their paychecks, and that means neither individual contributions nor union dues are available for the accumulation of strike funds.

The same dynamic is at work on the political level. While the transition from communism to capitalist democracy on the ideological level weakened labor by removing it as an ideological preoccupation of the regime, the economic collapse of Russia has done far more damage. Workers have lost the ability to threaten a "political strike" such as those of the late Soviet period. When coal miners went on strike in 1991, they threatened to paralyze the economy and shut down the country if their demands were not met, and they did in fact play a major role in Yeltsin's victory over Gorbachev. In today's Russia, workers cannot legitimately threaten to shut down an industrial economy that is already largely idle. The lack of resources that makes it problematic for unions to go on strike for any length of time also makes it difficult for workers and unions to organize and be active politically. Just as the Yeltsin regime effectively excluded labor from the process of structuring the economic policies of transition in 1992, so the structural effects of those policies continue to exclude labor from the political sphere. While some suggest that these economic conditions are temporary effects of the transition, they have only become more embedded in the system as the Yeltsin period has progressed. For the majority of Russia's workers, these conditions have become structural realities of the political economy of Yeltsinism.

Labor and the Politics of Privatization

Privatization was from the beginning a troubling issue for both workers and trade unions. There was little disagreement that property in post-Soviet Russia had to be denationalized, but the question of what form denationalization should take was left open. Some within the labor movement argued for strict equality of distribution to all working people, while others preferred giving the factories over to the existing management so that unions would know whom to fight. The majority presumed that they had a right to have some say over the fate of state property, but it was not clear how that right should be realized.[31] According to the government, privatization was necessary for economic and political reasons: private property was the basic prerequisite for a capitalist market economy, and giving the property to the people would draw them closer to the new regime and empower the population politically.

For a number of reasons, most workers chose to use their vouchers to buy into their own enterprises. First, the structure of the Soviet industrial system created extraordinary ties between a worker and a factory. The Soviet Union may have been run as "one giant corporation,"[32] but workers did not relate to state property in the abstract; rather, their relationship to that property was mediated by the enterprise that supplied them with work and the social infrastructure on which they relied. Second, workers' relative dependency on their enterprises made gaining control over them through Option Two privatization sensible from a purely material perspective. Finally, workers had little information about privatization in other regions, or of other enterprises. Even when they had little information about their own enterprise's situation, which was often the case, it still seemed better than the alternatives.

For most labor collectives and enterprise managers, privatization was initially a matter of gaining insider control at the expense of the state or outside investors.[33] In principle, at least, this put workers and their unions on the same side as management, and if viewed from the perspective of the putative results of the privatization program, employee ownership did quite well. In 1996, according to the Russian National Survey, 64.7 percent of private-sector corporations were majority employee owned, with the "rank and file" holding majority ownership in 30.5 percent of those corporations.[34] These numbers, however, do not reveal anything about the actual distribution of power between management and labor within the firms that were "employee owned," nor about the conflicts within the labor collectives that have emerged as a result of privatization.

The first and perhaps most obvious point is that majority employee ownership on paper does not translate in Russian enterprises into employee control over the firm. It is much more difficult for workers, who individually own only a handful of shares at most, to organize and vote those shares as a unified bloc than it is for management or outside firms to do so. This is a particularly vicious collective-action problem. Even with the will to organize and no free-rider problem, three major factors would make such organization a Herculean task: namely, the structure of diffused shares, the fact that some worker/shareholders have since been fired or put on administrative leave, and the reality of managerial control over information (particularly regarding the financial condition of enterprises), employment, and social benefits. Directors use their power to advantage by getting lower-level managers to convince workers to sign proxies. As Blasi explained in *Kremlin Capitalism,* workers "who did vote their own shares found it impossible to hide their identities, for over a quarter of the companies voted by a show of hands, and those that used paper ballots required a signature. The boss was watching." It is strange that the authors of *Kremlin Capitalism* implicitly blame workers and trade unions for this turn of events. "In what traditional free market economy," they ask, "could workers in most large factories belong to trade-unions, own the majority of their companies' shares, yet never elect an independent representative to the board of directors?"[35] But that is precisely the point: Russia was not and is not a "traditional free market economy." By adopting policies designed for a market economy in a country with the legacy of communism (which Blasi discusses in reference to trade unions), the leadership of Russia and its advisers, not least of all Blasi himself, bear more of the blame for the poverty and powerlessness of Russia's workers than do the workers who fear losing their jobs, homes, and health insurance.

In some cases it never got to the point of directorial divide and rule; the process of selling shares was itself the battleground among workers, managers, and the state. In the aviation industry, delaying the actual sale of shares to the end of the voucher privatization period gave management and the state a chance to profit at workers' expense. According to the head of the pilots' union, at Sheremet'evo airport and a number of other aviation enterprises delaying privatization meant that "people who received these vouchers were afraid that they would end up wasting them, and the majority of the representatives of the airline labor collectives used their vouchers to buy into any bank, factory, or joint-stock company they could find." As a result, by the final meeting on privatization, all but a handful of the enterprises' workers had sold their vouchers. The government then stepped in and announced that half the shares had to be purchased with vouchers, which the workers no longer had. The pilots' union then decided to buy vouchers "for all twenty-five thousand Sheremet'evo workers—four apiece at market prices. A voucher that had been worth 10,000 now cost 35,000. That meant that the government took 140,000 rubles off every worker." The president of the union continued, "why should I have to buy these bits of paper from the government rather than using the money to buy shares directly in the enterprise where I work, so that the money would stay in the company? This was robbing the people yet again."[36] Being forced to use available union funds for the purchase of vouchers, which was necessitated by the delays of management and the state in the first place, also meant that workers did not have the resources to buy enough shares to give them a say in running the company. At Sheremet'evo the process was limited to financial maneuvering; at other airports, representatives of workers who tried to organize vouchers during privatization were attacked on at least eight occasions, in one case fatally.[37]

One could argue that these events were not due to the specifics of the privatization program and that, as General Buck Turgeson contended in *Dr. Strangelove,* one should not condemn an entire program because of a few slipups. The privatization program, however, was carried out before any legal or institutional safeguards had been put in place, without the provision of the information necessary for workers to make informed choices, and in a time frame that made organizing the potential power of workers with vouchers virtually impossible. There are a series of arguments as to why speed was necessary, why workers' control was a bad idea, and why the process, flawed as it was, will be beneficial in the long term,[38] but workers understandably viewed the procedure as a betrayal that deprived them of their perceived right to have some control over the disposition of what had been "the property of the whole people."

The struggle for influence over the operation of enterprises, however, did not end for workers with the initial privatization process. There are cases across Russia of workers attempting to organize worker/shareholders into voting blocs and of unions trying to use their power as representatives of worker/shareholders to influence enterprise management boards. The cases of two large industrial concerns, Severstal' and Norilsk Nickel, are emblematic of the dynamics of privatization after the initial sale of shares.

At Severstal', one of the organizers of an independent trade union started a club called Defense, the goal of which was to organize workers with shares to vote as a bloc. The powerlessness of individual workers was clear to the organizer: he figured that to have even a 10 percent vote at a shareholders' meeting, he would have to control three hundred thousand voting shares. On average, a worker at the enterprise owned ten. His mechanism for attempting to organize three thousand workers was the trade union leaflet, the only resource he had available.[39] By this means, the organizers of Defense were attempting to convince each worker to give his proxy to the independent trade union, rather than to management.

The case of Severstal' was made more interesting by the emergence of another group called Shareholder, which was organized by the FNPR union in the enterprise. The conflict between the independents and the FNPR found yet another outlet in the politics of privatization. The independent union argued that the FNPR union was attempting to organize workers on behalf of management, and the FNPR union responded that the independent union was trying to "frighten the proletariat with stories of nomenklatura privatization."[40] As a result, the workers remained divided and management controlled the board of directors.

The case of Norilsk Nickel is more widely known because the battle over control there pitted the powerful directorate at the concern against the major Russian financial group ONEKIMbank.[41] The workers and trade unions were drawn into the struggle because of conditions in the region—at the enterprises attached to the concern—and once again because of inter-union conflicts. Norilsk Nickel is a huge set of industrial enterprises located above the Arctic circle in northern Siberia; it employs over one hundred thousand people, and over three hundred thousand depend on the concern for jobs, social services, pensions, vacations, and health care. It is in many ways an extreme example of the factory town approach to Soviet industrial planning, but it shares its basic features with hundreds of enterprises across Russia.

At the time that the struggle for control broke out in January 1996, workers had not been paid since October of the previous year. In the settlement of Talnakh, where many of the miners who work at Norilsk live, "for the past number of winters workers have had a unique survival experience, living without heat, water, or electricity. Many apartments have been frozen solid and abandoned because the entryways were made impassible by stalagmites and stalactites of ice."[42] Social services were falling apart, and the enterprise was trying to pass them off to the local government, which was ill equipped to meet the needs of the population. To further set the scene for labor's involvement in the struggle at Norilsk, the concern boasted several trade unions representing workers in various professions (and some in the same profession—for example, there were two miners' unions), some FNPR and some independent.

From the beginning, privatization at Norilsk was considered by some to be a scandal; as *Izvestiia* reported, it was notable for its haste, the lobbying involved, and the lack of thought that went into it. The board of directors consisted of ten current and former government officials, five representatives of the boards of subsidiary enterprises, and four representatives of labor councils.[43] Among the government officials on the board of Norilsk Nickel was Al'fred Kokh, the deputy director of the government committee on privatization. The state gave the director of Norilsk Nickel, Anatolii Filatov, a blank check to run the concern as he pleased: he was president of Norilsk Nickel, chairman of the board, and general secretary of the Norilsk industrial complex. The shares were parceled out so that the "labor collective" controlled 51 percent and the state held the remainder. Filatov effectively controlled over half the shares himself, since the state's shares were votes he could count on.

Workers at Norilsk Nickel were totally dependent on the enterprise, and yet the enterprise was ignoring its obligations, the legal ones as well as those implicit in the "social contract" of the Soviet period. The situation got bad enough in 1996 that the state decided to sell its shares, and this ignited another scandal. The share auction was awarded by the committee on privatization to ONEKIMbank, and it just so happened that ONEKIMbank itself won the share auction after disqualifying a bid for the shares that was twice its own. In the wake of the sale, representatives of the bank wanted to replace

Filatov and the board of directors, which they eventually did, but not before a major struggle.[44]

Although this struggle was primarily between ONEKIMbank and the existing management at Norilsk Nickel, workers and unions were drawn into the fray in two ways. First, the situation in the region had become so difficult in material terms that miners were going on hunger strikes in an attempt to get paid. ONEKIMbank promised immediate back pay if the workers would support its position in the fight against Filatov. In response, workers represented by two of the unions at Norilsk Nickel stated that "they were prepared to participate in the emergency meeting of the shareholders . . . in order to provide normal working conditions, social guarantees, and suitable pay for the workers of the complex."[45] In essence, all the workers could do with their "majority shares" was to vote to give the bank power in exchange for what was theirs by law: full pay distributed on time.

As in the case of Severstal', the conflict between the bank and management split the trade unions and ended any chance of solidarity across the enterprises that made up Norilsk Nickel. The familiar divide between the FNPR unions and the independents raised its head again, with "the independent union of mineworkers, judging by the comments of its leadership, in essence backing the bank, while other trade union bosses from the coordinating council of labor collectives and the council of trade union organizations of the joint-stock company supporting the director and the administration."[46] In the end, ONEKIMbank won the battle for Norilsk Nickel, but wage arrears remain unpaid and neither set of trade unions, much less the majority of workers, benefited from the change in leadership.

In case after case, the instrument that was intended, according to Yeltsin and his advisers, to create a "people's capitalism" ended up enriching one sector of the elite or another, sometimes in succession, and leaving workers with less power over the fates of their enterprises than they had before privatization began. If reactions of trade union leaders and rank-and-file workers are any indication, the experience of privatization was an embittering one that undermined the workers' faith not only in Yeltsin and his government, but in the entire concept of democratization of which privatization was presented as an integral part.

Conclusion

The policies that structure the political economy of Yeltsinism underscore the point that there is no such thing as purely economic or purely political reform. Too often the literature on transitions and democratization focuses on one element of this interconnected pair at the expense of the other, and in so doing obscures the effect that simultaneous transformation of the political economy has on the societies in question. More than that, the literature is analytically misleading. The labor legislation of the Yeltsin period is a case in point. The procedural norms and rights delineated in the labor laws created a formal, relatively democratic and inclusive framework for labor participation in the system, but this in itself does not make the laws important. The lack of resources for workers and the lack of enforcement of the laws that are structural features of Russia's postcommunist political economy make it virtually impossible for workers to assert those rights and follow the procedural norms. The adoption of laws without substance is not evidence of democratization.

Similarly, the language of social partnership present in many recent Russian laws and pronouncements could well be viewed as an example of "pacting," if disassociated from its context. In this case, the fiction is fairly obvious: government and management never took social partnership seriously because they did not have to. Voucher privatization functioned in a very similar way, using the language of democratization to mask what amounted to the transformation of the ruling elite into the ruling class through a massive transfer of property. This may represent the transition from one system to another, but it is not evidence of democratization.

Aleksandr Zolin, an adviser to Moscow mayor Iurii Luzhkov, said in 1996 that people who could not afford to live in Moscow should be forced to leave, stating that "there is no freedom without financial means."[47] However harsh the comment seems, Zolin was simply reiterating one of the fundamental postulates of democratic theory. "Political sociologists since Aristotle have argued that the prospects for effective democracy depend on social development and economic well-being," writes Robert Putnam in *Making Democracy Work*. "Contemporary democratic theorists, too, like Robert A. Dahl and Seymour Martin Lipset, have stressed various aspects of modernization . . . in their discussions of the conditions underlying stable and effective democratic government."[48] On these grounds, given the condition of labor in the political economy of Yeltsinism, the working class in Russia enjoys little freedom and has even less opportunity for effective participation in the putatively democratic institutions of Russia's political system.

Examining the fate of the Russian working class since 1992 helps to explain why so many of the indicators of democratization that Western transition theorists—who focus on the political realm narrowly defined—expect to see in Russia are absent. Why, for example, are political parties ineffective and underinstitutionalized, why have "civil society" groups failed to coalesce, and why has a law-based state failed to emerge despite reams of legislation designed to establish one? In large part, it is because the working class, which makes up the bulk of Russian society, has neither the resources nor the conditions of life to effectively participate. The state and economic elites that ignore rules and procedures at their whim do so because there is no countervailing social force powerful enough to stop them. Yeltsin's policies have seen to that.

The size and social weight of the working class, its comparative powerlessness in the present system, and the relatively unfettered power of the state and the economic elite in Russia are direct living legacies of the Soviet system and the transition policies adopted to deconstruct that system. The Soviet working class grew in response to the Communist Party's developmental priorities and ideological preoccupations. Industrial workers were the economic foundation of the Soviet state, but they were also dependent on that state and the factories where they worked. When the new leadership in Russia, with its own priorities and ideological preoccupations, decided to bring down the Soviet system using shock therapy and nomenklatura privatization, it was inevitable that the industrial working class—and therefore the majority of Russian society—would be brought down with it. It also meant that the state and the managerial class would be freed from even the limited social contract that once bound the Soviet regime to the populace.

The unique nature of the communist social formation continues to affect the process of transition in Russia and the debates on Russia's future. As much as many Russian and Western specialists contend that marketization and privatization were necessary because of the nature of the Soviet system, many others see the methods as unjust and the outcome destined to be contested. As a member of the forecasting laboratory of the Russian Academy of Sciences argued, "It is impossible to believe that the privatization process that has been carried out has once and for all resolved the question of the rights of 150 million Russian citizens to what was once the property of the whole people. The victims of three generations of every Russian family stand for these rights."[49] To paraphrase Marx, the political economy constructed by past generations continues to weigh, for some as a nightmare, on the political economy of the living.[50]

Conclusion

Labor Politics, Reform in Russia, and Democratization Theory

In early 1992, Boris Yeltsin and Egor Gaidar, of their own volition and on the advice of Western specialists, introduced shock therapy to Russia, promising that the inevitable hardships associated with it would be relatively fleeting. Six years later, Russia's neo-liberal experiment had driven the country to the brink of collapse. In October 1998, Russia was confronted with crises in industry, finance, trade, the political system, and society, in addition to the worst harvest in years and the specter of having to ask for aid from the West in order to avert shortages of basic foodstuffs as winter approached. While the crises of 1998 were of Yeltsin's own making in many respects, he inherited a country already traumatized by six years of reform under Gorbachev: perestroika had promised much but failed in the end to resolve its own contradictions. Both programs for extricating the Soviet Union and Russia from their authoritarian communist pasts, in Gorbachev's case toward democratic socialism and in Yeltsin's toward capitalist democracy, led to general crises. In the case of perestroika, this was due to Gorbachev's unwillingness or inability to fully implement the program that the logic of democratic socialist reform dictated. In the case of shock therapy, it was due to the basic incompatibility of the neo-liberal project with the political, socioeconomic, and cultural history and structures of Russia.

The case studies and more general analyses of labor politics and trade unions that make up the bulk of this book are a narrative of the partial empowerment but ultimate frustration and anger of workers under Gorbachev and the disenfranchisement and growing bitterness of workers under Yeltsin. Economist Paul Gregory asked rhetorically at the end of 1997 whether

Russia's transition has really been such a failure.[1] If viewed from the perspective of workers, who still make up the majority of Russian society, the answer is unquestionably yes. The issue of unpaid wages, which gets most of the attention of Western analysts when they consider labor at all, is only the most visible manifestation of the frankly disastrous effects of Russia's transition on workers. Regular paychecks, health care, pensions, paid personal and family vacations, job security, and working conditions have all been either lost or compromised. Just as Yeltsin's economic policies undermined the relatively advantaged position that Russia's industrial workers enjoyed under the Soviet system, his political program also destroyed the ideological claims that made workers so central to the politics of the Soviet Union. In their haste to carve out a new basis of legitimacy for themselves as anticommunists, Yeltsin and his allies—including some in the labor movement—effectively denied that labor politics had any role in a postcommunist system. As a result, workers have been politically marginalized, their organizations crippled, and their resources stripped away. Perhaps some would view this as a victory for the neoliberal model of transition, but it is difficult to see how destroying one of the most important bases for civil society helps the cause of democracy or economic stability in postcommunist Russia.

The structural disadvantages and social and economic hardships faced by workers did not, however, lead labor to acquiesce to the emerging system of political economy in Russia. The year 1998 was a time of upheaval in Russia, involving not only numerous changeovers in government and the collapse of the financial system, but increasing labor unrest as well. The actions of workers in 1998 were at times dramatic, as when miners blocked the Trans-Siberian Railroad, but their actions do not constitute evidence that contradicts the arguments made above about labor's structurally weak position in postcommunist Russia. Rather the strikes and blockades of 1998 throw into relief all of the major contradictions facing Russia and the labor movement caused by the neo-liberal experiment of the Yeltsin period.

As has been the case since perestroika began, the most restive as well as the most visible and organized group among Russia's workers was the miners. While strikes had been going on throughout the year, by May 1998 the actions of workers became more coordinated. In a typical pattern, the miners' demands began with economic issues and ended with political ones, from payment of back wages to the resignation of the government and the president. These strikes, however, had a new and potentially more radical aspect compared to the strikes of previous years. As noted above, in May and June of 1998 the miners in the Kuzbass, Vorkuta, Inta, and the Donbass went beyond holding meetings, curtailing production, and going on hunger strikes. They extended their tactics to shutting down the main railway lines and highways linking Moscow to the regional coal centers.[2] For part of May and June, the miners effectively cut the country apart, blocking the overland delivery of goods to Moscow from the north, from Siberia, from southern Russia, and from the Caucasus.[3]

The gravity and implications of the miners' actions were apparent in the response of local and regional officials to the blockade. Initially, they attempted to undercut the strike by arguing, as local officials had done on previous occasions, that the miners were primarily hurting other workers whose factories would have to shut down due to lack of fuel. Beyond that, regional governors in the Kuzbass and elsewhere declared states of emergency and took control of water and power stations and enterprises with continuous production cycles. It was perhaps an overstatement on the part of one commentator that "the levers of administration of a significant part of the country were concentrated in the miners' hands,"[4] but the strike and blockade did send shock waves throughout the country, the likes of which had not been felt since the strikes of 1989 and 1991. The miners and their supporters combined these actions with the maintenance of a permanent protest in Moscow, putting pressure on the government and the Duma alike to resolve the outstanding issues. As a result, the government took rapid steps to meet the most immediate of the miners' demands regarding wages, even as the unrest helped to undermine the new administration of Sergei Kirienko.

The central question is how to interpret the events of the summer and early fall of 1998 in terms of their implications for workers and the labor movement in Russia. The recent historical record suggests that signal events such as these have had a profound effect, particularly on the processes of political change in the Soviet Union and Russia, as well as on the nature of the labor movement. On the other hand, after the rise in influence of Soviet labor in the late Gorbachev period, the power and influence of workers and unions has taken a continuous downward curve. While it is too early to tell at the time of this writing what the long-term effects of the events of 1998 might be, the strikes did reveal certain trends within the labor movement that have very mixed implications for its future.

The first trend concerns the position of unions toward the government and reform, and in particular the stance of the Independent Union of Mineworkers and its leader Aleksandr Sergeev. The trade unions have had a complicated relationship with the Yeltsin government, with the FNPR being generally more critical and the independents being more supportive while all of them have tried to cut deals most advantageous to themselves. During the 1998 strikes and blockades, the miners' union finally broke with the Yeltsin government and its position on economic policy. Sergeev, who had been a member of the presidential council, finally quit the post, denounced Yeltsin, and demanded his resignation. Referring to plans to shut down more coal mines, the miners' union then released an acerbic announcement challenging the government: "The powers that be intend to close unprofitable industries. So why do they plan to retain the most unprofitable enterprise in all of Russia—themselves?"[5] The importance of this statement should not be underestimated, both because the miners' union is one of the most powerful in the country and because symbolically the miners' union in many ways stands for the workers of Russia. The NPG was the first independent union, it challenged the Communist Party and was crucial to Yeltsin's success in 1991. Many in the labor movement look to the miners for their lead, and a decisive break with the current leadership by the NPGR will affect the position of other workers and labor organizations.

The second major trend that these strikes revealed was the growing coordination of action between miners and other groups of workers in various parts of the country, including doctors, teachers, pilots, and railroad workers. In addition, there was evidence of increasing mutual support between members of the Russian intelligentsia and the labor movement, a cooperation that has not been much in evidence in the past several years. Again, it is too early to tell if this coordination will continue, either through trade union associations or more broadly based political movements such as Andrei Isaev's Union of Labor. If it does continue, it will be a major advance for the labor movement, because lack of unity and access to the broader political system has been one of labor's central liabilities since 1992.

Third, the strikes of 1998, particularly the blockades of major roads and railways, served as a reminder for workers and for the government that coordinated, radical action on the part of labor can have an immediate and noticeable impact on Russia, and that labor is a force to be reckoned with even in its weakened state. For the labor movement, it was a welcome victory of sorts after years of defeats at the hands of the ideologists of neo-liberal reform. This victory consisted not so much in meeting workers' immediate demands as in reaffirming on an individual and institutional level the potential of collective action. For the government at many levels, it was a wake-up call that the famed patience of Russia's people is not unlimited, and that more attention and resources had to be directed toward social questions if serious social upheaval was to be avoided. Evgenii Primakov's government seemed to be heeding that call by October 1998, at least on a rhetorical level, although little of substance has been accomplished.

While all of these trends were positive signs for the labor movement in Russia, the strikes also reinforced the analytical importance of two other features of Russia's postcommunist political economy that were serious liabilities for labor. First, the fact that these actions, like most of their predecessors, were reactive is not in itself surprising: most strikes are responses to the actions or plans of management or the state, in Russia and elsewhere. The central problem for labor remained the lack of institutional positions and interunion cooperation that would allow workers to influence socioeconomic policy or put forward their own credible initiatives prior to the next crisis that demanded industrial action. As the analysis in preceding chapters indicates, this situation was mainly due to the choices made by Yeltsin and his allies regarding political structures and institutions that effectively disenfranchised labor along with the rest of Russian society in 1992–1993. It was also the result, however, of the choices that trade unions and workers made in the late Soviet and post-Soviet periods. Expending so much energy on internecine conflict and on attempts to carve spaces for individual unions at the expense of broad political organizing proved extremely costly for the labor movement. The events of the summer of 1998 may prove in the long run to be a crucial juncture in the consolidation of labor as a political force, but conflicts among unions and workers in different economic sectors remained a problem in 1998. If anything, the roots of these conflicts grew stronger as the neo-liberal project evolved and as industrial sectors and their workers fought each other over resources in desperate attempts to survive Russia's economic implosion. The 1998 strikes and blockades did not change the structural factors that had led to these conflicts in the first place.

The second factor also is linked to the effects of neo-liberalism on the Russian political economy. The strikes and blockades demonstrated once again that the cycle of economic crisis, nonpayment of wages, labor unrest, and temporary government bailout of particular sectors remained in place. The workers' cutting off of major internal access routes to Moscow did not cause the government to change course, nor did it affect the attitudes of Russia's major creditors and suppliers of aid regarding Russia's need to continue on the path of neo-liberal reform. This was not particularly surprising either, because the causes of this cyclical pattern could not be addressed by tinkering with the implementation of neo-liberalism—better tax collection, lower taxes, and so on—to create a better structural adjustment program. Six years of such tinkering had done nothing to stem Russia's socioeconomic decline. Until and unless the underlying structural problems facing workers that resulted from shock therapy and privatization are addressed—namely, labor's lack of resources and its political marginalization—the labor movement will find it impossible to break out of this cycle regardless of how organized and coordinated it becomes.

The industrial actions of 1998 further exemplified the potential strengths and structural weaknesses of the Russian labor movement discussed in the previous chapters. Workers and their allies were becoming more organized and "solidaristic" due to Russia's deepening systemic crisis, even as the emergent system created structural barriers to organization and solidarity. Labor organizations demonstrated that they were a force to be reckoned with on a day-to-day basis, but at the same time their impact on the politics and economic policy of Russia was circumscribed by the cycles of crisis that were the long-term effect of neo-liberalism. The relative correlation of forces still ran against labor in spite of some favorable trends. Increasing cooperation in a system designed to divide and localized power in a system designed to disempower defined the Russian labor movement after six years of neo-liberal experimentation.

These six years under Yeltsin, preceded by six years of socialist reform under Gorbachev, shattered much of the labor relations system within which Russia's workers have to try to survive. Much of this book has been concerned with the question of how workers attempted to navigate the currents of change, but the broader question is: what do the attempts to reform the labor relations system since 1985 demonstrate about the process of reform in

Russia? The question can be viewed in three distinct ways. First, it is a question about the role of labor relations reform in the greater scheme of perestroika and glasnost, of shock therapy and building democracy, and what these reforms had in common, both positively and negatively, with other reforms of the two periods in question. Second, it is a question about the role that the attempted reforms of the labor relations system have played in the fate of Russia's ongoing transition from authoritarianism. Third, it is a question about the lessons to be drawn from the specific features of the reform process in industry for the continuing processes of change in Russia and other state-socialist systems.

As mature policies, perestroika and glasnost were designed to be mechanisms that would empower civil society at the expense of conservative elites and serve to ensure the continued stable development of Soviet society under the leadership of reform-minded Soviet elites. The reform of the labor relations system was of a piece with many other reform policies: the law on cooperatives, the reduction and then elimination of censorship, electoral reform, reform of the Party, and new thinking in foreign policy, to name a few. All of these policies were designed to "bring society back in": to give groups within society previously excluded from political life access to the system and to political resources. The argument that these policies were designed simply to keep the existing elites in power is only half true, and not particularly illuminating. It reveals nothing about the actual effects of the policies on the political and economic positions of social groups within the system.

In whatever other ways the policy of worker self-management in the labor relations reform program failed, it succeeded in bringing workers back into the political process. Like the other policies of these years, particularly glasnost and electoral reform, Gorbachev's initiatives did politically reanimate large sectors of the Soviet population. Insofar as this is true, it is simply wrong to argue, as most Russian and Western analysts do, that Gorbachev and perestroika failed. Unlike any previous reforms in the history of Russia, Gorbachev's programs helped create stable social constituencies for democratic reform, especially among significant sectors of the labor force.

In another important sense, of course, perestroika did fail: Gorbachev did not succeed in creating strong constituencies in support of his vision of democratic socialism and his leadership of the reform process. The reason these constituencies failed to emerge, however, is not that Gorbachev's reforms were too radical, but that they were not radical enough. The *LSE* left far too much power in the hands of the managerial and ministerial elites to make the self-management provisions included in the law truly effective. If a form of self-managed, democratic, and economically dynamic socialism was what Gorbachev actually intended, nothing less than the transfer of property rights from the state to the enterprise collectives, in conjunction with inclusive democratic political institutions, would have sufficed. This type of policy, however, would not only have challenged the ruling elites' control over the system, it would have made such control largely unnecessary and any role for large parts of the Soviet elite superfluous. Such a predicament had been the conundrum of Soviet reform since Khrushchev; in the end, Gorbachev apparently had neither the will nor the power to enact such a policy in the industrial realm, or any other.

This central dilemma was the main cause of the contradictions that were exhibited in virtually every piece of important reform legislation of the Gorbachev years. In terms of the ultimate fate of perestroika, however, the fact that the dilemma remained unresolved in the sphere of industrial labor relations was more important than in any other area of policy making save policy on the national question. The question of the relationship between workers, the labor relations system in which they lived, and the reform process was crucial because it addressed a key transitional issue: the relationship between property and power.

The labor relations reform policy of the Gorbachev years never resolved the issue of who controlled property or who had the power to make decisions regarding its disposition: the power of entrenched elites was never completely broken and workers were never sufficiently empowered to make such a resolution possible. The resulting stalemate within the industrial system served to alienate both workers and elites from perestroika and the Gorbachev leadership. Ultimately, it exacerbated the existing economic crisis by politicizing the production process without giving any side the power to resolve the political questions about control over industry that Gorbachev's labor relations policy raised.

Any answer to the question of whether policies could have been designed differently in order to avoid these contradictions—given the distribution of forces in society that faced Gorbachev when he took office—must of course remain speculative. Events surrounding the reforms that were enacted, however, suggest two further conclusions about the process of reform in Russia that remain important for the future of democratization. The first is that, however fraught with the potential for instability it might be, extensive social mobilization and popular involvement in the reform process is crucial to the extension of democratic reforms. For reformers within the political system, support from below is the only reliable basis for democratization. In the case examined here, the elites—charged with the task of assisting workers in the development of self-management institutions—for the most part either failed to do so or endeavored to sabotage the efforts of workers and managers who tried to change the system.

As to the problem of excess militancy contributing to the breakdown of the democratization process—discussed by transition theorists—in the case of Soviet and Russian industry since 1987, it has been precisely from the sectors demonstrating the greatest militancy that the democratization process has benefited the most. Soviet miners, as the direct and indirect result of their strikes, succeeded in advancing the democratization of the trade union system by creating their own unions—serving as an example to workers in other sectors, and pressuring the official unions to become more responsive. The strikes also helped workers and reform-minded local and regional officials to gain more control over the economic decision-making process in their regions. In regard to the effects of this militancy, one must distinguish between what any particular leader or analyst might regard as legitimate forms of democratization and the fact that elements of civil society in Russia gained more power in their respective areas because of the militancy of their political actions. Gorbachev may have been toppled in part by the process of social mobilization he set in motion, but given the nature of Soviet and Russian state-socialism and the reforms he set out to accomplish, he had no choice. One might fault him for his execution, but certainly not for his instinct. Gorbachev relied, in the end, too much on the apparatus of power that the logic of his reforms demanded be undermined.

Yeltsin, on the other hand, adopted a different and far more dangerous strategy. From the summer of 1992, Yeltsin relied on a series of economic policies, derived from Western political and economic systems, that severed the fundamental links between political, social, and economic reform and that virtually excluded from the reform process social mobilization and societal involvement. The separation of the privatization process from the process of restructuring the socioeconomic infrastructure of industrial cities was emblematic of this approach. Such an approach could only alienate further an already demoralized population and undermine the confidence of the Russian people—perhaps workers most of all—that democratization was worth the cost.

Whatever one thinks about shock therapy and nomenklatura privatization as economic policy, their mode of introduction was politically debilitating for the process of democratization in Russia. In the Russian Federation in 1992, democratic norms and procedures were relatively new and structurally weak, while interest in and disagreements about the future socioeconomic formation of the country were high. This was also a country in which a societal belief—particularly among the working class—in the people's right to have some say over the nature of social and economic change ran deep. In this context, Yeltsin and his government presented society with a socioeconomic fait accompli. It smacked of the type of "revolution from above" that Russian society had seen many times before, with all the attributes of authoritarian politics associated with such a state-driven approach.

To argue that Yeltsin has followed in the authoritarian footsteps of his predecessors is not to ignore the political context in which he was operating. It is true that the Russian Parliament gave Yeltsin extraordinary powers in 1991 to implement economic and social policy. It is also true that there was widespread support in parliament in late 1991 and early 1992 for the type of policy initiatives that Yeltsin introduced. It is further at least arguable that the Russian Parliament was not adequately democratic or representative, and therefore lacked legitimacy. On the other hand, the parliament never permanently waived its right to be involved in the making of policy; constitutionally, the power it gave to Yeltsin it also had the right to take away. It is also true, however, that support for Yeltsin's policies eroded in parliament in 1992, and calls for discussion and reconsideration of those policies mounted, setting the stage for the constitutional crisis of 1993. Finally, if one argues that the parliament lacked legitimacy, it could be argued that the powers parliament gave Yeltsin were illegitimate.

Once elected and empowered by parliament, Yeltsin behaved as if he were not subject to any democratic norms, procedures, or even expectations. He refused to negotiate with parliament, he did not try to build consensus around his reforms with either elite groups or society, and he ended up acting outside the constitution. To argue as some have that the Soviet-era constitution then in force was outdated, undemocratic, and amended beyond recognition is beside the point: as transition theorists never tire of pointing out, norms and procedures, flawed as they might be, are in part what democracy is about. Yeltsin's exclusion of the political representatives of Russia, compromised though they might have been, set the tone for the increasingly authoritarian turn of Russia's political life from that point on.

Beyond the confines of elite politics, Yeltsin's exclusion of society from the process of debate and policy making corroded democratization even further. It is ironic that Yeltsin's victory over Gorbachev relied on the very social mobilization that Yeltsin's policies undermined after 1991. In the case of labor, Yeltsin and his government made a conscious choice to exclude workers and their unions from genuine participation in the momentous choices that were being made. The effects of those choices continued through 1998 to destroy the ability of virtually all social groups to effectively participate in Russia's political life. Just as Gorbachev attempted, after much hesitation, to encourage social mobilization in order to carry out economic reform and erode the power of the more authoritarian wing of the Communist Party, Yeltsin rejected social empowerment and mobilization—just as many Western analyses of transition would have advised him to do—as a threat to his economic policies. In so doing, he provided solace and support for the more authoritarian part of the Russian political establishment, new and old. If Yeltsin's time in office illustrates anything clearly, it is that democracy cannot be built by the storied "iron fist" of Russia's political past.

This last point leads directly to the issue of reform and Russian political culture. The wariness about social mobilization and societal involvement in the reform process—exhibited by both Gorbachev and Yeltsin to varying degrees—reflects certain assumptions held by Russian elites, by others in Russian society, and by many in the West regarding the nature of this culture: namely, that Russians are not ready for democracy or are somehow inherently given to authoritarian political institutions. There is little evidence that suggests either is the case.

When given the opportunity to elect their own managers, workers as a general rule did not elect either yes men or tyrants. Where genuine elections in fact took place, competent managers were elected in the vast majority of cases, first and foremost because workers knew that it was in their best interest to elect them. Similarly, when the miners and those who sympathized with them went on strike, they did not do so in the tradition of the anarchistic Russian peasant rebellion. For the most part, order was maintained by the workers themselves, and strikes were selective so as not to cripple the day-to-day lives of the people in cities affected. The behavior of the leaders of the attempted putsch, the internecine warfare between Yeltsin and Gorbachev, the eventually bloody confrontation between Yeltsin and the leaders of the Russian Parliament, and the blatant disregard for law and democratic norms exhibited by the Russian government, legislature, regional and local officials, and economic elites suggest that if political immaturity and anarchistic tendencies are a problem in Russia, the problem lies more with the rulers than with the ruled.

There is little question that many Russians admire the "iron fist." For the majority of Russians, however, the pull of authoritarianism is based on a desire for order and stability that they have been denied for decades. It has become a commonplace, for instance, to point out that many workers continued to support the old system of labor relations, the old unions, and the existing forms of nationalized industry after Yeltsin's rise to power. For most workers, however, the attachment to the old system was not principled, but pragmatic. A well-designed program of reform addressing political, social, and economic issues, and carried out at a pace that actually allowed for a transition, rather than for shock without therapy, would have enjoyed significant support—not only among workers, but in society at large. It was the structure of the reform program, not the nature of the political culture, that in large part has determined the fate of democratization in Russia. Yeltsin may have succeeded in building a truncated form of capitalism in Russia, but that capitalist edifice continues to cast a long shadow of authoritarianism over the Russian political landscape.

Labor Relations in Russia and Models of Democratization

Most analysts would accept the argument that the structure of a reform program, rather than political culture or individual leaders, ultimately will determine the fate of democratization. The argument that democratization programs that have worked in the West could not have worked in Russia, due to the political, social, and economic structures of Russia's state-socialist system, is more controversial. The critique of Western models is grounded in an examination of the workers' relationship to democratization not only because all models of transition politics view this relationship as crucial, but also because workers—for historical, ideological, and economic reasons—remain the largest single socioeconomic group in Russia. Directly and indirectly, they have played a central role in postrevolutionary Soviet politics.

Existing models of transitions make a number of assertions about workers and democratization. The first and most important assertion—from which all the others follow and on which the entire case regarding labor rests—is that labor, to quote Guisseppe Di Palma, "has a vested interest in democracy," because as part of civil society labor cannot struggle for its economic or political interests in a nondemocratic system. The assumption therefore is that labor's support for democratization is not problematic: such support can be assumed, it need not be actively enlisted, negotiated, or nurtured.

One of the most important lessons for democratization theory that the study of Russian labor relations imparts is that in state-socialist systems this assumption is demonstrably false. Russian workers, like the society at large, are neither inherently authoritarian nor inherently anarchistic; they are not inherently democratic either. Russian workers had a great deal to lose by supporting democratization, including but not limited to their jobs and standard of living, because democratization entailed fundamental changes in the economic structures of the command-administrative system that were the legacy of the Soviet period. These economic changes required equally dramatic changes in the social infrastructure of Russian society. As long as it appeared—as it did under both Gorbachev and Yeltsin—that the government had no overall strategy for reform that would encompass the political and socioeconomic issues that inextricably bind together the shop floor, the apartment building, the hospital, the grocery store, the daycare center, city hall, and the voting booth, many workers inevitably remained either passive or even antagonistic toward democratization for entirely rational social and material reasons.

If Western scholars have not paid enough attention to the contradictions of the democratization process in Russia, it is mainly because models of transitions from authoritarianism have been far too focused on institution building in the narrow sense of that concept. This is not to downplay the importance of writing good constitutions, or building parliamentary systems that guarantee a workable division of powers, or devising electoral mechanisms that provide for equal and just contestation between competing parties and groups. All of these forms of institution building are necessary for a successful transition, but in Russia they would not be sufficient even if they had been accomplished.

In the Russian case, two other elements are of equal importance. First, having good institutions is of very little use unless there are groups within society that have been sufficiently empowered to actually take advantage of them. The analysis in the preceding chapters of the lack of progress in the development and strength of the labor movement since 1992, and of its political position, casts serious doubt on claims of democratization and the growing importance of civil society in Russia. While it is possible to view the development of labor unions and other social movements as a sign of democratization in and of itself, one needs to discriminate between the mere existence of nonstate controlled actors and their ability to act politically as determined by the political and economic structures of the country in question. Analyzing these movements in relation to the state and to those who control the economic system provides a better sense of the actual progress of democratization than examining institution building in the narrow sense.

The obverse side of this issue is equally important: the analytical question here is how the government went about the process of "destatization" of the Russian economy and polity. Again, Western analysts tend to view privatization and other forms of denationalization as prima facie evidence of democratization. In the Russian case, however, such actions merely transferred control over resources to existing elites, thereby making what was their contingent power under the old system permanent power in the "new" system. This was done without a commensurate strengthening of those groups within society over which these elites exercise control, and therefore it is difficult to argue that such actions should be viewed as democratization. The form of "destatization," rather than the mere fact of it, should be the determining factor in judging the progress of democracy, as the cases of Norilsk Nickel and the Soviet airline industry discussed in chapter 6 make all too clear.

Second—and in keeping with the argument that democratization in Russia is an inseparably political, social, economic, and cultural process—the traditional focus of democratization theorists on the problem of "crafting" national political institutions must be balanced by an equal emphasis on the complexities of rebuilding Russia's political, social, economic, and cultural life in the localities and provinces. It is the factories, the farms, the institutes—in short, the places of work—that serve as the center of the socioeconomic infrastructure in post-Soviet Russia. Any program for democratization in Russia that focuses narrowly on issues such as central political institutions and on privatization programs will accomplish little in terms of building democracy. And any analysis that separates these issues from the broader political and socioeconomic context of Russia's transition from authoritarianism will be severely distorted at best. Many specialists on Russia and the individual states of the former Soviet Union have done tremendous work that ties these issues together. Unfortunately, most Western transitologists and democratization theorists who have conceptually traveled to the East—and even more dangerously most Western politicians who make policy regarding Russia—continue to operate on the assumption that Russia is "conceptually equivalent" to Chile, the Philippines, Brazil, or Spain. Quite apart from the highly controversial history of structural adjustment and democratization in many of these countries,[6] the argument that the neo-liberal policies that some contend worked so well in Europe and in Latin America will also save Russia flies in the face of the post-Soviet Russian experience.

Even after six years of doling out money to Russia in exchange for "acceptable policies" and seeing the economy, polity, and society continue to implode, Clinton and other Western leaders proceeded in the fall of 1998 to tell Russia to stay the neo-liberal course of reform. But as Stephen F. Cohen has asked, why call it reform?[7] It seems that Western leaders could give no better advice than to persevere on the ruinous path that Russia was already following. Relying on Western assumptions has led to faulty analysis and continues to encourage the West to give Russia bad advice. It is truly disheartening that Russia's leaders up to the fall of 1998 seemed all too willing to accept such advice.

Western leaders, the International Monetary Fund, and those with financial interests in Russia immediately criticized the Primakov government, members of Russia's opposition groups, and those Russian economists and social scientists who suggested more state intervention and control over the country's political economy. Talk of the Russians rolling back the clock and engaging in Soviet-era planning, combined with the appropriate level of disapprobation of such methods and complaints that Russians still do not understand the global market, were a staple of Western commentary in late 1998. These views reflect a mixture of selective myopia and an almost willful misunderstanding of Russia and what has happened there since Yeltsin came to power.

The stark reality is that the intervention of the Russian state in the economy never withered away; the Russian state bureaucracy was larger by 1998 than it had ever been. What changed was the nature of state intervention, and whose interests that intervention served. The Russian state since 1991, from its adoption of shock therapy to privatization to banking and labor laws, has done everything in its power to make the country safe for domestic and foreign capital; if it failed to do so it was not for want of trying. Yeltsin and his advisers, domestic and foreign, attempted to shape policies to the advantage of entrepreneurs and investors on the theory that this was the only road to prosperity and democratic stability. In practice, such state intervention proved lucrative for a small minority and detrimental to society as a whole, while democratic stability was nowhere in sight.

The supposed debate over state intervention or nonintervention has always been a spurious one, in Russia and everywhere else. The issue for Russia remains how the state should intervene. The trends in Russia's political economy at the end of 1998 suggested that if anything but the extractive sector of Russia's industrial plant was going to be saved, the state would have to take over a large number of industries regardless of ideological objections. Many of the plants that were privatized have been stripped of assets or allowed to collapse, capital flight has been immense, and the lifeblood of many Russian cities has been drained as a result. At the end of 1998, the basic choice for the state lay between either responding to crises by taking over enterprises and other parts of the economy by default or planning steps to be taken, including renationalization, to pull Russia out of its crisis. After six years of corrupt privatization and crony capitalism, the latter seems the more promising and realistic option, particularly as foreign and domestic investors have little interest in saving what is left of Russia's economy.

The choice confronting Russia and the West after the collapse of neo-liberalism in 1998 was not between free-market democracy on the one hand and a return to communism on the other. Both choices were bankrupt and most people in Russia and the West knew it, in spite of rhetoric to the contrary. The real choices, equally stark in one sense, were more complicated. The least likely scenario is for Russia to accept its emerging role as basically a raw material and extractive-industry appendage of the West in the economic sphere while remaining a formally democratic but highly elite-centered and authoritarian political system. The latter might be acceptable to many in Russia, but one need not be an ardent Russian nationalist to reject the former. More likely for Russia is a turn to nationalist and populist leaders, such as Aleksandr Lebed or even Iurii Luzhkov, who might well behave in an autarkic and simultaneously aggressive manner toward the West while undoing the policies, if not the effects, of neo-liberalism. The third possibility is for Russia to reverse some of the policies of neo-liberalism, in particular privatization, to make its political system more inclusive, and to try to implement the model of social partnership that Yeltsin abandoned in 1992. While speculation is dangerous, by late 1998 the choice seemed to be a Russian Peronism or social democracy.

In either case, the political economy of the country would have to change if Russia were to survive as a stable and influential state. As quoted in chapter 6, Oleg Pchelintsev noted that few in Russia accepted the outcome of privatization, and that control over the national wealth remains the key issue. It would be a powerful argument for a populist demagogue to agitate for stripping the "new Russians" and foreigners of property, which would then be administered of course by the leader in the name of the people. More difficult would be a national debate and ultimate negotiation among groups over how to dispose of and then rebuild Russia's infrastructure. Some of the challenges this would raise were touched on in previous chapters of this book in relation to workers and managers. These challenges would be magnified when regional and ethnic groups within the Federation are taken into account.

"Restatization" and other "interventionist" policies would only be a prelude to closing down obsolete factories, which everyone agrees needs to be done. It should also be a prelude, however, to saving viable industries and constructing new enterprises where necessary. This should entail conscious, well-articulated, and popularly agreed-upon programs for rebuilding the social infrastructure—from housing to medicine to education—that has been so damaged during the last several years. I have argued in this book that Russia's communist experience created structures and attitudes that are far more "collective," for want of a better word, than those that exist in the West. For this reason, and because of the scarcity of capital in Russia, it seems likely that there will be more public and state-owned property in Russia than Western governments and business would like or even deem acceptable.

To put it bluntly, the West had best get used to the idea. Furthermore, it would be in the West's interests not only to accept such an outcome but to help Russia carry out the changes that Yeltsin's policies have made virtually unavoidable. As far as Russia is concerned, the West's fundamental interests are not financial, but political, strategic, and humanitarian, particularly after the events of late 1998. It is true that restatization or resocialization of large sectors of the Russian economy would hurt European and American companies in the short run. But why should Western governments care? When considered as a portion of the West's economic activity, Russia is inconsequential, and Western governments should not let the economic interests of a relatively small number of businesses dictate policy. The more significant argument is that the consolidation of capitalism and the progress of democracy are integrally linked; this has been the leitmotif of Western policy since 1992. Such linkage in the Russian case, however, is not merely misguided but positively harmful to the prospects of a stable, democratic Russia. Much more important is the reality that Russia has thousands of nuclear weapons, a large yet unstable military, and more than enough anti-Western ideologues to go around. The West needs a stable Russia, but Russia has to become stable on its own terms. If Russia is to stabilize in a democratic way, it will be on the basis of a more socially oriented, or even socialist, set of economic and political arrangements than the West is accustomed to.

The Russian leadership and the West must examine a much wider range of issues that pertain to rebuilding post-Soviet Russia than the economic and political nostrums of the past six years have allowed for, and must include the role of labor as a key player in any democratic outcome. Western countries have a wealth of experience in areas such as job retraining and placement, organization of unemployment benefits, labor arbitration, and regulation of workplace safety and environment, all of which postcommunist Russia lacks. If Western governments and the International Monetary Fund, in coordination with a committed Russian government, earmarked monies to restructure the labor relations system and social infrastructure, the funds might actually do some good. This would certainly be more productive than past policies of encouraging private enterprise and foreign investment, and unquestionably more useful than throwing additional money at Russia in an attempt to save an ailing and corrupt system. Such policies would not only serve the cause of economic and political stabilization: they might help undo the damage that neo-liberalism has done and genuinely further the cause of democratization in Russia.

Notes

Abbreviations of Russian Archives

f.   fond—main subject or personal file
op.   opis—secondary subject list
d.   delo—individual subject file containing documents
l. and ll. list and listi—page number(s)
ob   obratnaia storona—reverse side of page

Chapter 1: Restructuring State Socialism

1. For diverse views on this question, with varying emphases on leadership, ideology, class struggle, society, totalitarianism, and nationalism, see Archie Brown, *The Gorbachev Factor* (Oxford: Oxford University Press, 1996); Donald Filtzer, *Soviet Workers and the Collapse of Perestroika* (Cambridge: Cambridge University Press, 1994); Jerry Hough, *Democratization and Revolution in the USSR, 1985–1991* (Washington, D.C.: The Brookings Institution, 1997); Boris Kagarlitsky, *The Disintegration of the Monolith* (London: Verso, 1992); Moshe Lewin, "Society, Past and Present, in Interpreting Russia," in *Beyond Soviet Studies,* ed. Daniel Orlovsky (Washington, D.C.: Woodrow Wilson Center Special Studies, 1995), 56–71; Martin Malia, "From under the Rubble, What?" *Problems of Communism* 41, no. 1–2 (1992): 89–106; Ronald Grigor Suny, *The Revenge of the Past* (Stanford: Stanford University Press, 1993).

2. See, in particular on the economic debate, Anders Aslund, *How Russia Became a Market Economy* (Washington, D.C.: The Brookings Institution, 1995); Joseph Blasi, Maya Kroumova, and Douglas Kruse, *Kremlin Capitalism: Privatizing the Russian Economy* (Ithaca: Cornell University Press, 1997); and Lynn D. Nelson and Irina Y. Kuzes, *Radical Reform in Yeltsin's Russia* (Armonk, N.Y.: M. E. Sharpe, 1995); for more general arguments, see Michael McFaul, "State Power, Institutional Change, and the Politics of Privatization in Russia," *World Politics* 47, no. 2 (January 1995): 210–43, and his *Russia between Elections* (Washington, D.C.: Carnegie Endowment, 1996); and Robert C. Tucker, "Post-Soviet Leadership and Change," in *Patterns in Post-Soviet Leadership,* ed. Timothy J. Colton and Robert C. Tucker (Boulder: Westview Press, 1995), 5–28.

3. The flora and fauna issue is a reference to the debate of Philippe C. Schmitter

and Terry Lynn Karl with Valerie Bunce in the pages of *Slavic Review,* a debate emblematic of a broader fissure in the field. See Philippe C. Schmitter and Terry Lynn Karl, "The Conceptual Travels of Transitologists and Consolidologists: How Far to the East Should They Attempt to Go?" *Slavic Review* 53, no. 1 (spring 1994): 173–85; Valerie Bunce, "Should Transitologists Be Grounded?" *Slavic Review* 54, no. 1 (spring 1995): 111–27; Terry Lynn Karl and Philippe C. Schmitter, "From an Iron Curtain to a Paper Curtain: Grounding Transitologists or Students of Postcommunism," *Slavic Review* 54, no. 4 (winter 1995): 965–78; and Valerie Bunce, "Paper Curtains and Paper Tigers," *Slavic Review* 54, no. 4 (winter 1995): 879–987. See also Andrea Chandler, "The Interaction of Post-Sovietology and Comparative Politics: Seizing the Moment," *Communist and Post-Communist Studies* 27, no. 1 (March 1994): 3–18.

4. Giuseppe Di Palma, *To Craft Democracies* (Berkeley and Los Angeles: University of California Press, 1990), 44.

5. The term is taken from Michael Saward, "Democratic Theory and Indices of Democratization," in *Defining and Measuring Democracy,* ed. David Beetham (London: Sage Publications, 1994), 13–14; see also Robert Dahl, *Democracy and Its Critics* (New Haven: Yale University Press, 1989).

6. Saward in Beetham, *Defining and Measuring Democracy,* 13–14.

7. Geraint Parry and George Moyser, "More Participation, More Democracy?" in ibid., 44–62.

8. The sign read "Luchshe uzhasnii konets, chem uzhas bez kontsa." The discussions of the placard, the strike, and the problems they addressed took place on 15 and 16 April 1991.

9. See, for example, *Pravda,* 3 February 1996, 1; *Nezavisimaia gazeta,* 15 February 1996, 4.

10. For a variety of views on this subject, see Michael Burawoy, "From Sovietology to Comparative Political Economy," in Orlovsky, *Beyond Soviet Studies,* 72–102; Beverly Crawford, "Explaining Political and Economic Change in Post-Communist Eastern Europe," *Comparative Political Studies* 28, no. 2 (July 1995): 171–99; Stephen Hanson, "The Leninist Legacy and Institutional Change," *Comparative Political Studies* 28, no. 2 (July 1995): 306–14; Andrei Kuznetsov, "Economic Reforms in Russia: Enterprise Behaviour as an Impediment to Change," *Europe-Asia Studies* 46, no. 6 (1994): 955–70; Andrei Andreev, "Sobstvennost', vlast', i politicheskaia reforma v Rossii," *Moskva* 9 (1993): 141–48.

11. See Schmitter, Karl, Bunce, McFaul, and others cited above for particular iterations on this theme.

12. *Izvestiia,* 25 November 1993.

13. Bunce, "Should Transitologists Be Grounded?" 119.

14. Alfred Stepan, "Paths toward Redemocratization: Theoretical and Comparative Considerations," in *Transitions from Authoritarian Rule: Prospects for Democracy,* ed. Guillermo O'Donnell, Philippe C. Schmitter, and Laurence Whitehead (Baltimore and London: Johns Hopkins University Press, 1986), 65.

15. Ibid., 72.

16. O'Donnell, Schmitter, and Whitehead, *Transitions from Authoritarian Rule,* 19.

17. See Adam Przeworski, "Democracy as a Contingent Outcome of Conflicts," in *Constitutionalism and Democracy,* ed. Jon Elster and Rune Slagstad (Cambridge: Cambridge University Press, 1988), 79.

18. Schmitter and Karl, "Conceptual Travels of Transitologists," 184.

19. Adam Przeworski, *Democracy and the Market* (Cambridge: Cambridge University Press, 1988), 139–46.

20. Di Palma, *To Craft Democracies,* 13.

21. Schmitter and Karl, "Conceptual Travels of Transitologists," 179.

22. Ibid., 179–80.

23. Di Palma, *To Craft Democracies,* 78.

24. Przeworski, *Democracy and the Market,* 143.

25. Bunce, "Should Transitologists Be Grounded?" 120–21.

26. O'Donnell, Schmitter, and Whitehead, *Transitions from Authoritarian Rule,* 52–53.

27. Di Palma, *To Craft Democracies,* 97; and Adam Przeworski, "Some Problems in the Study of the Transition to Democracy," in O'Donnell, Schmitter, and Whitehead, 63.

28. See Przeworski, *Democracy and the Market,* 143 for examples.

29. See Philippe C. Schmitter, "Still the Century of Corporatism?" in *The New Corporatism,* ed. Fredrick Pike and Thomas Stritch (Notre Dame: Notre Dame University Press, 1974), 85–131; and O'Donnell, Schmitter, and Whitehead, *Transitions from Authoritarian Rule,* 52–53.

30. O'Donnell, Schmitter, and Whitehead, *Transitions from Authoritarian Rule,* 52–53.

31. Ibid.

32. Michael Burawoy, *Manufacturing Consent: Changes in the Labor Process under Monopoly Capitalism* (Chicago: University of Chicago Press, 1979), and his *Politics of Production* (London: Verso Press, 1985); see also Donald Filtzer, *Soviet Workers and De-Stalinization* (Cambridge: Cambridge University Press, 1992), and his *Soviet Workers and the Collapse of Perestroika.*

33. There are significant exceptions, the majority of which focus on Eastern Europe, such as the work of David Ost and the more empirical work of Adam Przeworski on Poland. Lynn Nelson and Irina Kuzes have done some of the best work on Russia in this regard.

34. Stephan Haggard and Robert R. Kaufman, *The Political Economy of Democratic Transitions* (Princeton: Princeton University Press, 1995), 3–4.

35. Ibid., 6–7.

36. Burawoy, in Orlovsky, *Beyond Soviet Studies,* 78.

37. Tucker, "Post-Soviet Leadership and Change," 6–7.

Chapter 2: The Dictatorship and the Proletariat

1. *Sed'moi s"ezd professional'nykh soiuzov SSSR* (Moscow, 1927), 49–50.

2. See Lewis Siegelbaum, *Stakhanovism and the Politics of Productivity in the USSR, 1935–1941* (New York: Cambridge University Press, 1988), 18; Hiroaki Kuromiya, *Stalin's Industrial Revolution* (Cambridge: Cambridge University Press, 1988), 88; Moshe Lewin, *The Making of the Soviet System* (New York: Pantheon, 1985), 225; I. A. Gladkov, ed., *Istoriia sotsialisticheskoi ekonomiki SSSR* (Moscow: Izdatel'stvo "Nauka," 1976), 3:124. The discrepancy in the figures is because the industries included in the calculation vary; the general parameters of the increase are similar in all sources.

3. See Kuromiya, "The Crisis of Proletarian Identity," in *Stalin's Industrial Revolution,* 78–107; William Chase, "Thoughts on Changing Relations between the

Working Class and the Party," in *Workers, Society, and the Soviet State: Labor and Life in Moscow, 1918–1929* (Urbana: University of Illinois Press, 1990), 293–304; Lewin, "Society, State, and Ideology during the First Five-Year Plan" and "Social Relations inside Industry during the Prewar Five-Year Plans, 1928–41," in *The Making of the Soviet System*, 209–40, 241–57.

4. Moshe Lewin comments that "NEP was a time when the workers, although quite poor and far from happy when facing the new breed of Nepman or state bosses ostentatiously enjoying the better things in life, were still the regime's favorites," which he argues was reflected in promotion campaigns and reserved places for admission to the Party (*Making of the Soviet System*, 247). While it is true that as individuals workers at times prospered during NEP, and (more important) still had rights that they exercised and unions that were semi-autonomous, the administrative structure of NEP in industry did relegate them to a subordinate position; this was increasingly the case as NEP progressed.

5. Siegelbaum, *Stakhanovism*, 23–39.

6. Quoted in Jeremy Azrael, *Managerial Power and Soviet Politics* (Cambridge, Mass.: Harvard University Press, 1966), 247–48.

7. See Lewin, *Making of the Soviet System*, 251–52, on the new powers of management and the implications thereof. On complaints that the unions were not doing their job in carrying out the party directive on one-man management, see Tsentral'nii Gosudarstvennii Arkhiv Oktiaber'skoi Revolutsii (TsGAOR), Moscow, f. 5451, op. 14, d. 197, ll. 1–6, 36–36ob, 39–41.

8. TsGAOR, f. 5451, op. 10, d. 197, l. 1.

9. See Siegelbaum, *Stakhanovism*, 27–30; Kuromiya, *Stalin's Industrial Revolution*, 272–86; Kendell Bailes, *Science and Technology under Lenin and Stalin* (Princeton: Princeton University Press, 1978), 173–87.

10. Chase, *Workers, Society, and the Soviet State*, 256–92.

11. See Kuromiya, *Stalin's Industrial Revolution*, 115–35.

12. See Kuromiya, *Stalin's Industrial Revolution;* Siegelbaum, *Stakhanovism;* Francesco Benenuti, *Stakhanovism and Stalinism, 1934–1938,* CREES Discussion Papers, SIPS Series No. 30 (Birmingham, England: University of Birmingham, 1989). This is not to say that there was no coercion involved; there certainly was. But for all those being coerced there was someone doing the coercing, and the evidence indicates that workers were as likely to coerce other workers as the Party or their unions were.

13. The phrase is Kuromiya's. See *Stalin's Industrial Revolution*, 78.

14. Siegelbaum, *Stakhanovism*, 184–90, and TsGAOR, f. 5451, op. 19, d. 233, l. 20; Rossiiskii Tsentr Khraneniia i Izucheniia Dokumentov Noveishei Istorii (RTsKhIDNI), Moscow, f. 17, op. 125, d. 310, ll. 33–34.

15. RTsKhIDNI, f. 85, op. 10, d. 130, l. 31.

16. Siegelbaum, *Stakhanovism*, 7.

17. TsGAOR, f. 5451, op. 15, d. 251, ll. 37–39; f. 5451, op. 15, d. 263, l. 14; f. 5451, op. 16, d. 555, ll. 1–8 and 21–29; f. 5451, op. 17, d. 292, l. 4; RTsKhIDNI, f. 85, op. 29, d. 99, ll. 1–2; f. 85, op. 29, d. 130, l. 86.

18. See Kuromiya, *Stalin's Industrial Revolution*, 129–35; Lewin, *Making of the Soviet System*, 255–56; Siegelbaum, *Stakhanovism*, 190–204; Isaac Deutscher, *Soviet Trade Unions* (London: Oxford University Press, 1950), 114–16. The introduction of comrades' courts in 1930 was designed to help in overcoming the "still insufficiently conscious relationship of the backward group of workers and employees to socialist forms of labor," and one of the powers of the courts was to punish workers for

"acts undermining socialist competition and shock-work." See TsGAOR, f. 5451, op. 15, d. 181, l. In the Western literature, Siegelbaum gives the most nuanced account of workers' reactions to shock workers. See Siegelbaum, *Stakhanovism,* 190–204; also Isaac Deutscher, *Soviet Trade Unions* (London: Oxford University Press, 1950), 114–16; Kuromiya, *Stalin's Industrial Revolution,* 129–35; Lewin, *Making of the Soviet System,* 255–56.

19. See Kuromiya, *Stalin's Industrial Revolution,* 320; Seigelbaum, *Stakhanovism,* 45; Gladkov, *Istoriia sotsialisticheskii ekonomiki SSSR,* 3:145; TsGAOR, f. 5451, op. 14, d. 239, l. 5; RTsKhIDNI, f. 85, op. 29, d. 130, l. 12. For a similar set of numbers in the coal industry, see TsGAOR, f. 5451, op. 14, d. 191, l. 4.

20. The phrase is taken from Veblen, via Siegelbaum, but the concept is well known in the industrial relations literature. See Burawoy, *Manufacturing Consent,* 77–94.

21. TsGAOR, f. 5451, op. 14. d. 197, l. 3.

22. Burawoy, *Manufacturing Consent,* 46–73.

23. Ratchet planning was a system by which, if a factory overfulfilled its plan targets by, say, 10 percent, the next set of plan targets would be 10 percent higher, such as in "ratchet up the pressure."

24. See Mark R. Beissinger, *Scientific Management, Socialist Discipline, and Soviet Power* (Cambridge, Mass.: Harvard University Press, 1988), 264–69, on what he describes as "the indulgency pattern" of the late Brezhnev era.

25. Filtzer, *Soviet Workers and De-Stalinization,* 59.

26. Arvid Brodersen, *The Soviet Worker* (New York: Random House, 1966), 139.

27. These laws were overturned by the Supreme Soviet; see "Ob otmene sudebnoi otvetstvennosti rabochikh i sluzhashchikh za samovol'nyi ukhod s predpriiatii i iz uchrezhdenii i za progul bez uvazhitel'noi prichiny," *Vedemosti Verkhovnogo Soveta SSSR,* no. 10, 1956, art. 203.

28. *Sbornik zakonodatel'nykhaktov o trude* (Moscow: "Iuridicheskaia literatura," 1984), 546; Mary McAuley, *Labour Disputes in Soviet Russia, 1957–1965* (Oxford: Oxford University Press, 1969), 66, particularly 139–203.

29. See Filtzer, *Soviet Workers and De-Stalinization,* 38–41.

30. Ibid., 92.

31. As Filtzer points out in *Soviet Workers and De-Stalinization,* workers in disadvantaged industries, such as textiles and other light industries, saw their wages increase, but the reform did nothing to alter the disparity between them and workers in heavy industries. This reflected the difficulty that Khrushchev encountered in his attempt to shift the weight of Soviet investment capital from "Group A" industries to "Group B" industries. See Karl Linden, *Khrushchev and the Soviet Leadership, 1957–1964* (Baltimore: Johns Hopkins University Press, 1966), particularly 58–71.

32. Filtzer, *Soviet Workers and De-Stalinization,* 93–95. The "progressive piece-rate" system was one in which workers received progressively higher bonuses the more they overfulfilled output quotas or plan targets. The base wage was set so low that workers could not live on it, and therefore had to exert themselves to an ever greater degree in order to earn a living wage. This system, however, could also be used by managers and workers to substantially enhance wage levels if norms were set artificially low, as they often were, thus leading to massive overexpenditure of wage funds (see Siegelbaum, *Stakhanovism,* 89–90). Thus, eliminating progressive piece rates was not necessarily an entirely altruistic policy decision.

33. Filtzer, *Soviet Workers and De-Stalinization,* 115; McAuley, *Labour Disputes in Soviet Russia,* 90–95.

34. See Filtzer, *Soviet Workers and De-Stalinization,* 102–15; McAuley, *Labour Disputes in Soviet Russia,* 88–95.

35. See Blair Ruble, *Soviet Trade Unions* (Cambridge: Cambridge University Press, 1981), 31–35.

36. For divergent views on the subject, see Brodersen, *The Soviet Worker;* Emily Clark Brown, *Soviet Trade Unions and Labor Relations* (Cambridge, Mass.: Harvard University Press, 1960); Robert Conquest, *Industrial Workers in the USSR* (London: Bodley Head, 1967); Filtzer, *Soviet Workers and De-Stalinization;* Roy Godson, *The Kremlin and Labor* (New York: Crane, Russak, 1977); D. C. Heldman, *Trade Unions and Labor Relations in the USSR* (Washington, D.C.: Council on American Affairs, 1970); Ruble, *Soviet Trade Unions.*

37. Ruble makes a similar argument in *Soviet Trade Unions,* 34.

38. The response of the Soviet authorities during this period to any manifestations of independent worker actions was invariably swift and harsh; the best-known case surrounded events in Novocherkassk in June 1962. See P. P. Siuda, "Krovavyi opyt sovetskikh rabochikh," *Nasha gazeta,* 29 May 1990, 4–5.

39. Alec Nove, *An Economic History of the USSR* (London: Lane, 1969), 362–67.

40. Ruble, *Soviet Trade Unions,* 40–44.

41. See Beissinger, *Scientific Management, Socialist Discipline,* 177.

42. Nove, *Economic History,* 367.

43. On the failures of the Kosygin reforms, see A. Kolganov, "Protivorechie tsentralisma i samostoiatel'nosti," *Voprosi ekonomiki* 9 (1986): 73; V. Radaev, "Khozraschetnaia samostoiatel'nost' predpriiatii," *Voprosi ekonomiki* 1 (1985): 29; Anders Aslund, *Gorbachev's Struggle for Economic Reform* (Ithaca: Cornell University Press, 1991), 12–15; Ed Hewett, *Reforming the Soviet Economy* (Washington, D.C.: The Brookings Institution, 1988), 230–45; Peter Rutland, "Productivity Campaigns in Soviet Industry," in *Labour and Employment in the USSR,* ed. David Lane (Brighton: Wheatsheaf Books, 1986), 204–5; Peter Rutland, *The Myth of the Plan* (La Salle, Ill.: Open Court, 1985), 120–22.

44. Nove, *Economic History,* 371–76; James Millar, "The Little Deal," *Slavic Review* 44, no. 4 (1985): 694–706.

45. Walter D. Conner, *The Accidental Proletariat* (Princeton: Princeton University Press, 1991), 70–72; Murray Yanowitch, "Pressures for More 'Participatory' Forms of Economic Organization in the Soviet Union," *Economic Analysis and Workers' Management* 3–4 (1978): 404–6.

46. V. A. Iadov, "Orientatsiia: tvorcheskaia rabota," in *Obshchestvo i molodezh',* ed. G. M. Gusev (Moscow, 1968).

47. Joel Moses, "Worker Self-Management and the Reformist Alternative in Soviet Labour Policy, 1979–1985," *Soviet Studies* 39, no. 2 (April 1987): 205–28.

48. Millar, "The Little Deal," 700–706.

Chapter 3: The Revolution Delayed

1. Conner, *Accidental Proletariat;* Gertrude Schroeder, "Anatomy of Gorbachev's Economic Reform," in *Milestones in Glasnost and Perestroyka: The Economy,* ed. Ed A. Hewett and Victor Winston (Washington, D.C.: The Brookings Institu-

tion, 1991), 204–24; Giulietto Chiesa, *Transition to Democracy: Political Change in the Soviet Union, 1987–1991* (Hanover, N.H.: University Press of New England, 1993).

2. The Kama Association for the Production of Heavy Transport Vehicles (KamAZ) is located in Naberezhnye Chelny in Tatarstan (Russian Federation); the Makhachkala Priboro-Stroitelnyi Zavod is located in Makhachkala, Dagestan (Russian Federation); and the Shakhta imeni Gorkogo is located in Donetsk (Ukraine).

3. "Osnovy zakonodatel'stva Soiuza SSR i Soiuznykh Respublik o Trude," and "Kodeks zakonov o trude RSFSR," in *Sbornik normativnykh aktov o trude* (Moscow: "Iuridicheskaia literatura," 1984), 1:12–112.

4. Dr. E. [Evgenii] P. Torkanovskii, Institute of Economics of the AN USSR, interview by author, Moscow, 18 December 1990.

5. Gennadi Kirilov, brigadier and labor organizer from the foundry factory of KamAZ, interview by author, Naberezhnye Chelny, 28 March 1991.

6. Nail' S. Nurmukhamedov, interview by author, Naberezhnye Chelny, 1 April 1991. See also Yegor K. Ligachev, *Inside Gorbachev's Kremlin* (New York: Random House, 1993), 15.

7. Mikhail Aleksandrov, "Zavodskie ispytaniia," *Moskovskie novosti* 34 (20 August 1989): 5.

8. For a good overview of the structure of the "association" in the Soviet industrial system, see Alec Nove, *The Soviet Economic System* (Boston: Allen and Unwin, 1986), 69–74.

9. Interview by author with shop foremen and division heads from the KamAZ foundry in Naberezhnye Chelny, 27 March 1991. See also the "series" that appeared in *Pravda*: "Shtrafnoi udar," 17 February 1988, 2; "A tabachok—vroz'," 21 March 1988, 2; "'Davaite schitat'," 22 March 1988, 2; and "Ne raznesut li po 'brevnyishku'," 30 April 1988, 2.

10. Interview by author with a division head of the KamAZ foundry factory, Naberezhnye Chelny, 27 March 1991.

11. Nurmukhamedov interview.

12. Nurmukhamedov interview. Similar comments were made by Valentin Landik, general director of the Nord Association, in an interview by author at Nord Association offices, Donetsk, 6 April 1991.

13. The typical argument of those who opposed the election of leading managerial personnel was that workers were not "mature" enough to elect responsible leaders. The comments of workers about what kind of person was needed to manage a factory belie that suggestion; see "Ia—'nachal'nik tsekha'," *Rabochii Kamaza,* 19 October and 4 December 1990, 1.

14. Il'giz T. Akhmetov, interview by author, Naberezhnye Chelny, 27 March 1991.

15. Kirilov interview.

16. See "Zakon o gosudarstvennom predpriiatii (ob"edinenii)," *Izvestiia,* 1 July 1987, 2.

17. V. Korol', "Dat' dorogu modernizatsii," *Rabochii Kamaza,* 13 April 1990, 3; Akhmetov interview.

18. O. Zakamskii, Iu. Astankov, and N. Aver'ianov, "Rabotat' na ravnykh," *Rabochii Kamaza,* 21 February 1990, 3.

19. "Perspektivna li rabota tsentra?" *Rabochii Kamaza,* 13 April 1990, 3.

20. This means that if the piece rate for the production of brake shoes, for

example, is ten rubles and the production norm is thirty brake shoes per shift, then a worker would receive ten rubles apiece for the first thirty brake shoes produced, and then fifteen rubles apiece for each brake shoe over thirty that she or he produced in a given shift. This rate is known as a coefficient of .5.

21. "Perspektivna li rabota tsentra?" 3.

22. "Rabotat' na ravnykh," *Rabochii Kamaza*, 21 February 1990, 3.

23. V. Khlystov, "V tsentralizovannii tupik?" *Rabochii Kamaza*, 13 April 1990, 1.

24. "Perspektivna li rabota tsentra?" 3.

25. Korol', "Dat' dorogu modernizatsii," 3.

26. The information in the preceding paragraphs is taken from S. Isichko, "Poshchechina kollektivu," *Rabochii Kamaza*, 17 April 1990, 3.

27. Kirilov interview.

28. Isichko, "Poshchechina kollektivu," 3.

29. "Kollektivnyi dogovor," *Rabochii Kamaza*, 7 February 1990, 1.

30. "Bol'she sprosa," ibid.

31. S. Isichko, "Khozhdenie v narod," *Rabochii Kamaza*, 22 August 1990, 2.

32. Kirilov interview.

33. Leonid Komm, "Interview," *Rabochii Kamaza*, 29 June 1990, 2. See also Z. Gorbunkova, "Aktsii kamaza," *Rabochii Kamaza*, 18 May 1990, 1.

34. "AO—puti k razvitiiu v usloviiakh rynka," *Rabochii Kamaza*, 27 September 1990, 1–2.

35. In both the commentary by managers and the articles by journalists on this issue, no distinctions were made between "KamAZ" and the "labor collective of KamAZ" or between the "management of KamAZ," "KamAZ," and the "labor collective of KamAZ," except when they were speaking of the division of the 25.5 percent of the government shares "controlled by KamAZ," when the distinction became clear.

36. Komm, "Interview."

37. A. Kosenkov, "Byt' khoziainom svoei sud'by," *Rabochii Kamaza*, 16 November 1990, 2.

38. This is Kirilov's estimate, based on discussions with other workers in his own factory and members of his group from other factories within the KamAZ association.

39. See "Aktsii Kamaza," *Rabochii Kamaza*, 18 May 1990, 1; "AO—put' k razvitiiu," 1; and "Na puti neformal'nogo razvitiia," *Rabochii Kamaza*, 12 May 1990, 2. The latter article was notable because during a meeting of the conference of brigadiers, N. Bekh stated that "the joint-stock company KamAZ will be directed by a management board. The leadership of the association thinks that one of the members of this board should be the president of the council of brigadiers." I heard two interpretations of this proposal by Bekh. First, management felt that since brigadiers were generally speaking experienced workers and close to the factory floor, the president of the council could represent the workers' interests on the management board. Second, management wanted to ensure the support of the brigadiers for the transition to an AO *(aktsionernoe obshchestvo)*. Insofar as brigadiers are viewed by many workers as the lowest rung on the managerial ladder and a key element of the "KamAZ labor aristocracy," many workers believed that this cooperation would be naturally forthcoming if management guaranteed the interests of the brigadiers, and would be particularly important in ensuring the success of the transition in a form that was amenable to management's interests.

40. "Interes k Kamazu rastet," *Rabochii Kamaza*, 12 October 1990, 2.

41. Isichko, "Khozhdenie v narod," 2.

42. L. Fedotova, "Eksperiment na agregatnom," *Rabochii Kamaza,* 30 November 1990, 1.

43. E. Shaidullova, quoted in ibid.

44. "Stolknulis' dve tochki zreniia," *Rabochii Kamaza,* 13 July 1990, 2. These disputes are classic examples of the issue of workers' control over production processes and the ability of workers to "withdraw their efficiency" as a means of leverage vis-à-vis management.

45. See "Proekt: kollektivnyi dogovor," *Rabochii Kamaza,* 21 November 1990, 1–2.

46. V. N. Istoman, interview by author, at the administrative offices of the MPSZ, Makhachkala, Dagestan, 8 January 1990.

47. Factory newspaper *Etalon* 1–2 (7 November 1988): 3.

48. Interview by author with workers, including the leaders of the factory's informal workers' group, in Makhachkala, 8 January 1991. Their account was indirectly confirmed by Istoman himself during our interview, but he was less willing to speak ill of his predecessor than were the workers.

49. V. N. Istoman, interview by author, Makhachkala, 7 January 1991.

50. Sh. N. Mishiev, interview by author, Makhachkala, 7 January 1991.

51. Meeting of author with managers and workers, Makhachkala, 7 January 1991.

52. Survey, conducted the first week of January 1991.

53. Interview by author of workers from the informal workers' group, 8 January 1991.

54. Survey, conducted the first week of January 1991.

55. Survey by the MPSZ Komsomol committee, results provided by Oleg B. Aliev, Moscow Institute of Management.

56. Meeting between management and workers, attended by author, Makhachkala, 8 January 1991.

57. Istoman interview, 7 January 1991.

58. *Etalon* 3 (13 January 1989): 1; *Etalon* 15 (7 April 1989): 2; *Etalon* 24 (2 June 1989): 2.

59. Abdul Nidapeirov, a member of the informal workers' group, interview by author, Makhachkala, 8 January 1991.

60. Mishiev interview.

61. The following material is derived from my discussion with the workers involved, as well as from copies of the original letter and the response of the Dagestan oblast trade union committee, which were obtained for me by the leaders of the informal workers' group. These letters will be referred to hereafter as the Dagoblsovprof letters.

62. Dagoblsovprof letters, 1–3; *Etalon* 12 (23 March 1990): 1.

63. Interview by author with the leaders of the informal workers' group, Makhachkala, 8 January 1991.

64. "Kodeks zakonov o trude RSFSR," 111.

65. Meeting of managers and workers, Makhachkala, 8 January 1991.

66. "Kodeks zakonov o trude RSFSR," 51–52.

67. Meeting of managers and workers, Makhachkala, 8 January 1991.

68. Interview by author with the leaders of the informal workers' group, Makhachkala, 8 January 1991.

69. Tizutdin Adip'gereev, interview by author, Makhachkala, 8 January 1991.

70. Valerii Miller, chairman of the official trade union at Gorky, interview by author, Donetsk, Ukraine, 16 April 1991; in separate interviews, the co-chair of the Donetsk strike committee and the co-chair of the Council of Workers' Committees of the Kuzbass supported Miller's characterization of the process, Donetsk, 13 April 1991.

71. Interview by author with the head engineer of the Gorky mine, Donetsk, 16 April 1991.

72. Interview by author with co-chair of the Donetsk strike committee and other miners, Donetsk, 13 April 1991.

73. Miller interview.

74. S. N. Vasiliev, president of the Gorky mine STK (Sovet Trudovogo Kollektiva, or Council of the Labor Collective), interview by author, Donetsk, 16 April 1991.

75. Miller interview.

76. Ibid. For coal-mining regions taken together, on average 80 percent of all members were replaced in the post-strike elections.

77. Vasiliev interview.

78. Miller interview.

79. Ibid.

80. Ibid. Miller's account was confirmed by both the head engineer and the STK president at Gorky, as well as by Victor V. Solomikhin, a member of the economics department of Donetsk State University.

81. Miller interview; the co-chair of the Donetsk city strike committee recounted the events in similar language.

82. Vasiliev interview.

83. This disillusionment, which for some bordered on betrayal, was reflected in the discussions and documents that emerged from the first Congress of Miners in Donetsk in 1990. See *Pervyi s"ezd shakhterov SSSR* (Donetsk: Otraslevoi rabochii komitet pri p/o "Donetskugol'," 1990), parts 1 and 2 (the official record of the congress); "Rezoliutsiia ob otnoshenii k deistvuiushchemu trudovomu zakonodatel'stvu" (a resolution passed by the congress and then "published" in photocopies). V. V. Komarovskii wrote an article for the miners at the congress, which the miners then published in a small run (they still had litle access to presses at that time): *Bor'ba shakhterov: nekotorye prichiny i usloviia (Otchet,* 1990*)*.

84. Torkanovskii interview.

85. Managers conveying this attitude toward the policy included the following: factory directors Istoman of the MPSZ, Landik of Nord, and Sobstel' of the Opytnyi zavod Sibirskogo otdeleniia AN SSSR(OZ SO AN SSSR); assistant directors Ivanova of Gazapparat, Nurmukhamedov of KamAZ, and Tret'iakov of OZ SO AN SSSR. For more detailed survey data see Ia. S. Kapeliush, "Vybornost' rukovoditelei: vchera i segodnia," *Sotsiologicheskie issledovaniia* 2 (1988): 44–49; and T. I. Bagaeva, "Nado li vybirat' rukovoditelei?" *Sotsiologicheskie issledovaniia* 1 (1990): 71–74.

86. Torkanovskii interview. See also Leonid Abalkin, *Ne ispol'zovannyi shans* (Moscow: Politizdat, 1991), 247.

87. Interview by author with STK president at Sibselmash, Novosibirsk, 24 April 1991.

88. Torkanovskii interview.

89. Kirilov interview.

90. Viktor Kozhemiako, "Pravo na vybor," *Moskovskie novosti* 8 (22 February 1987): 9; A. Speranskii, "Za zakrytoi dver'iu," *Pravda,* 1 April 1988, 2; Mikhail Cher-

niak, "Mnogim sperva eto kazalos' spektaklem," *Moskovskie novosti* 17 (24 April 1988): 9.

91. The argument was reminiscent of that made during the drafting of the *LSE*. Most of the evidence points to the fact that when unqualified people did run for senior management posts, they invariably lost. See, for example, the report on the election of the general director at AvtoVAZ, KamAZ's sister factory, in "Chetvertii direktor," *Moskovskie novosti* 1 (1989): 12.

92. Interview by author with workers at Sibselmash, Novosibirsk, 24 April 1991.

93. Torkanovskii interview.

94. Mikhail Kisliuk, interview by author, Kemerovo, 29 April 1991.

95. Boris Kurashvili, "Direktiva o direktore," *Moskovskie novosti* 9 (28 February 1988): 9; Evgenii Torkanovskii, "Demokratiia dlia direktora?" *Moskovskie novosti* 21 (22 May 1988): 2; and Lev Don, "Upravlenie samoupravleniem," *Moskovskie novosti* 29 (17 July 1988): 2.

96. Iuri Grafskii, "Uchit'sia upravliat' samim," *Nedelia* 49 (5–11 December 1988): 6–7.

97. A. Speranskii, "Za zakrytoi dver'iu," *Pravda,* 1 April 1988, 2; A. Vorotnikov, "Konflikt nazreval," *Pravda,* 13 April 1988, 2; G. Trigub, "No gorispolkom protiv," *Izvestiia,* 8 May 1988, 2; Iu. Vorob'evskii and N. Zagnoiko, "Demokratiia s kisloi minoi," *Sovetskaia rossiia,* 13 August 1988, 1.

98. See A. Konikov, "Shtrafnoi udar," *Pravda,* 17 February 1988, 2; I. Pestun and V. Shirokov, "Isk bez pred'iavleniia," *Pravda,* 17 March 1988, 4; V. Badov, "A Tabachok—vroz'," *Pravda,* 21 March 1988, 2; M. Berger and A. Pashkov, "Delo uralmasha," *Izvestiia,* 23 March 1988, 3; V. Baturin et al., "Predpriiatie pribyl'noe, a ego likvidiruiut," *Pravda,* 6 April 1988, 1; M. Bublichenko, "A rabochikh ne sprosili," *Pravda,* 8 April 1988, 2.

Chapter 4: Class Power and Power Politics

1. M. S. Gorbachev, "Novogodnee obrashchenie k sovetskomu narodu," in *Izbrannye rechi i stat'i,* 7:222.

2. Evgenii Ambartsumov, "Razmyshleniia pered s"ezdom profsoiuzov," *Moskovskie novosti* 8 (22 February 1987), 3; Alexander Auzan, "Zachem nam nuzhen profsoiuz?" *Sotsialisticheskaia industriia,* 1 May 1989, 2; Iu. Artem'ev, "Vykhozhu iz profsoiuza," *Gudok,* 20 May 1989. Some of the material used in this chapter was provided to the author by Russko-Amerikanskii Fond Profsoiuznykh Issledovanii i Obucheniia in the form of photocopied collections of newspaper articles from the central and regional Soviet press. These collections did not always include the page numbers on which the articles in the newspapers appeared. In those instances here and below where this is the case, it will be indicated by the letters "n.p." after the citation.

3. Gorbachev, *Izbrannye rechi i stat'i,* 7:221.

4. Aleksandr Susoev, "Komu nanosit ushcherb zabastovka," *V boi za ugol',* 16 January 1990, 6.

5. Linda J. Cook, "Lessons of the Soviet Coal Miners' Strike of Summer 1989," *Harriman Institute Forum* 4, no. 3 (March 1991): 2–3; *Ekonomicheskaia gazeta* 27 (1989): 5; Elizabeth Teague, "Miners' Strike in Siberia Winds Down, Strike in Ukraine Spreads to Other Areas: A Status Report," *RL 334/89,* 20 July 1989, 4; V. Andriianov, "Gornyi udar," *Dialog* 1 (1990): 61. The strikes were not limited to coal

mines. Iuri Tepliakov, "Chrezvychainoe proisshestvie," *Moskovskie novosti* 42 (18 October 1987): 8–9; Leonid Kapeliushnyi, "Predel neterpeniia," *Moskovskie novosti* 27 (3 July 1988): 12.

6. For an excellent account of the day-to-day events of the strike, see Viktor Kostiukovskii, *Kuzbass: zharkoe leto 89-go* (Moscow: "Sovremennik," 1990).

7. Interview by author with co-chair of the Donetsk city strike committee, Donetsk, 13 April 1991; Aleksandr Aslanidi, co-chair, Council of the Workers' Committees of the Kuzbass, interview by author, Kemerovo, 26 April 1991; Andriianov, "Gornyi udar," 62; Kostiukovskii, *Kuzbass,* 8, 10; "Dialogi vokrug sobytii," *Moskovskie novosti* 32 (6 August 1989): 8; N. Chentsov, "Zabastovki moglo ne byt'," *Dialog* 1 (1990): 69.

8. Cook, "Lessons of the Soviet Coal Miners' Strike," 5; Kostiukovskii, *Kuzbass,* 101–6.

9. Quoted in Kostiukovskii, *Kuzbass,* 8–9.

10. Interview by author with members of the Donetsk strike committee, 13 April 1991; Aslanidi interview.

11. Kostiukovskii, *Kuzbass,* 45.

12. Ibid., 124–42.

13. Ibid., 13.

14. During a meeting with the local Communist Party *aktiv,* Shchadov announced that the following day he was going to issue an order to all mines that striking workers were not to be paid and that they would be posted as "absent without reasonable cause." This latter formulation was grounds for dismissal under Soviet law.

15. Kostiukovskii, *Kuzbass,* 20–21, 92–98.

16. Ibid., 101–6; Andriianov, "Gornyi udar," 60–61; A. Susoev, "Komu nanosit ushcherb zabastovka?" 6.

17. "Iz obrashcheniia Kemerovskogo obkoma KPSS, oblispolkoma, oblsovprofa i obkoma VLKSM k trudiashchimsia Kuzbassa," reprinted in Kostiukovskii, *Kuzbass,* 37.

18. Why other sectors of the Kuzbass working class did not go on strike has been questioned by a number of scholars and analysts both in Russia and the West. Some thought these workers illustrated a classic example of a collective-action problem. While not dismissing such a perspective entirely, the fact that workers' committees from other industrial sectors sent messages to the miners' strike committees asking whether they too should go on strike—particularly since in some cases votes had already been cast in support of strike action—makes this view doubtful. The coordination of strike action appears to have been well thought out and carefully organized. Insofar as this is true, lack of action by other sectors of the workforce was an indication of collective action, not its absence.

19. Kostiukovskii, *Kuzbass,* 20–21, 29–30.

20. Kisliuk interview.

21. Kostiukovskii, *Kuzbass,* 92–98; Vladimir Gurevich, "Ugol' i reforma," *Moskovskie novosti* 31 (30 July 1989): 9; Iuri Tiurin, "Shakhory zhdut peremen," *Moskovskie novosti* 36 (3 September 1989): 15; Elizabeth Teague, "Miners' Strike in Siberia Winds Down," *Radio Liberty Report on the USSR,* 28 July 1989, 15–19; Lewis Siegelbaum, "Behind the Soviet Miners' Strike," *Nation,* 23 October 1989, 451–56.

22. Kostiukovskii, *Kuzbass,* 170.

23. Donetsk city strike committee co-chair interview; Miller interview. For details on reelection meetings, see Seigelbaum, "Behind the Soviet Miners' Strike," 454–55.

24. "Profsoiuzy: pobedivshie ili pobezhdennye?" *Moskovskie novosti* 32 (6 August 1989), 8.

25. In an extensive survey conducted by the Institute of the International Workers' Movement of the USSR Academy of Sciences in January 1990, miners indicated that they had the greatest level of confidence in the brigade-level STKs, followed by the strike committees, the mine STKs, and finally the trade unions and party organizations. V. Komarovskii, "Bor'ba shakhterov: nekotorye prichiny i usloviia," p. 7 of text and p. 14 of raw data printouts. Internal document of the regional workers' committees.

26. Andriianov, "Gornyi udar," 63.

27. *Nedelia* 10 (5–11 March 1990): 2.

28. "Bol'she organizovannosti i poriadka v bor'be za perestroiku: Vstrecha v TsK KPSS," *Pravda,* 25 September 1989, 1–2.

29. P. Slezko, "Sindrom zabastovki," *Nedelia* 10 (5–11 March 1990): 3.

30. Len Karpinskii, "Konsolidatsiia cherez konflikt," *Moskovskie novosti* 31 (30 July 1989): 8; Kostiukovskii, *Kuzbass,* 143–60.

31. Kostiukovskii, *Kuzbass,* 145.

32. Aslanidi interview; Kostiukovskii, *Kuzbass,* 171–85.

33. These papers included *Nasha gazeta* and *Iiul'* in the Kuzbass, *Narodnaia gazeta* in the Donbass, *Birlesu* in Kazakhstan, and a number of "mnogotirazhni" in the mines and other factories.

34. Interview by author with the editors of *Nasha gazeta,* Kemerovo, 26 April 1991.

35. The paper received permission to publish in mid-February 1990; on the mood that the dispute had created, see Vasilii Popok et al., "Kak i pobedim," *Nasha gazeta,* published under the aegis of *Elektromotor* O, no. 9 (13 February 1990): 1. (Issues were numbered with "O" to indicate that, as yet, it was not officially recognized.)

36. Interviews with the editors of *Nasha gazeta,* Aslanidi, and Kisliuk confirm this trend and the importance of the "press war" for it. The ongoing battles over the legal status of the paper are chronicled in detailed if rather sensationalist terms in the early issues of the paper published under the banners of factory newspapers. See "K chitateliu," *Khimik,* 11 December 1989, 1; "K chitateliu" and "<<Karbolit>>: Vstupaem v Soiuz," *Stroitel',* 20 December 1989, 1; and Iurii Chun'kov, "Nashi pervoocherednye zadachi," *Zheleznodorozhnik kuzbassa,* 30 December 1989, 3.

37. M. Kisliuk, "Proshai, regional'nyi khozraschet? Proshai, protokol?" *Stroitel'—Soiuz trudiashchikhsia kuzbassa,* 20 December 1989, 1.

38. Viacheslav Golikov, "Malen'kie khitrosti," *Stroitel'—Soiuz trudiashchikhsia kuzbassa,* 20 December 1989, 1.

39. "Obrashchenie sovmestnogo soveshchaniia predstavitelei rabochikh komitetov, obkoma KPSS, oblispolkoma, oblsovprofa k pravitel'stvu SSSR i trudiashchimsia kuzbassa," *Zheleznodorozhnik kuzbassa—Soiuz trudiashchikhsia kuzbassa,* 30 December 1989, 3; "Predvybornaia platforma," *Za bol'shuiu khimiiu,* 10 January 1990, 3.

40. For the text of the agreement, see "Soglashenie . . . ," *Zheleznodorozhnik kuzbassa,* 23 January 1990, 2; also V. Kostiukovskii, "Kuzbass . . ." *Sovetskaia Rossiia,* 17 January 1990, 2.

41. "Chevo dobilis', chevo ne dobilis'. . . ," *Nasha gazeta,* 6 February 1990, 2.

42. "Profsoiuz shakhterov," *Nasha gazeta,* 1 May 1990, 1.

43. According to the records of the congress, there was only one worker elected

to the central committee of the union. "Pochemu ushli iz s"ezda," *Izvestiia*, 1 April 1990, 1.

44. "Deklaratsiia osnovnykh printsipov Konfederatsii Truda," *Nasha gazeta*, 15 May 1990, 2. The discussion of the first congress that follows is based on material taken from this document.

45. "Resoliutsii 1 [pervogo] S"ezda Konfederatsii Truda," *Nasha gazeta*, 8 May 1990, 3.

46. V. Loktev and A. Skrypnik, "Na ostrie," *Pravda*, 4 June 1990, 3. Melnikov's term "the union" referred to the Union of Workers of the Kuzbass, which he saw as being behind the Confederation of Labor.

47. V. Kostiukovskii, "Zharkoe leto v Kuzbasse," *Izvestiia*, 18 June 1990, 2.

48. David Remnick, "Soviet Miners Vow to Form Own Union," *Washington Post*, 16 June 1990, 16, 19; "O polozhenii v strane," *Nasha gazeta*, 3 July 1990, 2; "Kto zhe byl v Donetske?" "Resoliutsiia po voprosam sotsial'no-ekonomicheskogo polozheniia, vypolneniiu postanovleniia No. 608, perspektivam perekhoda k rynku," and "Rezoliutsiia o podgotovke k sozdaniiu nezavisimogo profsoiuza," *Narodnaia gazeta*, 13 July 1990, 2–3.

49. Stephen White, *Gorbachev and After* (Cambridge: Cambridge University Press, 1992), 172.

50. Yeltsin, speaking during a meeting with representatives of the Council of Workers' Committees of the Kuzbass, 23 June 1990; the stenographic record of the meeting was reprinted in *Nasha gazeta*, 26 June 1990, 4.

51. "Chto reshat shakhtery," *Izvestiia*, 6 July 1990, 2; Mikhail Loginov, "Shakhtery: My ustupim tol'ko rynku," *Literaturnaia gazeta*, 7 July 1990, 9; and extensive material in *Nasha gazeta*, 10–24 July, particularly "Zabastovka v Kuzbasse," *Nasha gazeta*, 17 July 1990, 1–5.

52. "Kakim byt' soiuzu trudiashchikhsia Kuzbassa?" *Nasha gazeta*, 18 September 1990, 6; "V konferentsii: predstoit novyi povorot rabochego dvizheniia Kuzbassa," *Nasha gazeta*, 25 September 1990, 3; "V konferentsii rabochikh komitetov Kuzbassa," *Nasha gazeta*, 2 October 1990, 1; Aleksandr Zamogil'nov, "Kto my? Chto my? Zachem my?" *Nasha gazeta*, 2 October 1990, 5; and V. M. Golikov, "Rabochee dvizhenie: sovremennaia politicheskaia situatsiia, otchet o prodelannoi rabote i zadachi na blizhaishee vremia," *Nasha gazeta*, 9 October 1990, 4–6.

53. Gertrude E. Schroeder, "*Perestroyka* in the Aftermath of 1990," in Hewett and Winston, *Milestones in Glasnost and Perestroyka*, 459–69.

54. Both Ryzhkov and Primakov, for example, spoke of the dangers of what the former termed "economic separatism" and the latter referred to as "'economically absurd' regional self-sufficiency" at the twenty-eighth party congress in July 1990. See White, *Gorbachev and After*, 178.

55. "Sovet rabochikh komitetov Kuzbassa: Nuzhny li segodnia rabochie komitety?" *Nasha gazeta*, 25 December 1990, 1; "Chleny soveta rabochikh komitetov Kuzbassa vstretilis' s Borisom Yeltsinym," *Nasha gazeta*, 1 January 1991, 1.

56. D. Shagiakhmetov, "Itak zabastovka ne sostoilas'," *Nasha gazeta*, 22 January 1991, 1–2; "Neobol'shevism ne proidet!" *Nasha gazeta*, 25 January 1991, 1; Vladimir Shishvatov, "Ianvar' 91-go: uroki nesostoiavsheisia zabastovki," *Nasha gazeta*, 29 January 1991, 1, 3.

57. Nadezhda Stepanova, "Nachinaetsia? 'Biriulinskaia' pered zabastovkoi?" and Anatolii Malykin, "Ukraina pered zabastovkoi?" both in *Nasha gazeta*, 26 February 1991, 1; similar demands came from Karaganda, "Karaganda:

zabastovka 1 Marta," *Nasha gazeta,* 1 March 1991, 1.

58. "Obrashchenie k shakhteram strany," *Nasha gazeta,* 1 January 1991, 6; for full text of draft, see "General'noe tipovoe tarifnoe soglashenie mezhdu pravitel'stvom soiuza SSR i federatsiei nezavisimykh profsoiuzov gorniakov," *Nasha gazeta,* 8 March 1991, 3–6.

59. Interview with Vyacheslav M. Golikov and Aleksandr Aslanidi, "4 Marta—sutochnaia politicheskaia zabastovka," *Nasha gazeta,* 1 March 1991, 2.

60. L. N. Lopatin et al., "Neskol'ko tezisov o rabochem dvizhenii Kuzbassa," *Nasha gazeta,* 7 May 1991, 9.

61. See particularly the newspaper *Kuzbass* from the first week of March to the end of April. The fate of metallurgical plants was particularly sensitive, because a shutdown in one of these plants threatened to do permanent harm to the coke batteries and casting machinery. Such interviews were virtually nightly fare on the evening news in these regions.

62. The co-chair of the Donetsk city strike committee and Aslanidi in particular mentioned these tactics as a problem about which the workers' committees were particularly sensitive. The issue arose on numerous occasions during interviews with workers not connected to the mine industry in Donetsk and Kemerovo, who mentioned that "government attempts to split the workers have been common throughout the strike." They mentioned not only the mass media, but also attempts by Party and even trade union officials from the factories, who during factory meetings used the miners' strike demands as a means of causing tension among the workers. The workers concerned were employed in steel production, textiles, and on the railroad in varying capacities from repair workers to locomotive engineers. The results differed from factory to factory. A significant amount of antipathy toward the miners was found at Gazapparat, a consumer goods production facility in Donetsk; among the railroad workers, on the other hand, the level of support was quite high, such that workers joined the strike meetings on a shift-by-shift basis.

63. *Nasha gazeta,* for the period March–April 1991; the paper published a record regularly, under a number of headlines, usually either "Bastuem" or "Zabastovka prodolzhaet."

64. This was particularly important in the Kuzbass, because at the time the newspaper of the workers' committees was busy trying to avoid being shut down by the regional Party and state institutions. First Secretary Aleksandr Melnikov and Soviet Chairman Aman Tuleev were attempting to prohibit *Nasha gazeta* from using state-owned printing presses and had also brought suit against the editors for libel and defamation of character. I discussed this in detail with the newspaper's editors and Aslanidi. Neither Melnikov nor Tuleev agreed to be interviewed.

65. "Khronika sobytii," *Nasha gazeta,* 5 March 1991, 1–2. According to Aslanidi, coal production at the height of the strike stood at 83 percent of its pre-strike level. Local officials and Soviet scholars corroborated the claim by the workers' committees that the limited nature of the strike was by design, but there were also numerous cases in which miners' collectives decided to stay at work despite the request of the strike committees.

66. "Vystuplenie Borisa Yeltsina pered chlenami zabastovochnykh komitetov Kuzbassa," *Nasha gazeta,* 4 May 1991, 2–4. An arrangement such as this had been worked out on 15 April for the Raspadskaia mine by the president of the RSFSR Council of Ministers Ivan Siliev. *Nasha gazeta,* 19 April 1991, 3.

67. Gorbachev, *Izbrannye rechi i stat'i,* 4:100.

68. S. Chugaev, "Profsoiuzy staviat usloviia," *Izvestiia,* 30 June 1990, 1; Ye. Sorokin, "Accord Reached," *Pravda,* 11 February 1990, 2.

69. The new charter was published in *Trud,* 22 May 1990.

70. "Kak eto bylo...," *Rabochii Kamaza,* 15 November 1990, 2.

71. White, *Gorbachev and After,* 59.

72. "Ustav (Deklaratsiia) Federatsii professional'nykh soiuzov RSFSR," *Rabochii Kamaza,* 7 March 1990, 2.

73. "Pervymi v Rossii," *Rabochii Kamaza,* 10 April 1990, 2; Andrei Dudnikov, "Ostalos' nemnogo smenit' vyveski," *Nasha gazeta,* 14 December 1990, 4.

74. Elizabeth Teague, "Organized Labor in Russia in 1992," *RFE/RL Research Report* 2, no. 5 (29 January 1993): 38; Jennifer Gould, "Union Dues," *Moscow Times,* 16 June 1992, 1, 4.

75. For example, the FNPR alone represented the interests of Russian workers during negotiations over the Agreement on Labor and Socioeconomic Issues for 1991 conducted between the USSR Council of Ministers and the VKP (Vseobshchaia Konferentsiia Profsoiuzov) in April 1991. See *Trud,* 26 April 1991, 1, 2 for the text of the agreement.

76. Viktor Utkin, the president of the NPG, interview by author, Moscow, 23 April 1992.

77. A. N. Erokhin and A. M. Stepanov, "Strakh i sotsstrakh: Gosprofsoiuzy dezinformiruiut trudiashchikhsia," *Nasha gazeta,* 11 December 1990, 6; "Uchreditel'naia konferentsiia nezavisimogo profsoiuza gorniakov Kuzbassa," *Nasha gazeta,* 18 June 1991, 1, 4; Aleksandr Sergeev, "Obman po-gosprofovski, ili skol'ko zhe nalogov platit rabochii v nashem gosudarstve," *Nasha gazeta,* 28 June 1991, 3; V. Komarovskii, "Deviat' tezisov o rabochem i profsoiuznom dvizhenii v Rossii," *Polis* 3 (1992): 124–25.

78. Komarovskii, "Deviat' tezisov," 125.

79. N. Kuznetsov, "Aviadispetchery govoriat: Khvatit!" *Nasha gazeta,* 21 May 1991, 1; "Zabastovka aviadispetcherov skoree vsego sostoitsia," *Nasha gazeta,* 9 August 1991, 1; and "Lokomotivshchiki Topok preduprezhdaiut: gotovy ostanovit' poezda," *Nasha gazeta,* 9 August 1991, 3.

80. Vladimir Volin, "Stat'ia zakona," *Moskovskie novosti* 25 (18 June 1989), 15; Sergei Khramov, president of Sotsprof, interview by author, Moscow, 22 April 1992.

81. "Informatsionnoe soobshchenie," *Rabochaia sila* 1 (April 1991): 1.

82. Komarovskii, "Deviat' tezisov," 125.

83. "Ustav ob"edineniia profsoiuzov SSSR Sotsprof," sections 2.2 and 3.1, pp. 4 and 5–6 respectively.

84. In 1992 Sotsprof began forming all-Russia unions, which made the maintenance of localist principles very difficult, particularly because Sotsprof and the other independent unions collided more and more often with the FNPR unions when the former tried to expand their membership.

85. Khramov interview, 1992.

86. P. N. Taletskii discusses Sotsprof's difficulties, in *Eto trudnoe profsoiuznoe remeslo* (Moscow, 1992), n.p.

87. V. Lisakov, "Nakonets-to nachalos'," *Moskovskaia pravda,* 23 July 1991, 1–2; "Profsoiuzy priglashaiut na piket," *Kuranty,* 24 October 1991; "Osennee nastuplenie profsoiuzov," *Delovoi mir,* 25 October 1991, 1; Irina Demchenko, "Profsoiuzy preduprezhdaiut pravitel'stvo," *Izvestiia,* 11 January 1992, 2.

88. V. Komarovskii, "S kem i o chem nameneno dogovarivat'sia pravitel'stvo," *Rossiiskaia gazeta,* 7 February 1992.

89. "Osennee nastuplenie profsoiuzov," 1; "Profsoiuzy preduprezhdaiut pravitel'stvo," 2; Teague, "Organized Labor in Russia in 1992," 38.

90. Komarovskii, "S kem i o chem namereno dogovarivat'sia pravitel'stvo." 91. Ibid.

Chapter 5: Disempowering Labor

1. The idea of this particular trade-off is common in the democratization literature. See Di Palma, *To Craft Democracies;* Przeworski, *Democracy and the Market;* Haggard and Kaufman, *Political Economy of Democratic Transitions.*

2. Aslund, *How Russia Became a Market Economy;* Blasi, Kroumova, and Kruse, *Kremlin Capitalism;* Egor Gaidar, "Rossiia i reformi," *Izvestiia,* 19 August 1992, 3.

3. Luiz Carlos Bresser Pereira, Jose Maria Maravall, and Adam Przeworski, *Economic Reforms in New Democracies: A Social Democratic Approach* (Cambridge: Cambridge University Press, 1993); Beverly Crawford, ed., *Markets, States, and Democracy* (Boulder: Westview Press, 1995); Nelson and Kuzes, *Radical Reform in Yeltsin's Russia;* Kazimierz Poznanski, *The Evolutionary Transition to Capitalism* (Boulder: Westview Press, 1995).

4. Aslund, *How Russia Became a Market Economy,* 188; Michael Mandelbaum, "By a Thread," *New Republic,* 5 April 1993, 18–23.

5. Nelson and Kuzes, *Radical Reform in Yeltsin's Russia,* 26.

6. Richard Jackman, "Economic Policy and Employment in the Transition Economies of Central and Eastern Europe: What Have We Learned?" *International Labour Review* 3 (1994): 329–30; Blasi, Kroumova, and Kruse, *Kremlin Capitalism,* 13–49, table 2 (190); "Zaniatost' i rynka truda," *Voprosi ekonomiki* 12 (1993): 53–105.

7. Aslund, *How Russia Became a Market Economy;* Blasi, Kroumova, and Kruse, *Kremlin Capitalism;* Roman Frydman, Andrzej Rapaczynski, and John Earle, *The Privatization Process in Russia, Ukraine, and the Baltic States* (London: Central European University Press, 1993); Lynn D. Nelson and Irina Y. Kuzes, *Property to the People: The Struggle for Radical Economic Reform in Russia* (Armonk, N.Y.: M. E. Sharpe, 1994); Andrei Shleifer and Maxim Boycko, "The Politics of Russian Privatization," in *Post-Communist Reform: Pain and Progress,* ed. Olivier Blanchard (Cambridge, Mass.: MIT Press, 1993).

8. In *Kremlin Capitalism,* Blasi, Kroumova, and Kruse give a detailed description of the options available.

9. VTsIOM Intertsentr, *Ekonomicheskie i sotsial'nye peremeny: monitoring obshchestvennogo mneniia* 5, no. 25 (September/October 1996): 61–66.

10. Beverly Crawford and Arend Lijphart, "Explaining Political and Economic Change in Post-Communist Eastern Europe: Old Legacies, New Institutions, Hegemonic Norms, and International Pressures," *Comparative Political Studies* 28, no. 2 (July 1995): 195.

11. Michael Urban, *The Rebirth of Politics in Russia* (Cambridge: Cambridge University Press, 1997), 287.

12. Linda Cook, "Workers in the Russian Federation," *Communist and Post-Communist Studies* 28, no. 1 (1995): 30–34.

13. Mikhail Shmakov, *Material otchetnogo doklada Predsedatelia FNPR M. V. Shmakova na III s"ezde Nezavisimykh Profsoiuzov Rossii,* 25 (draft version).

14. Ibid., 26; L. [A.] Gordon, E. Klopov, V. Komarovskii, and V. Gimpel'son,

"Rabochee dvizhenie v sovremennoi Rossii: ravnovesie perspektiv," in *Sotsial'no-tru-dovye issledovaniia,* vol. 1, *Rabochee dvizhenie v segodniashei Rossii: stanovlenie, sovremennye problemy, perspektivy,* ed. Gordon et al. (Moscow: IMEMO-RAN, 1995), 62–89.

15. Irina Ledeneva, assistant to President Misnik of PGMPR, interview by author, Moscow, 22 June 1994.

16. Shmakov, *Material otchetnogo doklada,* 24.

17. Ibid., 18, 22. Italics added.

18. Sergei Magaril of the Russian Social Democratic Party, interviews by author, Moscow, 23 June 1994 and 16 December 1996.

19. V. Komarovskii, "3-i S"ezd NPG (Nekotorye itogi sotsiologicheskogo oprosa uchastnikov)," in L. A. Gordon, E. Klopov, V. Komarovskii, and V. Gimpel'-son, *Sotsial'no-trudovye issledovaniia, vyp. II: Profsoiuznoe dvizhenie: tendentsii i problemy perekhodnogo perioda* (Moscow: IMEMO-RAN, 1995), 53–57.

20. Leonid A. Gordon, V. E. Gimpel'son, E. V. Klopov, and V. V. Komarovskii, *K izucheniiu obshchestvennykh problem truda v Rossii pervoi poloviny 90-kh godov* (Moscow: IMEMO-RAN, 1996), 39.

21. For a typical example, see "Ustav Rossiiskogo profsoiuz lokomotivnykh brigad zheleznodorozhnikov," *Rossiiskii profsoiuz lokomotivnykh brigad zheleznodor-ozhnikov (RPLBZh), Rossiiskii Komitet* (Moscow: RPLBZh, 1994), 11.

22. Sergei Khramov, "My pravy siloi nashego profsoiuza," *Advokat* 5 (May 1996): 86–95; Gordon et al., *K izucheniiu obshchestvennykh problem,* 46. Sotsprof president Sergei Khramov made this claim in the *Advokat* interview and in an interview by the author, Moscow, 21 November 1996. According to VTsIOM data, 68 percent of workers identified themselves as FNPR members and 9 percent as members of independent unions.

23. Prior to 1994, NORP was known as the Confederation of Free Trade Unions of Russia (KSPR).

24. Gordon et al., *K izucheniiu obshchestvennykh problem,* 43.

25. According to one survey in 1995, 12 percent of workers felt that trade unions played a positive role in society; 9 percent that they played a negative role, and 64 percent that they played no important role at all. Gordon et al., *K izucheniiu ob-shchestvennykh problem,* 28. See also Aleksandr Buzgalin and Andrei Kolganov, "Russia's Trade Union Movement Today," *Jamestown Foundation Prism* 3, no. 16, pt. 3 (10 October 1997): 3.

26. Boris Misnik, "Govorim FNPR—podrazumevaem KPSS," *Izvestiia,* 21 October 1993, 5.

27. The relevant decree was dated 28 September 1993; see I. Shestakova, "Krakh fonda—udar po rabochemu," *Kiselevskie vesti,* 23 July 1994, for a detailed discussion.

28. Pavel Taletskii, "Smenili shantazh—pivnoi na sotsstrakhovskii," *Delo* 29 (1994), n.p.; Khramov interview, 21 November 1996; Anatoli Kocher, president of the Assotsiatsii letnogo sostava Rossii (Association of Flight Personnel of Russia), interview by author, Moscow, 22 June 1994; Andrei Shugaev, head of legal services for the Russian-American Fund for Trade Union Research, interview by author, Moscow, 29 June 1994.

29. Iurii Shatyrenko, "Fond bol'she ne budet kormushkoi," *Delo* 7 (1994), n.p.

30. Sergei Khramov, "Osnovnye principy deiatel'nosti organizatsii Sotsprof," *Rabochaia sila* 3, no. 12 (May 1995): 4.

31. Andrei Nikolaev, "Glavnyi konveier AZLK groziat ostanovit'," *Segodnia,* 3 April 1994, n.p.; Khramov interview, 21 November 1996.

32. Vladimir Veprev, "Blagami ukazami mostitsia doroga k bezzakoniiu," *Delo* 13 (March 1994), n.p. Italics are boldface in original.

33. Aleksandr Kalinin, "Privodnym remnem da po...," *Rossiia,* 19–25 December 1994, n.p.

34. A. Bol'shanin, "O tarifnom i kartel'nom soglasheniiakh i koe o chem es-hche...," *Kuzbass,* 9 September 1994, n.p.; Nataliia Dmitrieva, "Na chuzhoi karab-vai...," *V boi za ugol',* 23 June 1994, n.p.; Aleksei Kliushnikov, "Ezh v shtanakh," *Iunost* (Iaroslavl'), 22 September 1994, n.p.; Andrei Tarabrim, "Kak nam reorganizo-vat' rosugleprof?" *Na-gora,* 21–22 July 1994, n.p. See also the irregular issues of *Rabochaia sila* for 1995 and 1996.

35. Boris Kagarlitsky, "Profsoiuzy stoiat pered vyborom: kratkii kurs istorii i varianty povedeniia FNPR v novykh usloviiakh," *Golos Profsoiuzov* (Iaroslavl'), 5–12 October 1994.

36. Buzgalin and Kolganov, "Russia's Trade Union Movement Today," 3.

37. Khramov, "Osnovnye principy deiatel'nosti organizatsii Sotsprof," 4.

Chapter 6: Laboring under Illusions

1. L. D. Trotsky, *Moia Zhizn'* (Berlin, 1930), 2:64.

2. Viktor Komarovskii, "Rol' profsoiuzov v stanovlenii sistemy sotsial'nogo partnerstva v Rossii: sovremennoi sostoianie i perspektivy," in *Sotsial'no-trudovye issledovaniia,* vol. 2, *Profsoiuznoe dvizhenie: tendentsii i problemy perekhodnogo perioda* (Moscow: IMEMO-RAN, 1995), 11.

3. Ibid., 12.

4. Vladimir Varov, "Kto zhe navodit ten' na plentin'?" *Delo* 23 (June 1994), n.p.

5. *Chto mogut profsoiuzy* (Moscow: Bibliotechka "Rossiiskoi Gazety," 1996), 18:72 and 57–58, respectively.

6. Feliks Babitskii, "Profsoiuzy groziat voinoi—Administratsiia Prezidenta pred-pochitaet peregovory," *Rossiiskie vesti,* 16 August 1994, n.p.; Artem Gurstnyi, "Pod-pisyvat' ili net," *Solidarnost',* 9 (1994), n.p.; Andrei Nikolaev, "Profsoiuz mashinos-troitelei otkazalsia ot obshchestvennogo soglasiia," *Segodnia,* 26 July 1994, n.p.

7. Vladimir Grishchenko, "Ot deklaratsii k otvetstvennosti," *Delo* 12 (March 1994), n.p.

8. Ibid.

9. Evgenii Gontmakher, "Sotsial'naia politika dolzhna byt' politikoi shirokogo dialoga," *Profsoiuznoe obozrenie* 3 (1994): 25.

10. The locomotive engineers' union, Sotsprof, and many of the union associa-tions now provide labor organizers with model charters that have been tested for legal-ity in previous court cases.

11. Article 28 of the union law requires the administration to provide unions with the necessary space and equipment to function. See "Federal'nyi zakon Rossi-iskoi Federatsii o Professional'nykh soiuzakh, ikh pravakh i garantiiakh deiatel'nosti," *Chto mogut profsoiuzy,* vyp. no. 18:8–25.

12. Shugaev interview.

13. Ibid.

14. "Zakon o kollektivnykh dogovorakh i soglasheniiakh," *Chto mogut prof-soiuzy,* 30.

15. Ibid., 34.

16. "Zakon o poriadke razresheniia kollektivnykh trudovykh sporov," *Chto mogut profsoiuzy,* 55.

17. The relevant passages in the law are in article 16, section 3, and article 17, section 2.

18. Nikolai Miakinnik, "Luchshe samolet v nebe, chem sinitsa v rukakh minis-terstva," *Rossiiskie vesti* 19 (May 1994), n.p.; Andrei Nikolaev, "Letchiki ob"iavili bessrochnuiu zabastovku" and "Zabastovky letchikov sud priznal nezakonnoi," *Segod-nia,* 17 and 20 May 1994, n.p.

19. Viktor Kalashnikov, "Bastovat' mozhno, no luchshe dogovorit'sia," *Chto mogut profsoiuzy,* 59.

20. *Trud SSSR: statisticheskii sbornik* (Moscow, 1988), 26.

21. Bertram Silverman and Murray Yanowitch, *New Rich, New Poor, New Rus-sia* (Armonk, N.Y.: M. E. Sharpe, 1997), table 3.6 (51).

22. Gordon et al., *K izucheniiu obshchestvennykh problem,* 28.

23. Silverman and Yanowitch, *New Rich, New Poor, New Russia,* 46–46, 51–52.

24. Ibid., table 5.1 (84).

25. Ibid., 86.

26. Tony Weselowsky, "Russia: Workers Still Waiting to Be Paid," *RFE/RL,* document reference (www.rferl.org/nca/features/1998/02/F.RU.980211152221).

27. Tony Weselowsky, "Russia: Idle Workers Plague Industry," *RFE/RL,* docu-ment reference (www.rferl.org/nca/features/1998/02/F.RU.980211152324).

28. Gordon et al., *Sotsial'no-trudovye issledovaniia,* vol. 4, *Formirovanie rynka truda i sotsial'naia mobil'nost' v Rossii* (Moscow: IMEMO-RAN, 1996).

29. M. Kirilova, "Poisk raboty: sootnoshenie institutsional'nykh i nefor-mal'nykh mekhanizmov mobil'nosti," in Gordon et al., *Formirovanie rynka truda,* 51–66. Information on the effectiveness of employment service offices comes from my interviews with trade union leaders and representatives of the Free Trade Union Institute of the AFL-CIO, in Moscow, June 1994 and December 1996.

30. V. Gimpel'son, "Uvolnennye rabotniki na rynke truda," in Gordon et al., *Formirovanie rynka truda,* 18.

31. The first view was articulated by Abdullabek Khidirov of the Vorkuta Work-ers' Committee, the second by Sergei Khramov of Sotsprof (Khramov interview, 1996). Variations on these views were common throughout the labor movement. This was one issue that did not break down on strict FNPR/independent union lines. The interviews were conducted during May and June 1994, just as voucher privatization was ending.

32. Blasi, Kroumova, and Kruse, *Kremlin Capitalism,* 27.

33. Ibid., 51–61; Gordon et al., *K izucheniiu obshchestvennykh problem,* 108–9.

34. Blasi, Kroumova, and Kruse, *Kremlin Capitalism,* table 5 (193). Blasi does not explain how "rank and file" is defined in this survey.

35. Ibid., 106–7.

36. A. A. Kocher, president of the Association of Flight Personnel of Russia, and V. A. Kurochkin, president of the Locomotive Engineers' Union, interview by au-thor, Moscow, 22 June 1994.

37. Ibid.

38. Blasi, Kroumova, and Kruse, *Kremlin Capitalism,* 13–49; Aslund, *How Russia Became a Market Economy,* 223–71, 272–316.

39. "Klub 'Zashchita' reshil vziat' v odin kulak golosa kak minimum trekh tysi-

ach aktsionerov 'Severstali'," *Rech'* (Cherepovets), 12 May 1994, n.p.

40. Sergei Begliak, "Gonka startovala: priz—mesto v sovete direktorov AO 'Severstal'," *Rech'* (Cherepovets), 10 June 1994, n.p.

41. Maksim Filimonov, "Privatizatsiia v Rossii visit na voloske," *Nezavisimaia gazeta,* 25 January 1996, 4; Iaroslav Shimov, "V konflikt vokrug 'Noril'skogo nikelia' aktivno vmeshalis' profsoiuzy," *Izvestiia,* 27 January 1996, 2; Aleksei Tarasov, "Talnakh: podzemnyi bunt gorniakov," *Izvestiia,* 16 February 1996, 1–2, "Noril'skii shakhter nepreklonen," *Izvestiia,* 20 February 1996, 2, and "Zhizn' v 'zaloge'," *Izvestiia,* 12 March 1996, 5.

42. Tarasov, "Zhizn' v 'zaloge'," 5.

43. Ibid.

44. Blasi, Kroumova, and Kruse, *Kremlin Capitalism,* 75.

45. Filimonov, "Privatizatsiia v Rossii visit na voloske," 4.

46. Shimov, "V konflikt vokrug 'Noril'skogo nikelia' aktivno vmeshalis' profsoiuzy," 2.

47. Quoted in Silverman and Yanowitch, *New Rich, New Poor, New Russia,* 55.

48. Robert D. Putnam, *Making Democracy Work* (Princeton: Princeton University Press, 1993), 11.

49. Oleg Pchelintsev, "Revoliutsiia iarche, chem reforma," *Nezavisimaia gazeta,* 6 February 1996, 4.

50. Karl Marx, "The Eighteenth Brumaire of Louis Bonaparte," in *Karl Marx: Selected Writings,* ed. David McLellan (Oxford: Oxford University Press, 1977), 300.

Conclusion

1. Paul R. Gregory, "Has Russia's Transition Really Been Such a Failure?" *Problems of Post-Communism* 44, no. 6 (November/December 1997): 13–22.

2. For details on the strike action, see Zakhar Vinogradov, "Shakhterskii vzryv postavil stranu v samuiu krainiuiu situatsiiu," *Nezavisimaia gazeta,* 21 May 1998 (online NGA-No. 089).

3. See reports in ibid; and Aleksandr Zhelenin, "V Vorkute Shakhtery 'vzaili v plen' vse nachal'stvo," *Nezavisimaia gazeta,* 15 May 1998 (online NGA-No. 85).

4. Vinogradov, "Shakhterskii vzryv."

5. Aleksandr Zhelenin, "Shakhteram nadoel president," *Nezavisimaia gazeta,* 25 June 1998 (online NGA-No. 112).

6. Walden Bello, *Dark Victory* (London: Pluto Press, 1994).

7. Stephen F. Cohen, "Why Call It Reform?" *Nation,* 7/14 September 1998.

Select Bibliography

Archives

Rossiiskii Tsentr Khraneniia i Izucheniia Dokumentov Noveishei Istorii (RTsKhIDNI)
    Fond 17—Central Committee of the Communist Party of the Soviet Union
    Fond 76—Personal Files of Felix Derzhinskii
    Fond 79—Personal Files of Valerian Kuibyshev
    Fond 85—Personal Files of Grigorii (Sergo) Ordzhonikidze
    Fond 145—Personal Files of Viktor Nogin

Tsentral'nii Gosudarstvennii Arkhiv Oktiaber'skoi Revolutsii (TsGAOR)
    Fond 5451—All Union Central Council of Trade Unions

Interviews

Interviews with the following individuals and groups cited in this work were conducted by the author from December 1990 to June 1991, April 1992, June 1994, and December 1996.

Tizutdin Adip'gereev, founder of the informal workers group, Makhachkala Electronic Instrument Factory. Makhachkala, 8 January 1991.

Il'giz T. Akhmetov, factory division head, KamAZ. Naberezhnye Chelny, 27 March 1991.

Aleksandr Aslanidi, co-chair, Council of Workers' Committees of the Kuzbass. Kemerovo, 26 April 1991.

Aleksander V. Buzgalin, professor, Moscow State University.

Co-chair, Donetsk city strike committee.

Council of the Labor Collective, Siberian Agricultural Machines Production Association ("Sibselmash").

Editors, *Nasha gazeta*, Kemerovo.

Vladimir Gimpelson, Institute for International Economics and International Relations, Moscow.

Leonid Gordon, Center for Employment Studies, Moscow.

V. N. Istoman, director, Makhachkala Electronic Instrument Factory. Makhachkala, Dagestan, 8 January 1990. 7 January 1991.

Svetlana Ivanova, assistant director for economic questions, "Gazapparat," Donetsk.

Boris Kagarlitsky, Union of Labor, Moscow.

Sasha Karkots, member of the informal workers group, Makhachkala Electronic Instrument Factory.

Sergei Khramov, president, Sotsprof. Moscow, 22 April 1992 and 21 November 1996.

Gennadi Kirilov, brigadier and founder of the Temporary Workers' Group, foundry works, KamAZ. Naberezhnye Chelny, 28 March 1991.

Mikhail Kisliuk, vice president of the Kemerovo Regional Executive Committee (Oblispolkom). Kemerovo, 29 April 1991.

Svetlana Klimova, Institute for International Economics and International Relations, Moscow.

Anatoli Kocher, president of the Assotsiatsii Letnogo Sostava Rossii (Association of Flight Personnel of Russia), and V. A. Kurochkin, president of the Locomotive Engineers' Union. Moscow, 22 June 1994.

V. V. Komarovskii, Center for Employment Studies, Moscow.

Dr. Boris Kurashvili, Institute of State and Law, Academy of Sciences of the USSR, Moscow.

Valentin Landik, director, Nord Association, Dontesk. Dontesk, 6 April 1991.

Irina Ledeneva, assistant to President Misnik of GMPR. Moscow, 22 June 1994.

Sergei Magaril, Social Democratic Party of Russia. Moscow, 23 June 1994 and 16 December 1996.

Management and labor representatives, Makhachkala Electronic Instrument Factory.

Management board, experimental factory of the Siberian division of the Academy of Sciences of the USSR.

Roy Medvedev, Socialist Party of Russia, Moscow.

Valerii Miller, chairman, trade union council (of the VTsSPS union), Gorky mine. Donetsk, Ukraine, 16 April 1991.

Sh. N. Mishiev, trade union president, Makhachkala Electronic Instrument Factory. Makhachkala, 7 January 1991.

Victor R. Nekrasov, president, Seafarers Union of Russia.

Abdul Nidapeirov, member of the Informal Workers' Group, Makhachkala Electronic Instrument Factory. Makhachkala, 8 January 1991.

Nail S. Nurmukhamedov, vice director for social questions, KamAZ. Naberezhnye Chelny, 1 April 1991.

Iulia Promina, trade union president, Kamgasenergostroi.

Railroad engineers, Railroad-Car Repair Depot, Donetsk.

Nina G. Savitskaia, editor, newspaper Birlesu, Alma-Ata.

Mikhail N. Selikhov, producer, Gostelradio (State Television and Radio).

Andrei A. Shugaev, general manager, Juridical Program, Russian-American Fund for Trade Union Research. Moscow, 29 June 1994.

Dr. Viktor V. Solomikhin, Economics faculty, Donetsk State University.

Dr. E. P. Torkanovskii, Institute of Economics, Academy of Sciences of the USSR. Moscow, 18 December 1990.

Trade-union chairpersons, Federation of Independent Trade Unions of Russia (formerly VTsSPS), Novosibirsk Region.

Dr. Sergei Tsakunov, Center for Social-Strategic Research, Moscow.

Eduard Tsekhamov, member of the informal workers' group, Makhachkala Electronic Instrument Factory.

Viktor Utkin, president, Independent Union of Mineworkers. Moscow, 23 April 1992.

S. N. Vasiliev, president, Gorky mine Council of the Labor Collective. Donetsk, 16
    April 1991.
Workers on the first shift, Railroad-Car Repair Depot, Donetsk.
Alekansder Zamiatin, director, Juridical Program, Free Trade Union Institute, St. Pe-
    tersburg.

Newspapers and Journals

Individual source citations from newspaper articles are given in the notes to each
chapter.

Soviet and Russian

Birlesu
Chest' shakhtera
Delo
Delovoi mir
Dialog
Eko
Ekonomicheskaia gazeta
Elektromotor
Etalon
Golos profsoiuzov (Iaroslavl')
Gudok
Iiul'
Informatsionnyi biulleten
Iunost (Iaroslavl')
Izvestiia
Khimik
Kiselevskie vesti
Kommunist
Komsomolskaia pravda
Kuranty
Kuzbass
Literaturnaia gazeta
Moscovskaia pravda
Moskovskie novosti
Moscow News (English edition)
Moscow Times
Na-gora
Narodnaia gazeta
Nasha gazeta
Nedelia
New Times
Nezavisimaia gazeta
Novyi mir
Planovoe khoziaistvo
Pravda
Profsoiuznoe obozrenie
Rabochaia sila

Rabochaia tribuna
Rabochii Kamaza
Rech' (Cherepovets)
Rosseiskaia gazeta
Rossiia
Rossiiskie vesti
Rubicon
Segodnia
Solidarnost'
Sotsialisticheskii trud
Sotsiologicheskie issledovaniia
Sovetskaia rossiia
Sovetskoe gosudarstvo i pravo
Stroitel'
Trud
V boi za ugol'
Vedemosti Verkhovnogo Soveta SSSR
Voprosy ekonomiki
Za bol'shuiu khimiiu
Zheleznodorozhnik kuzbassa

Western

American Sociological Review
Communist and Post-Communist Studies
Comparative Political Studies
Economic Analysis and Workers' Management
Europe-Asia Studies
Foreign Broadcast Information Service
Nation
New Republic
New York Times
Problems of Communism
Problems of Post-Communism
Radio Liberty Research Report on the USSR
Slavic Review
Soviet Economy
Soviet Studies
Washington Post
World Politics

Articles and Books

Abalkin, Leonid. "Glavnoe napravlenie ekonomicheskoi politiki KPSS." *Kommunist* 5 (1986).
———. *Ne ispol'zovannyi shans*. Moscow: Politizdat, 1991.
———. "Uskorenie sotsial'no-ekonomicheskogo razvitiia: sushchnost' i istochniki." *Planovoe khoziaistvo* 3 (1986).
Afanas'ev, V. G. *Nauchnoe upravlenie obshchestvom*. Moscow, 1968.
Aganbegian, A. G. "General'nii kurs ekonomicheskoi politiki." *Eko* 11 (1985).

———. "Na novom etape ekonomicheskogo stroitel'stva." *Eko* 8 (1985).

———. "Perelom i uskoreniie." *Eko* 6 (1986).

Akhmeduev, A. "Predlozheniia po proektu zakona SSSR 'O gosudarstvennom pred-priiatii (ob"edinenii)." *Voprosy ekonomiki* 4 (1987).

Andreev, Andrei. "Sobstvennost', vlast', i politicheskaia reforma v Rossii." *Moskva* 9 (1993).

Andreev, V. "O polnomochiiakh soveta trudovogo kollektiva." *Kommunist* 5 (1987).

Andriianov, V. "Gornyi udar." *Dialog* 1 (1990).

"AO—put' k razvitiiu v usloviiakh rynka." *Rabochii Kamaza,* 27 September 1990.

Arnot, Bob. *Controlling Soviet Labor.* Armonk, N.Y.: M. E. Sharpe, 1988.

Aslund, Anders. *Gorbachev's Struggle for Economic Reform.* Ithaca: Cornell University Press, 1991.

———. *How Russia Became a Market Economy.* Washington, D.C.: The Brookings Institution, 1995.

———. "The Making of Economic Policy in 1989 and 1990." In Hewett and Winston, eds. *Milestones in Glasnost and Perestroyka.*

Azrael, Jeremy. *Managerial Power and Soviet Politics.* Cambridge, Mass.: Harvard University Press, 1966.

Bagaeva, T. I. "Nado li vybirat' rukovoditelei?" *Sotsiologicheskie issledovaniia* 1 (1990).

Bailes, Kendell. *Science and Technology under Lenin and Stalin.* Princeton: Princeton University Press, 1978.

Baranenkova, T. "Puti ukrepleniia trudovoi distsipliny." *Voprosi ekonomiki* 5 (1986).

Beetham, David, ed. *Defining and Measuring Democracy.* London: Sage Publications, 1994.

Beissinger, Mark R. *Scientific Management, Socialist Discipline, and Soviet Power.* Cambridge, Mass.: Harvard University Press, 1988.

Bello, Walden. *Dark Victory.* London: Pluto Press, 1994.

Benenuti, Francesco. *Stakhanovism and Stalinism, 1934–38.* University of Birmingham, CREES Discussion Papers, SIPS Series no. 30, 1989.

Berliner, Joseph. *Factory and Manager in the USSR.* Cambridge, Mass.: Harvard University Press, 1957.

———. *Soviet Industry From Stalin to Gorbachev.* Ithaca: Cornell University Press, 1988.

Black, Cyril E., ed. *Rebirth: A History of Europe Since World War II.* Boulder: Westview Press, 1992.

Blasi, Joseph, Maya Kroumova, and Douglas Kruse. *Kremlin Capitalism: Privatizing the Russian Economy.* Ithaca: Cornell University Press, 1997.

Bogomolov, G. and P. Vaniarkin. "Sotsialisticheskoe sorevnovanie i Shchekinskii method." *Sotsialisticheskii trud* 4 (1979).

Bresser Pereira, Luiz Carlos, Jose Maria Maravall, and Adam Przeworski. *Economic Reforms in New Democracies: A Social Democratic Approach.* Cambridge: Cambridge University Press, 1993.

Brodersen, Arvid. *The Soviet Worker.* New York: Random House, 1966.

Bronshtein, V. V. "O normakh i stimulakh." *Eko* 4 (1986).

Brown, Archie. *The Gorbachev Factor.* Oxford: Oxford University Press, 1996.

Brown, Emily Clark. *Soviet Trade Unions and Labor Relations.* Cambridge, Mass.: Harvard University Press, 1960.

Bulianda, A. "Samoupravlenie i tsentralizm." *Kommunist* 7 (1987).

Bunce, Valerie. "Paper Curtains and Paper Tigers". *Slavic Review* 54, no. 4 (winter 1995).

———. "Should Transitologists Be Grounded?" *Slavic Review* 54, no. 1 (spring 1995).

Burawoy, Michael. *Manufacturing Consent: Changes in the Labor Process under Monopoly Capitalism*. Chicago: University of Chicago Press, 1979.

———. *The Politics of Production*. London: Verso Press, 1985.

Burowoy, Michael, and Pavel Krotov. "The Soviet Transition from Socialism to Capitalism: Worker Control and Economic Bargaining in the Wood Industry." *American Sociological Review* 57, no. 1 (1992).

Buzgalin, Aleksandr, and Andrei Kolganov. "Russia's Trade Union Movement Today." *Jamestown Foundation Prism* 3, no. 16, pt. 3 (10 October 1997).

Carr, E. H. *The Bolshevik Revolution, 1917–1923*. New York: W. W. Norton, 1985.

———. *Socialism in One Country, 1924–1926*. London: Macmillan & Co. Ltd., 1958.

Chandler, Andrea. "The Interaction of Post-Sovietology and Comparative Politics: Seizing the Moment" *Communist and Post-Communist Studies* 27, no. 1 (March 1994).

Chase, William. *Workers, Society, and the Soviet State: Labor and Life in Moscow, 1918–1929*. Urbana: University of Illinois Press, 1990.

Chentsov, N. "Zabastovki moglo ne byt'." *Dialog* 1 (1990).

Cherednichenko, K. K., and I. I. Goldin. *Shchekinskii method*. Moscow, 1988.

Chiesa, Giulietto. *Transition to Democracy: Political Change in the Soviet Union, 1987–1991*. Hanover: University Press of New England, 1993.

Chto mogut profsoiuzy. Vol. 18. Moscow: Bibliotechka "Rossiiskoi Gazety," 1996.

Cohen, Stephen F. *Rethinking the Soviet Experience*. New York: Oxford University Press, 1985.

Colton, Timothy J., and Robert C. Tucker, eds. *Patterns in Post-Soviet Leadership*. Boulder: Westview Press, 1995.

Conner, Walter D. *The Accidental Proletariat*. Princeton: Princeton University Press, 1991.

Conquest, Robert. *Industrial Workers in the USSR*. London: Bodley Head, 1967.

Cook, Linda J. "Lessons of the Soviet Coal Miners' Strike of Summer 1989." *Harriman Institute Forum* 4, no. 3 (March 1991).

———. "Workers in the Russian Federation." *Communist and Post-Communist Studies* 28, no. 1 (1995).

Crawford, Beverly. "Explaining Political and Economic Change in Post-Communist Eastern Europe." *Comparative Political Studies* 28, no. 2 (July 1995).

———, ed. *Markets, States, and Democracy*. Boulder: Westview Press, 1995.

Crawford, Beverly, and Arend Lijphart. "Explaining Political and Economic Change in Post-Communist Eastern Europe: Old Legacies, New Institutions, Hegemonic Norms, and International Pressures." *Comparative Political Studies* 28, no. 2 (July 1995).

Dahl, Robert. *Democracy and Its Critics*. New Haven: Yale University Press, 1989.

Desiatii s"ezd RKP/b/: Stenograficheskii otchet. Moscow: Gosudarstvennoe izdatel'stvo politicheskoi literaturi, 1963.

Deutscher, Isaac. *Soviet Trade Unions*. London: Oxford University Press, 1950.

Di Palma, Giuseppe. *To Craft Democracies*. Berkeley and Los Angeles: University of California Press, 1990.

Elster, Jon, and Rune Slagstad, eds. *Constitutionalism and Democracy*. Cambridge: Cambridge University Press, 1988.

Filtzer, Donald. *Soviet Workers and De-Stalinization*. Cambridge: Cambridge University Press, 1992.

——. *Soviet Workers and Stalinist Industrialization*. London: The Pluto Press, 1986.

——. *Soviet Workers and the Collapse of Perestroika*. Cambridge: Cambridge University Press, 1994.

Fitzpatrick, Sheila. "Postwar Soviet Society: The 'Return to Normalcy,' 1945–1953." In Linz, ed. *The Impact of World War II on the Soviet Union.*

Fomin, V. A., ed. *Nekotorye voprosy nauchnogo upravleniia obshchestvom.* Moscow: "Nauka," 1967.

Gimpel'son, G. *Sovetskii rabochii klass, 1918-1920 gg., sotsial'no-politicheskie izmeneniia.* Moscow: Izdatel'stvo "Nauka," 1974.

Ginzburg, A. *Dlia chego nuzhny i kak dolzhny rabotat' proizvodstvennye soveshchaniia?* Moscow: Izdatel'stvo VTsSPS, 1926.

Gladkov, I. A., ed. *Istoriia sotsialisticheskoi ekonomiki SSSR.* Moscow: Izdatel'stvo "Nauka," 1976.

Godobreldze, S. *Proizvodstvennie i ekonomicheskie soveshchanie.* Tiflis: Izdatel'stvo soveta professional'nykh soiuzov Gruzii "Shrama," 1927.

Godson, R. *The Kremlin and Labor.* New York: Crane, Russak, 1977.

Gol'tsman, A. *Dorogu initsiative rabochikh.* Moscow: Moskovskii rabochii, 1929.

Gorbachev, Mikhail S. *Izbrannye rechi i stat'i.* Vols. 1–7. Moscow: Izdatel'stvo politicheskoi literatury, 1987–1990.

Gordon, Leonid A. *Rabochii klass SSSR.* Moscow: "Nauka," 1985.

——. "Sotsial'naia politika v sfere oplaty truda." *Sotsiologicheskie issledovaniia* 6 (1987).

Gordon, Leonid A., V. E. Gimpel'son, E. V. Klopov, and V. V. Komarovskii. *Formirovanie rynka truda i sotsial'naia mobil'nost' v Rossii.* Vol. 4 of *Sotsial'no-trudovye issledovaniia.* Moscow: IMEMO-RAN, 1996.

——. *K izucheniiu obshchestvennykh problem truda v Rossii pervoi poloviny 90-kh godov: sub"ekty i ob"ekty sotsial'no-trudovykh otnoshenii.* Moscow: Institute Mirovoi Ekonomiki i Mezhdunarodnykh Otnoshenii RAN, 1996.

——. *Krupnye promyshlennye predpriiatiia—perestroika upravleniia i trudovykh otnoshenii (monograficheskie issledovaniia 1992-1995 gg.* Vol. 3 of *Sotsial'no-trudovye issledovaniia.* Moscow: IMEMO-RAN, 1995.

——. *Profsoiuznoe dvizhenie—tendentsii i problemy perekhodnogo perioda.* Vol. 2 of *Sotsial'no-trudovye issledovaniia.* Moscow: IMEMO-RAN, 1995.

——. *Rabochee dvizhenie v segodniashnei Rossii: stanovlenie, sovremennye problemy, perspektivy.* Vol. 1 of *Sotsial'no-trudovye issledovaniia.* Moscow: IMEMO-RAN, 1995.

Gordon, Maks. *Uchastie rabochikh v organizatsii proizvodstva: ot rabochego kontrolia k proizvodstvennim soveshchaniiam.* Leningrad: Izdatel'stvo Leningradskogo gubprofsoveta, 1927.

Gregory, Paul R. "Has Russia's Transition Really Been Such a Failure?" *Problems of Post-Communism* 44, no. 6 (November/December 1997).

Gusev, G. M., ed. *Obshchestvo i molodezh'.* Moscow, 1968.

Haggard, Stephan, and Robert R. Kaufman. *The Political Economy of Democratic Transitions.* Princeton: Princeton University Press, 1995.

Hanson, Stephen. "The Leninist Legacy and Institutional Change." *Comparative Political Studies* 28, no. 2 (July 1995).

Hauslohner, Peter. "Democratization 'From the Middle Out': Soviet Trade Unions and Perestroika." *Harriman Institute Forum* 1, no. 10 (1988).

Heldman, D. C. *Trade Unions and Labor Relations in the USSR.* Washington, D.C.: Council on American Affairs, 1970.

Hewett, Ed. *Reforming the Soviet Economy.* Washington, D.C.: The Brookings Institution, 1988.

Hewett, Ed, and Victor Winston, eds. *Milestones in Glasnost and Perestroyka: The Economy.* Washington, D.C.: The Brookings Institution, 1991.

Hosking, Geoffrey. *The First Socialist Society.* Cambridge, Mass.: Harvard University Press, 1985.

Hough, Jerry. *Democratization and Revolution in the USSR, 1985–1991.* Washington, D.C.: The Brookings Institution, 1997.

Iadov, V. A. "Orientatsiia: tvorcheskaia rabota." In Gusev, ed. *Obshchestvo i molodezh'.*

Iarkin, Iuri. "Vybornost' i podotchetnost'." *Kommunist* 8 (1987).

Isichko, S. "Khozhdenie v narod," *Rabochii Kamaza,* 22 August 1990, 2.

———. "Poshchechina kollektivu," *Rabochii Kamaza* 17 April 1990, 3.

Iugai, T. "Struktura zaniatosti v usloviiakh intensifikatsii." *Voprosy ekonomiki* 11 (1986).

Jackman, Richard. "Economic Policy and Employment in the Transition Economies of Central and Eastern Europe: What Have We Learned?" *International Labour Review* 3 (1994).

Kagarlitsky, Boris. *The Dialectic of Change.* London: Verso, 1990.

———. *The Disintegration of the Monolith.* London: Verso, 1992.

Kalinin, S. A. "Bol'she doveriia kollektivu." *Kommunist* 6 (1987).

Kapeliush, Ia. S. "Obshchestvennoe mnenie o vybornosti na proizvodstve." *Informatsionnyi biulleten* 39 (1969).

———. "Vybornost' rukovoditelei: vchera i segodnia." *Sotsiologicheskie issledovaniia* 2 (1988).

Karl, Terry Lynn, and Philippe C. Schmitter. "From an Iron Curtain to a Paper Curtain: Grounding Transitologists or Students of Postcommunism." *Slavic Review* 54, no. 4 (winter 1995).

Khramov, Sergei. "My pravy siloi nashego profsoiuza." *Advokat* 5 (May 1996): 86–95.

———. "Osnovnye printsipi deiatel'nosti organizatsii Sotsprof." *Rabochaia sila* 3, no. 12 (May 1995): 4.

Khrishchev, E. I. and L. I. Kozhokar'. "Svet i teni kollektivnogo podriada." *Sotsiologicheskie issledovaniia* 4 (1986).

Kirichenko, V. "Perestroika sistemi upravleniia i tsentralizovannoe planirovanie." *Kommunist* 3 (1986).

Kirsch, Leonard J. *Soviet Wages: Changes in Structure and Administration Since 1956.* Cambridge, Mass.: MIT Press, 1972.

Klepatskii, L. "O voprose formakh organizatsii i upravleniia promyshlennosti v SSSR." In Fomin, ed. *Nekotorye voprosy nauchnogo upravleniia obshchestvom.*

"Kodeks zakonov o trude RSFSR." In *Sbornik normativnykh aktov o trude.* Moscow: "Iuridicheskaia literatura," 1984.

Kolganov, A. "Protivorechie tsentralisma i samostoiatel'nosti." *Voprosi ekonomiki* 9 (1986).

Komarovskii, V. V. *Bor'ba shakhterov: nekotorye prichiny i usloviia (Otchet),* 1991. Printed by the Independent Union of Miners (NPG) as a bound photocopy of Komarovskii's original manuscript for the internal use of the miners' union. A copy was provided to the author by the Donbass regional office of the NPG.

———. "Deviat' tezisov o rabochem i profsoiuznom dvizhenii v Rossii." *Polis* 3 (1992).

———. "Rol' profsoiuzov v stanovlenii sistemy sotsial'nogo partnerstva v Rossii: sovremennoi sostoianie i perspektivy." In *Sotsial'no-trudovye issledovaniia, vyp. 2: Profsoiuznoe dvizhenie: tendentsii i problemy perekhodnogo perioda* (Moscow: IMEMO-RAN, 1995), 11.

———. "S kem i o chem namereno dogovarivat'sia pravitel'stvo." *Rossiiskaia gazeta,* 7 February 1992.

Komm, Leonid. "Interview." *Rabochii Kamaza,* 29 June 1990, 2.

Kornai, Janos. *The Socialist System.* Princeton: Princeton University Press, 1992.

Korol', V. "Dat' dorogu modernizatsii," *Rabochii Kamaza,* 13 April 1990, 3.

Kosenko, V. "Rasshirenie prav ili ego imitatsiia?" *Kommunist* 8 (1987).

Kostakov, Vladimir. "Polnaia zaniatost': Kak my ee ponimaem?" *Kommunist* 14 (1987).

———. "Zaniatost': defitsit ili izbytok?" *Kommunist* 2 (1987).

Kostiukovskii, Viktor. *Kuzbass: zharkoe leto, 89-go.* Moscow: "Sovremennik," 1990.

Kotkin, Stephen. *Magnetic Mountain: Stalinism as a Civilization.* Berkeley and Los Angeles: University of California Press, 1995.

KPSS o profsoiuzakh. Moscow: Profizdat, 1967.

KPSS v resoliutsiiakh i resheniiakh s"ezdov, konferentsii i plenumov TsK. Moscow: Izdatel'stvo politicheskoi literatury, 1989.

Krotov, F. G. *Rabochii klass: vedushchaia sila stroitel'stva kommunisma.* Moscow: Izdatel'stvo "Mysl," 1965.

Kurashvili, Boris P. "Kontury vozmozhnoi perestroiki." *Eko* 5 (1985).

———. "Organizatsiia truda dlia budushchego." *Eko* 3 (1986).

Kurennoi, A. M. *Aktivnaia zhuznennaia pozitsiia sovetskogo rabochego.* Moscow: Profizdat, 1983.

Kuromiya, Hiroaki. *Stalin's Industrial Revolution.* Cambridge: Cambridge University Press, 1988.

Kuznetsov, Andrei. "Economic Reforms in Russia: Enterprise Behaviour as an Impediment to Change." *Europe-Asia Studies* 46, no. 6 (1994).

Lane, David, ed. *Labour and Employment in the USSR.* Brighton: Wheatsheaf Books, 1986.

Lenin, V. I. *Polnoe sobranie sochinenii.* Moscow: Izdatel'stvo politicheskoi literaturi, 1977.

Lewin, Moshe. *The Gorbachev Phenomenon.* Berkeley and Los Angeles: University of California Press, 1988.

———. *The Making of the Soviet System.* New York: Pantheon Books, 1985.

———. *Stalinism and the Seeds of Soviet Reform.* London: Pluto Press, 1991.

Ligachev, Yegor K. *Inside Gorbachev's Kremlin.* New York: Random House, 1993.

Linden, Karl. *Khrushchev and the Soviet Leadership, 1957–1964.* Baltimore: Johns Hopkins University Press, 1966.

Linz, Susan, ed. *The Impact of World War II on the Soviet Union.* Totowa, N.J.: Rowman & Allanheld, 1985.

Malia, Martin. "From under the Rubble, What?" *Problems of Communism* 41, no. 1–2 (1992).

Manevich, E. L. "Khoziaistvennyi mekhanism i ispol'zovanie trudovykh resursov." *Eko* 12 (1986).

McAuley, Mary. *Labour Disputes in Soviet Russia, 1957–1965.* Oxford: Oxford University Press, 1969.

McFaul, Michael. *Russia between Elections.* Washington, D.C.: Carnegie Endowment, 1996.

———. "State Power, Institutional Change, and the Politics of Privatization in Russia" *World Politics* 47, no. 2 (January 1995).

Miliukov, A. "Osnovnoe khoziaistvennoe zveno v sisteme upravleniia ekonomikoi." *Voprosy ekonomiki* 5 (1987).

Millar, James. "The Little Deal." *Slavic Review* 44, no. 4 (1985).

Moore, Barrington. *The Social Origins of Dictatorship and Democracy.* Boston: Beacon Press, 1966.

Moses, Joel. "Worker Self-Management and the Reformist Alternative in Soviet Labour Policy, 1979–1985." *Soviet Studies* 39, no. 2 (April 1987).

Nelson, Lynn D., and Irina Y. Kuzes. *Property to the People: The Struggle for Radical Economic Reform in Russia.* Armonk, N.Y.: M. E. Sharpe, 1994.

———. *Radical Reform in Yeltsin's Russia.* Armonk, N.Y.: M. E. Sharpe, 1995.

Noren, James H. "The Economic Crisis: Another Perspective." In Hewett and Winston, eds. *Milestones in Glasnost and Perestroyka.*

Nove, Alec. *An Economic History of the USSR.* London: Lane, 1969.

Odinnadtsatii s"ezd RKP/b/: stenograficheskii otchet. Moscow: Gosudarstvennoe izdatel'stvo politicheskoi literaturi, 1961.

O'Donnell, Guillermo, Philippe C. Schmitter, and Laurence Whitehead, eds. *Transitions from Authoritarian Rule: Prospects for Democracy.* Baltimore and London: Johns Hopkins University Press, 1986.

Orlovsky, Daniel, ed. *Beyond Soviet Studies.* Washington, D.C.: Woodrow Wilson Center Special Studies, 1995.

Osinsky, N. *Stroitel'stvo sotsializma.* Moscow, 1918.

"Perspektivna li rabota tsentra?" *Rabochii Kamaza,* 13 April 1990, 3.

Pervushin, S. P. "Pol'nyi khozraschet—organizatsionnye i metodicheskie osnovy." *Eko* 5 (1987).

Pervyi s"ezd shakhterov SSSR, parts 1 and 2. Donetsk: Otraslevoi rabochii komitet pri p/o "Donetskugol'," 1990.

Pike, Fredrick, and Thomas Stritch, eds. *The New Corporatism.* Notre Dame: Notre Dame University Press, 1974.

Poznanski, Kazimierz, ed. *The Evolutionary Transition to Capitalism.* Boulder: Westview Press, 1995.

Przeworski, Adam. *Democracy and the Market.* Cambridge: Cambridge University Press, 1988.

———. "Democracy as a Contingent Outcome of Conflicts." In Elster and Slagstad, eds. *Constitutionalism and Democracy.*

Putnam, Robert D. *Making Democracy Work.* Princeton: Princeton University Press, 1993.

Rabochii klass SSSR, 1955–1965. Moscow: "Nauka," 1969.

Rabochii klass SSSR, 1966–1970. Moscow: "Nauka," 1979.

Radaev, V. "Khozraschetnaia samostoiatel'nost' predpriiatii." *Voprosi ekonomiki* 1 (1985).

Rapaczynski, Andrezej, and John Earle. *The Privatization Process in Russia, Ukraine, and the Baltic States.* London: Central European University Press, 1993.

Ruble, Blair. *Soviet Trade Unions.* Cambridge: Cambridge University Press, 1981.

Rutland, Peter. *The Myth of the Plan*. La Salle, Ill.: Open Court, 1985.

———. "Productivity Campaigns in Soviet Industry." In Lane, ed. *Labour and Employment in the USSR*.

Ryzhkov, Nikolai. *Perestroika: istoriia predatel'stv*. Moscow: Novosti, 1992.

Rzhanitsyna, L. "Pooshchrenie rabotnikov v usloviiakh perestroiki." *Voprosy ekonomiki* 6 (1987).

Sbornik zakonodatel'nykh aktov o trude. Moscow: "Iuridicheskaia literatura," 1984.

Schmitter, Philippe C. "Still the Century of Corporatism?" In Pike and Stritch, eds. *The New Corporatism*.

Schmitter, Philippe C., and Terry Lynn Karl. "The Conceptual Travels of Transitologists and Consolidologists: How Far to the East Should They Attempt to Go?" *Slavic Review* 53, no. 1 (spring 1994).

Schroeder, Gertrude. "Anatomy of Gorbachev's Economic Reform." In Hewett and Winston, eds. *Milestones in Glasnost and Perestroyka*.

———. "Gorbachev: 'Radically' Implementing Brezhnev's Reforms." *Soviet Economy* 2, no. 4 (1986).

———. "*Perestroyka* in the Aftermath of 1990." In Hewett and Winston, eds. *Milestones in Glasnost and Perestroyka*.

Scott, James C. *The Moral Economy of the Peasant*. New Haven: Yale University Press, 1976.

Sed'moi s"ezd professional'nykh soiuzov SSSR. Moscow, 1927.

Selznick, P. *The Organizational Weapon: A Study in Bolshevik Strategy and Tactics*. New York: McGraw-Hill, 1952.

Shalaev, Stepan. "Sovetskii profsoiuzy v sisteme sotsialisticheskogo samoupravleniia." *Kommunist* 10 (1985).

Shcherbakov, V. I. "Kardinal'naia perestroika oplaty truda." *Eko* 1 (1987).

Shleifer, Andrei, and Maxim Boycko. "The Politics of Russian Privatization." In Oliver Blanchard, ed. *Post-Communist Reform: Pain and Progress*. Cambridge, Mass.: MIT Press, 1993.

Shmakov, Mikhail. *Material otchetnogo doklada Predsedatelia FNPR M. V. Shmakova na III s"ezde Nezavisimykh Profsoiuzov*. Draft version, courtesy of the FNPR, 1996.

Shmelev, Nikolai. "Avansy i dolgi." *Novyi mir* 63, no. 6 (1987).

Shmelev, Nikolai, and Vladimir Popov. *The Turning Point*. New York: Doubleday, 1989.

Siegelbaum, Lewis. "Behind the Soviet Miners' Strike." *Nation*, 23 October 1989.

———. *Soviet State and Society between Revolutions, 1918–1929*. Cambridge: Cambridge University Press, 1992.

———. *Stakhanovism and the Politics of Productivity in the USSR, 1935–1941*. New York: Cambridge University Press, 1988.

Silverman, Bertram, and Murray Yanowitch. *New Rich, New Poor, New Russia*. Armonk, N.Y.: M. E. Sharpe, 1997.

Skoblikov, E. A. "Vopreki instruktsiiam provodim eksperiment po khozraschetu." *Eko* 12 (1985).

Starodubrovskii, V. "Usilit' ekonomicheskuiu rol' predpriiatii." *Kommunist* 6 (1987).

Stepan, Alfred. "Paths toward Redemocratization." In O'Donnell, Schmitter, and Whitehead, eds. *Transitions From Authoritarian Rule: Prospects for Democracy*.

Suny, Ronald Grigor. *The Revenge of the Past*. Stanford: Stanford University Press, 1993.

Susoev, Aleksandr. "Komu nanosit ushcherb zabastovka." *V boi za ugol'*, 16 January 1990.

Taletskii, P. N. *Eto trudnoe profsoiuznoe remeslo*. Moscow, 1992.

Teague, Elizabeth. "Miners' Strike in Siberia Winds Down." *Radio Liberty Report on the USSR*, 28 July 1989.

———. "Miners' Strike in Siberia Winds Down, Strike in Ukraine Spreads to Other Areas: A Status Report," *RL 334/89*, 20 July 1989.

———. "Organized Labor in Russia in 1992." *Radio Free Europe/Radio Liberty Research Reports* 2, no. 5 (29 January 1993).

———. "Worker Unrest in 1989." *Report on the USSR*. Vol. 2, No. 4, 1990.

Temkina, Anna. "The Labor Movement of the Perestroika Period." *Russia and the West* 20 (1991).

Tikhomirov, Iu. A., and G. Kh. Shakhnazarov, eds. *Samoupravlenie: ot teorii k praktike*. Moscow: "Iuridicheskaia literatura," 1988.

Trotsky, L. D. *Moia Zhizn'*. Berlin, 1930.

Tsvetkov, S. "O chelovecheskom faktora sotsialisticheskogo proizvodstva." *Voprosy ekonomiki* 11 (1985).

Tsypkin, Mikhail. "Workers' Militia: Order Instead of Law?" *Radio Free Europe/Radio Liberty Report on the USSR*, 17 November 1989.

Tucker, Robert C. "Post-Soviet Leadership and Change." In Colton and Tucker, eds. *Patterns in Post-Soviet Leadership*.

Turysov, K. "Chelovecheskii faktor v strategii uskoreniia." *Eko* 2 (1987).

"Uchenye obsuzhdaiut zakona SSSR 'O gosudarstvennom predpriiatii (ob'edinenii).'" *Voprosy ekonomiki* 5 (1987).

Urban, Michael. *The Rebirth of Politics in Russia*. Cambridge: Cambridge University Press, 1997.

Vaipan, V. A. "Funktsii kollektivnogo dogovora skvoz' prizmu perestroiki." *Sovetskoe gosudarstvo i pravo* 5 (1988).

Voskresenskaia, M. A., and L. Novoselov. *Proizvodstvennie soveshchanie—shkola upravlenie, 1921–1965*. Moscow: Izdatel'stvo VTsSPS Profizdat, 1965.

Vozrastanie role trudovykh kollektivov v kommunisticheskom stroitel'stve. Irkutsk: Ministerstvo vyshego i srednego spetsial'nogo obrazovaniia RSFSR, 1973.

White, Stephen. *Gorbachev and After*. Cambridge: Cambridge University Press, 1992.

Yanowitch, Murray. "Pressures for More 'Participatory' Forms of Economic Organization in the Soviet Union." *Economic Analysis and Workers' Management* 3–4 (1978).

Zaslavskaia, Tatiana I. "Chelovecheskii faktor razvitiia ekonomiki i sotsial'naia spravedlivost'." *Kommunist* 3 (1986).

———. "Ekonomika skvoz' prizimu sotsiologii." *Eko* 7 (1985).

Index